"In *Homeric Moments,* Eva Brann lovingly leads us, as she has surely led countless students, through the gallery of delights that is Homer's poetry. Brann's enthusiasm is as infectious as her deep familiarity with the works is illuminating."

Rachel Hadas, Rutgers University–Newark
Author of *Halfway Down the Hall: New and Selected Poems*

"Eva Brann has a true aptitude for felicitous expression, and one can feel through her prose the presence of a great and patient teacher."

Dennis L. Sepper, University of Dallas
Author of *Descartes's Imagination*

"For anyone eager to experience the profundity and charm of Homer's great epic poems, Eva Brann's book will serve as a passionate and engaging guide. Brann displays a deep sensitivity to the cadence and flow of Homeric poetry, and the kind of knowing intimacy with its characters that comes from years of teaching and contemplation. Her relaxed but informative approach succeeds in conveying the grandeur of the great Homeric heroes, while making them continually resonate for our own lives. Brann helps us see that this poetry has an urgency for our own era as much as it did for a distant past."

Ralph M. Rosen, University of Pennsylvania
Author of *Old Comedy and the Iambographic Tradition*

"Brann invites us to enter a conversation in which information and formal arguments jostle with appreciations and frank conjectures and surmises to increase our pleasure and deepen the inward dimension of our humanity."

Richard Freis, Millsaps College

"This is a book of sustained love which has matured over fifty years. Eva Brann's series of vignettes on Iliadic and Odyssean themes serve as finely tuned apertures to Homeric art and portraiture. Her fresh perceptions will invite questions and discoveries from readers, new and old, and deserve our gratitude."

Stephen Scully, Boston University
Author of *Homer and the Sacred City*

"Eva Brann's collection of astute observations, unusual asides, and visual snapshots of the *Iliad* and the *Odyssey* reveals a lifelong friendship with the poet, and is as pleasurable as it is informative. *Homeric Moments* is rare erudition without pedantry, in a tone marked by good sense without levity."

Victor Davis Hanson, California State University, Fresno
Author of *The Other Greeks* and coauthor of *Who Killed Homer?*

"Eva Brann's splendid *Homeric Moments* offers the reader forty-eight clues to the delight to be taken in reading—and teaching—the Homeric poems for over fifty years. These clues, presented in a series of intricate vignettes, form an arabesque that allows Brann's reader and the reader of Homer to appreciate the depths of the Homeric *Odyssey* and *Iliad* and, more importantly, the fundamental complementarity of the two poems. The *Odyssey* and Odysseus are, appropriately, the focus of attention, for it is impossible to recognize the intellectual challenge of appreciating the artistry and moral universe of the *Odyssey* and Odysseus without knowing the more austere pleasures of the *Iliad*. This profound meditation on the Homeric epics is beautifully written and enhanced by citations of the poetry of poets who have shared the author's experience of Homeric delights. *Homeric Moments* will provide delight and insight for the reader who has read Homer for fifty years as well as the student who reads the *Odyssey* and the *Iliad* for the first time."

Diskin Clay, Duke University
Author of *Platonic Questions*

ALSO BY EVA BRANN

*Late Geometric and Protoattic Pottery, Mid 8th to
    Late 7th Century B.C.*

Paradoxes of Education in a Republic

The Past-Present

Trilogy of the Human Center

The World of the Imagination: Sum and Substance

What, Then, Is Time?

The Ways of Naysaying: No, Not, Nothing, and Nonbeing

TRANSLATED BY EVA BRANN

Greek Mathematical Thought and the Origin of Algebra
by Jacob Klein (from the German)

Plato's Sophist
(from the Greek, with Peter Kalkavage and Eric Salem)

Plato's Phaedo
(from the Greek, with Peter Kalkavage and Eric Salem)

HOMERIC

CLUES TO DELIGHT IN

AND THE ILIAD

EVA BRANN

PAUL DRY BOOKS

PHILADELPHIA 2002

MOMENTS

READING THE ODYSSEY

First Paul Dry Books Edition, 2002

Paul Dry Books, Inc.
Philadelphia, Pennsylvania
www.pauldrybooks.com

Text type: Sabon
Display type: Lithos
Composed by P. M. Gordon Associates
Designed by Adrianne Onderdonk Dudden

3 5 7 9 8 6 4
Printed in the United States of America

Library of Congress Cataloging-in-Publication Data

Brann, Eva T. H.
    Homeric moments : clues to delight in reading the Odyssey and the Iliad /
Eva Brann. — 1st Paul Dry Books ed.
        p. cm.
Includes bibliographical references.
    ISBN 0-9679675-6-2 (cloth : alk. paper) — ISBN 0-9679675-7-0 (pbk. :
alk. paper)
    1. Homer—Criticism and interpretation. 2. Epic poetry, Greek—
History and criticism. 3. Odysseus (Greek mythology) in literature.
4. Achilles (Greek mythology) in literature. 5. Trojan War—Literature
and the war. 6. Homer. Odyssey. 7. Homer. Iliad. I. Title.
    PA4037 .B64 2002
    883'.01—dc21

                                                                2002006003

ISBN 0-9679675-6-2 (cloth)
ISBN 0-9679675-7-0 (paper)

TO J.S.B.

CONTENTS

PREFACE

I WROTE THIS BOOK because after a half century of reading Homer, both by myself and with students, I was full of small discoveries and large conjectures. I hope that it will draw an audience either of first-time readers who are a little afraid to face Homer directly and would like some clues to approaching his poetry, or of readers who come away from their first reading of Homer with a strong sense that there is much more to the epics than early acquaintance reveals and who would like some help discovering what it might be. The book might also appeal to teachers who want to direct their students to some hidden treasures. It might even find favor with classicists who want to focus on the meaning of the poems rather than on ancillary learning, in order to make new discoveries or to have their wild surmises confirmed. In short, my ideal reader would be one who hopes that Homer might be wonderful in very precise ways and who does not want to be distracted from discovering these by circumstantial scholarship; with that sort of reader this book, which fits no ready-made niche, might find a home.

I shall be focusing on certain crucial and interpretable moments in the *Odyssey*, whose meanings are worked into the poetry by Homer with artful reticence. These moments cast a somber or hilarious or poignant light on the narrative; often they reveal that what transpires overtly is not what is really happening. Quite a few of these highlights are not common knowledge. There are no references to secondary works (though a doubting reader can check assertions from the references to the Homeric texts at the end of the book). For my purposes, the best commentary on the *Odyssey* is the *Iliad*, and the best commentators on both epics are Homer's fellow poets of all ages.

E. B.
Annapolis, Maryland 2002

HOMERIC MOMENTS

CLUES TO DELIGHT IN READING THE ODYSSEY

AND THE ILIAD

ACCOUNTING FOR THE TITLE

Homeric questions and answers
Moments and events
Clues and evidence
Delight and death
Reading and interpretation
Odyssey and *Iliad*

READING HOMER'S POEMS is one of the purest, most inexhaustible pleasures life has to offer—a secret somewhat too well kept in our time. The aim of this book is to tell anyone who might care—first-time, second-time, or third-time readers or people who have not yet laid eyes on the epics—some of the causes and details of that delight.

Why do these details need telling? There are two reasons, one happier than the other. The happier one is that readers like me, who have read Homer and talked about the poems with students and other friends and made hundreds of mental and marginal notes, are naturally bursting with discoveries which it is much less painful to communicate to the world than to hold in. The second reason is that, apart from the sad fact that there are certain prejudices abroad these days against old and great books—those "classics"—just because they are old and great, the approaches that are intended to introduce us to them are sometimes really derailments that deflect our attention from the poems themselves.

The title of this book is meant to announce the keywords for the notions that I want to put in service for Homer. This foreword will therefore be an amplification of the title; readers wanting to get on with it may wish to skip the whole thing and go to any one of the forty-eight little chapters that arouses their interest. For those readers, let me say upfront what my main notion is.

It is that there are two *Odysseys: Odyssey* straight and *Odyssey* cunning. The straight *Odyssey* is full of memorable incident and captivating beauty, but the cunning *Odyssey* is, once you've caught on, the marvel of the ages in its artfulness. Since the Homeric epics have in fact been the marvel of the ages, I am certain that other readers have always known, or at least sensed, the myriad of small revelations I am about to relate, though these readers—early on they were hearers—may not have been the type to make a book of their insights. Consequently, it would perfectly suit my hopes for this book if readers were to poke around in it to find encouragement and corroboration of their own wild surmises.

HOMERIC QUESTIONS AND ANSWERS

We are blessed in knowing almost nothing about the poet called Homer—blessed because we may concentrate on his poetry without distracting ourselves with information the poet himself did not think was relevant to the world he made for us. I would not want to claim that knowing things is not, on the whole, good—on the contrary, I will be implying continually that our whole experience is to be brought to bear on reading the epics—but to serve a good purpose, extraneous information always requires the graceful art of timely forgetting.

The sum of things unknown about Homer is called "the Homeric question." We do not know for sure when Homer lived, or if the name belongs to one man or if each of the two Homeric epics had its own Homer; in antiquity those who believed the latter were called the "Separators." Nor do we know whether each of the epics was composed—it is not known whether in oral or written form—by one poet or whether it was put together by a last collator out of many then current stories or lays; those who believed the latter were called in modern times the "Aggregationists." In fact we have no direct evidence that the author of the *Odyssey*, at least, was a man at all. Samuel Butler claimed in *The Authoress of the Odyssey* (1897), a book which is as perceptive in its reading of the poem as it is ridiculous in its conclusion, that the poet was Nausicaa, the young princess of the Phaeacian fairyland, who is unlike all Odysseus' other women in being just short of womanhood in age and like them in being very keen witted. This claim is like saying that that apotheosis of girlhood, Countess Natasha Rostov, is the authoress of Tolstoy's *War and Peace* because this novel, the modern counterpart of the *Iliad* and the *Odyssey* together, displays a "womanly instinct" in its apprehension of men.

The ancients thought that the war which is the setting, if not the subject, of the *Iliad* ended in 1183 B.C. with the sack of Ilium-Troy and that Homer composed his poems in the ninth or eighth century; moderns put him as late as 700 B.C. In the latter case, since a Greek adaptation of the Semitic alphabet was then coming into use, the poems might have been written down by their poet. In any case, the epics were completed when their events were distant memories, insofar as they were facts at all.

Homer—we do not know if "Homer," which means "Hostage" or "Pledge," was a nickname, and if so, for what he was hostage or to whom he was pledged—may have been born in

Ionia, on the coast of Asia Minor, though in antiquity seven cities claimed him. He was always said to have been blind, an apprehension I will make the most of below (19).*

The reading of the Homeric epics presented in the forty-eight chapters of this book is not helped much by the two and a half thousand years of ingenious speculation on the Homeric question, but it might, quite incidentally, add one more opinion to them. Besides eliciting the significance of Homer's blindness, I will work on the hypothesis that the two epics taken together are tightly complementary and that taken separately each is an intricately tight-woven whole—and this surmise will be fruitful. At a time when the Separators and Aggregators were passionately at work, Goethe wrote a poem equally passionate (though of no great lyrical beauty) called "Homer Against Homer," in which he rebels against the acute-mindedness of those "who liberated us from all reverence / So that we affirmed far too freely / That the *Iliad* is only a patchwork." This present reading is not liberated from all reverence.

Whoever Homer was, we may confidently say this of him: He was not a literary man. He had, I think, never read a book about books, if he ever read a book at all. But he did, evidently, have a long poetic tradition behind him, a tradition largely lost, of lays, legends, folktales, war stories, together with a poetic diction and a prosody, that is, a metric system. It was the heroic hexameter, a line unvaryingly of six feet, composed basically of dactyls, a metrical foot named from *dāktўlŏs*, "finger." For each of them, another type of foot, a spondee (⁻ ⁻) might be substituted; the term signifies a libationary foot, because at libations slow solemn rhythms were in order. The last foot was a spondee or a trochee (⁻ ˘), the "running" foot. Modern readers will take the longs as *stressed*, the shorts as

---

* Numbers in parentheses refer to chapters in the text.

more tripping; in ancient Greek, longs actually had a *duration* double of shorts. Here is the first line of the *Odyssey:*

Ān- dră mŏı | ēn- nĕ- pĕ, | Mōu- să, pŏ- | lў- trŏ- pŏn | hōs mă- lă | pōl- lă.

It is a regular heroic line, in which the fifth foot is normally a dactyl. To have a spondee there indicates some sort of solemn havoc; it is a metric subtlety Homer uses with impressive effect. For example, the *Odyssey* has a villainous, draft-dodging antihero, Aegisthus, who conspires with his mistress, Agamemnon's wife, Clytemnestra, to murder the returning commander in chief of the Trojan expedition. This deed dominates the consciousness of all the "Returns." (The word is capitalized because it is almost a technical term in the *Odyssey* (15).) Hear how heavyheartedly proceeds and ends the line that, early on, concludes the introduction of his baneful name:

hōs ĕ- phăth´ | Hēr- mēı- | ās āll´ | ou phrĕ- năs | Āı- gı- | sthōı- o.

The lines preceding are also heavily spondaic, but none as discombobulatingly so as the ones whose fifth foot is, against ordinary usage, a spondee.

A long oral tradition of hexametric recital would surely prepare a professional poet for wielding a standard line with so much flexibility, and so would the memory training required to hold in mind the twenty-seven thousand eight hundred and two lines of the two epics, later on divided into twenty-four books each. And hold them in mind he did, both he and his audience, for his control of significant detail over thousands of lines is demonstrable (10, 12, 14, 18, 19, 25, 36, 48). In his Latin poem "On the Poetic Art" Horace says in humorously awed censoriousness: "I feel indignant when good Homer nods / But truly in so long a work it is permissible for sleep to creep in." I too am the proud discoverer of more than one such lapse. For example, when Aeneas and Achilles do battle Achilles sends his spear right through Aeneas' shield, which he is holding over his head, so that it fixes itself in the ground behind him; some fifty lines on, a rescuing god draws that same spear out of that same shield. So what?

Homer, then, used the not-so-raw materials of his tradition as Shakespeare used the *Chronicle* of Hollingshed for his history plays and Bach the chorales of his church for his Passions and cantatas, and with these they all worked a sea change into something rich and strange.

But while Homer did not have a literary, that is a written, tradition behind him, he most certainly had one ahead of him, since he himself became the source of literature. For if there actually is a something to be called "literature," aside from a catalogue of belles-lettres, it must manifest itself as a cohesive texture of influences on a literate reader and writer, and there Homer is first in time, first in enduring effect, first in breadth of use, first in force of inspiration. Think not only of Latin and English epic: Virgil's *Aeneid,* which is at once the continuation and the rival of the Homeric epics, and Milton's *Paradise Lost,* which appropriates Homeric heroes to populate Hell. Think also of the multitude of lyric poems—some of which will be called in as aids to interpretation in this book—and of all the stories abstracted from Homer's poetry and absorbed even now as "myth" in prose and pictures. As Whitehead said that all philosophy was a footnote to Plato, so we might say that all Western literature is a footnote to Homer—literature, that is, insofar as it is indeed a tradition.

Homer, then, is first to us, though he was not first to himself. That is the way great traditions seem to work: They are not just smoothly continuous manifestations of excellence but include sudden irruptions of truly miraculous moments which, eclipsing what is behind them, seem like abrupt beginnings.

Thus those wonders of frieze painting found in the caverns of Lascaux were preceded by gifted Neolithic paintings twice their age but nonetheless seem to their modern viewers like primally ultimate exemplars of visual representation, which in their subtle exploitation of the billowing cave walls, the unhesitating perfection of their line, the sophistication of their coloration, the grandeur of their composition, and the sheer "thereness" of their animal figures seem at once the unsurpassable finale and the very beginning of the art of painting. My mind ran to the Rotunda of the Aurochs at Lascaux because the poet Homer seems to me to have had a painter's vision not dissimilar in the sheer presence of his epic shapes (19). But my main point is that Homer seems to be such a sudden peak in the high country of human artistry, one whose poetry rises from the roots provided by nameless poets before him and whose poems are themselves the quarry of all the authored literature thereafter.

I shall, consequently, take "Homer" as the name of the one poet (or of two who were each other's alter ego) who composed the *Iliad* and the *Odyssey.* This point is worth making because it entitles me to suppose that behind the epics there is *one* poetic intention and that clues found far apart in the forty-eight books of both epics were put there by one author, the responsible progenitor, who had in his mind what we may notice. Thus *we* may ask what *he* intended, an approach disallowed by some theorists of literature. But here it will be adopted.

MOMENTS AND EVENTS

The *Iliad* and the *Odyssey* are both extended narratives, long-breathed relations. The *Odyssey* particularly tells of ten years of time passing. We might even say that time passing and how things come to pass in time are its narrative form insofar as Homer makes carefully intricate compositions of temporal sequences and parallelisms (5, 25, 36, 47). So why speak of Homeric *moments?*

I think that Homer's alleged blindness betokens the extraordinary visual acuity of his poetry, the sharply detailed inner visions he constructs for us in words. Such sights of the imagination tend toward a kind of vivid momentariness, a pregnant momentousness. Much later Aristotle will bring into use a word very familiar to us in its modern adaptations: *energeia,* often translated "activity." For us energy is the capacity for being actively at work, but *energeia* is the fulfillment itself of that capacity, expressed not in locomotion but as a kind of vibrant stasis, when any being is fully at work just being itself, being what it was meant to be.

Into the dynamic, temporally flowing narrative of the epics are set these stations of activity, when the tale comes to its fulfillment in a high point, a moment of summary significance. These moments are often primarily visual, in the sense that the words set the scene, and we are responsible for turning their indications and intimations into the picture that shows the meaning. For example, Homer leads us into the scene where Penelope and Odysseus, faithful wife and returning husband, sit face-to-face in private over their own hearth for the first time in twenty years. The manner and mode of their mutual acknowledgment remains unsaid, by them or by Homer, but it is nonetheless *shown* (45), for it is a remarkable fact (and one of the ultimate mysteries of human nature) that words spoken over many passages can converge to concreteness in an internal picture that carries conviction.

Homer, we might say, is self-illustrating. Perhaps it is not altogether mannerly to fix on his high moments—a little like picking the raisins you like out of a cake or the eight measures that ravish you out of a cello sonata. But in truth, these moments are so artfully enmeshed in the surrounding narrative, which leads up to them by hints and then slopes away from them laden with meaning, that attention to them is not really sensation hunting; in any case, they are, intentionally, the foci of this book. Incidentally, not every visual effect is narratively revealing; Homer delights in painting for our simple delectation sharply molded, detailed landscapes and artifacts (18).

And, of course, there are many such moments, when time stops and something becomes manifest, which are purely verbal, when we are meant to hear an arresting, even heart-stopping word-sound. For example, when Achilles mourns his dearest friend, Patroclus, whom he has sent into battle as his surrogate, he cries out: "I have lost him." But the Greek word for "lost" can also be heard thus: "I have *destroyed* him," and as in one of those optical illusions where a figure suddenly shifts meaning, the *Iliad* suddenly emits a more flickering, somber light (10, 26).*

This is the time to reveal a—poorly—hidden agenda of this book: to snaffle at least a few readers into learning Greek. What else, after all, is so important, once livelihood is assured and the family launched and leisure left over? For reading Homer, happily not much is needed. Truth to tell, most of us who learned Greek in college can't really sight-read very competently, so that running over a dozen lines of hexameter is like a toboggan ride: down the chute and you are lucky if you aren't spilled onto the icy bank and arrive at the bottom with only one loosely dragging accusative. But the rush is marvelous, and the rewards of slow reading, of enforced attention to formal detail, helped by any one of the unceasing stream of

---

* All translations of the *Odyssey*, the *Iliad,* and all other works are mine, except where noted. Sometimes I have translated the same line in different ways to bring out particular meanings.

fine translations, each of which preserves different features of the original, are really great.* I will not hesitate to draw the reader's attention to Homer's Greek when he does something wonderful with it, but always in transliteration and with a translation.

It hardly needs saying that, the word "moment" having numerous significations, I'll be using it for Homeric moments other than those just delineated, such as "in Homer's epics even the most minor characters have their moments of distinction" or "the levity of the Homeric gods is of great moment to the gravity of men."

CLUES AND EVIDENCE

From the fact that there is a unifying intelligence of enormous memorial capacity informing the poems comes a certain confident alertness to clues and cues: clues that lead to the story behind the story, cues that signal some strange business about to go on.

There is a convenient notion going around that an ingenious professional reader may say almost anything, may play any half-plausible riff off the text, improvise brilliantly way beyond the poet's provable intention, because that text has in fact floated free of its maker and an authorial intention is indiscernible in principle. The Greek word for a "maker" is *poietes,* and what is being denied in this postmodern mode is that poems are by poets. The gist of my approach will be as follows:

---

* There is something to be said for learning Greek quite apart from the reading of authors. My father, a physician who was educated in a German classical gymnasium, cherished the following story: His Greek professor, bidding goodbye to a student being withdrawn by his father for a business apprenticeship, was heard to say sorrowfully: "What a pity he couldn't stay for the irregular verbs! One more month and he'd have had something to sustain him in life."

While the poet's specific personal circumstances are neither here nor there, it is a reasonable faith that there is a responsible author, a maker, who leaves an inexhaustible wealth of intentional small signs *meant* to be picked up by any reader as evidence *from* the lines of what is being said *beyond* and between the lines. These intimating clues take the form not only of metric anomalies, signifying visualizations, and double meanings already exemplified, but also of apparently misapplied epithets (21), homonyms, that is, words having the same sound but different meanings (35), suggestive descriptions (24), and dozens of other devices, but, above all, of pregnant silences and significant omissions. For example, never till the very end of the *Odyssey* is a fact explicitly mentioned that casts a darkish light over Odysseus' Return: that the wooers who are beleaguering his son and wife are the children of a generation of Ithacans whom Odysseus has deployed into oblivion (26, 43).

My reverent faith in the poet Homer is not, I hasten to say, some antecedent stance or, God forbid, a literary theory. It is rather a consequence of reading the poems, sprung from the fact that there seems to be no end of telling particulars that ask to be listened to, that the text seems to be teeming with yet more indices at every fresh reading, so that an ardent and trusting attention to this poet of poets is continually rewarded, and discoveries seem minimally subjective and even demonstrable. Let me put it this way: If I were, by a fate beyond my deserts, translated to the Elysian Fields, there to be admitted to conversation with the Immortals (as Plato's Socrates hoped to be and Swift's Gulliver in fact was), and if I there heard Homer discourse so as to show him a simpler man than I thought and my readings to be mere inventions, I would be not only sadly deflated but *very* surprised.

It is, then, my sense of Homer's inexhaustibility that encourages me to take up once again preoccupations that have filled libraries with books for ages and filing cabinets with articles for centuries, and to find the thought of all that unread material not burdensome but buoyant. It bears saying twice, too, that I cannot believe that the discoveries made explicit here haven't been apprehended implicitly by Homer lovers through the millennia and that many others haven't been captivated by the sense that there is more going on than meets the word-reading eye.

The evidence being in the lines, the references for each claim are given at the end of the book for the suspicious to check out and the persuaded to follow up—for, of course, I am anxious for these pages to lead their readers back to Homer's poems.

DELIGHT AND DEATH

In mathematics a postulate is a proposition the student is asked to agree with whether or not it seems quite self-evident —else nothing can go forward. Let me say then that the possibility of pleasure to be gotten from reading the epics is my second postulate (the first being the requirement of attentive trust in the text). I want to call the pleasure peculiar to reading Homer "delight." Candor requires me to admit that it is with the reading of Homer as with all the other self-endorsing pleasures of life—those, that is, in which genuine enjoyment is attended by a sense of self-approval: we do not do most incessantly what we are most pleased with ourselves for being pleased by, and many easier books get read before Homer is taken up once again—but then always with an acute sense of homecoming.

Nevertheless this epic pleasure, like tragic pleasure, poses a problem—a problem felt, I think, by all readers who really give themselves over to the experience. The *Iliad* is a book of battles; long stretches in its early, middle, and final phases consist of nothing but one death or wounding, one pitiless killing and graphic piercing of eye, gullet, chest, and bowel after the other. And there are deaths out of battle, like the sacrificial manslaughter of the twelve Trojan boys by an Achilles beside himself with raging grief for his dead friend Patroclus.

Homer, to be sure, does everything a poet can do to make these horrors palatable. The surfeit of killing is perhaps mitigated by the fact that each recital is a remembrance: that this dead warrior has his name, ancestry, place of origin, and manner of armament forever set in the greatest of all war poems, which is thus also a tremendous war memorial. There are few mass carnages; most battles are single combat in which two "forefighters" (*promachoi*), often nobodies never heard of before or after, emerge from the troops, sometimes racing forward on chariots, and stand forth, like sudden coagulations of warriorhood, briefly here and now:

> And, as imagination bodies forth
> The forms of things unknown, the poet's pen
> Turns them to shapes, and gives to airy nothings
> A local habitation and a name.

The most beautiful similes are, moreover, reserved for this deadly combat—and the most poignant ones. There is, for example, one Gorgythion, an undistinguished youngster, a side-son of Priam, King of Troy, who is hit in the chest by an arrow meant for Hector, Priam's best son:

> And like a poppy he let fall his head to one side, a poppy that
>   is in a garden,
> Laden with fruit and the showers of spring,
> So he bowed to one side his head made heavy with helmet.

Behind almost every battle or casualty Homer puts a relieving picture of peace or nature (20).

It helps, but not enough. To attend to all the gore is gruesome, but not to attend puts the reader in the false situation of being bored by fatalities. Aristotle, a keen literary critic, says outright that the *Iliad* is simple and concerns suffering, while the *Odyssey* is complex and concerns character, and that is certainly a summary of the reasons this book is more about the *Odyssey* than the *Iliad*.

But the *Odyssey* too has its share of brutality that casts a grimly dark light on its perpetrators. Its first ending—like a Beethoven symphony this poem has concluding climax upon concluding climax (14)—relates the great, unforgiving slaughter of Penelope's wooers and the mass hanging of the faithless serving women. Before that dozens of sailors are eaten by monsters and swallowed by the sea. And although these deaths are perhaps not meant to have much gravity, there is no evading the fact that what would be plain bad in life—to hear of death nonchalantly or with pleasure—falls under the postulate of pleasure in reading epic. I think that fact can cease to be a perplexity only when poetry ceases to be wholeheartedly experienced. So when in Plato's *Republic* Socrates bans the poets, and Homer in particular, from his political community for making what ought to be excruciating to an audience pleasant to it, he does so not because he is deaf to poetry but because he is alive to it. He is only facing squarely *the* ethical problem of the arts: the surreptitious pleasure of representational excruciation, the inherent sadism of esthetic contemplation.

It does not really resolve the perplexity—it only states it— to say that while it is the part of a citizen of life to intervene by action, it belongs to a reader of fiction to be a very attentive bystander; that dictum just defines what is called the "esthetic pleasure," the pleasure that is the problem. There are, however, different kinds of esthetic pleasure. In the broadest sense it is the encompassing delight in imitation itself: "For we delight in contemplating accurate images of disgusting beasts and corpses, which are themselves painful to see," says Aristotle. He explains the reason—there is pleasure, the pleasure of learning, just in recognizing a likeness: I *know* the man Odysseus. It may be a true but it is also a dangerous doctrine that every decoding of a representation is a learning experience: it gives license to every kind of image viewing. Special among the pleasures of imitation watching is the "tragic pleasure" which Aristotle is deeply interested in delineating; it is that famous "purification of affections through pity and fear."

This exoneration of esthetic pleasure as a kind of learning, and of tragic pleasure in particular as a kind of cleansing of the passions, is an answer to Socrates who thinks that, on the contrary, by such engagement with imitations our passions are excited to excess, and we are incited to passionate conduct. Homer is for Socrates, who has from childhood on loved and reverenced him, "the leader (*hegemon*) of all those beautiful tragedians" and so to be regarded as responsible for the tragic dramas that put before us living imitations of terrifying events. And in fact, the epics contain within themselves all the chief tragic plots; for example, of Oedipus who married his mother, of Ajax who committed suicide (6), and above all, of Agamemnon whose murder (or execution) by his wife, Clytemnestra, looms behind the *Odyssey;* the epics are the treasure house of tragic myth (32).

Aristotle tacitly protests this lumping together of tragic and epic pleasure. And indeed, nothing defines the epic mode better than to contrast it with tragedy. Tragedy is in the present tense, spoken by impersonating actors; it is fast-paced, taking place, by a very apt Greek convention, within one day; it is tightly focused on one action, and it usually ends in the hero's death, preceded by excruciating events and dramatically drawn out reverses and recognitions.

Although Aristotle does not work out the pleasure proper to epic (since he thinks tragedy the better genre), its modes and tempos and its specific pleasure can be delineated by contrast. To begin with, epic is told in the past tense and not enacted; it is long-breathed and can encompass a decade and narrate events twenty or a hundred years distant, and its wide focus encompasses the known earth and beyond. In neither of the Homeric epics does the chief protagonist die, and tension does not gather toward a late recognition and reversal, but something much more subtle is afoot (45). Whoever needs a plot driving straight to a denouement will not be able to tolerate epic, which requires not so much a patient as a laid-back listener. The ample telling of the tale, that Homeric time-taking (47), not only affects the reader but also the people of the epic. Tragic heroes tend to undergo sudden catastrophic shifts of fortune—their fate—which leave them transformed but also dead; Odysseus, at least, undergoes a multitude of experiences, vicissitudes that leave him more like himself than ever and very much alive.

The pleasure is correspondingly different. Tragedy may effect a purification of the passions, but the pity and fear will tend to induce grave and dark ponderings, whereas epic calls for nimble and delicious discovery. Tragedy is brief, forceful, close-up, dramatic—"drastic" one might say; epic is extended, insinuating, wide viewed—contemplative in the sense of expansive viewing. Epic-telling—the word "epic" is the adjective from *epos*, the "uttered word," thence the "told tale"—is leisurely yet incident laden, wide-ranging yet purposeful, objective yet feeling-laden, stately yet immediate. Of the Homeric poems, Wordsworth's definition of poetry seems to me fairly accurate: Poetry is "the spontaneous overflow of powerful feelings; it takes its origin from emotion recollected in tranquility." While acted tragedy has what we call a "dramatic" impact (*drama* being the Greek word for "deed"), epic, which has only told words, possesses a counter-quality I think of as absorbability, the slowly emergent, detailed, inward refiguring of an event. The slow past-tense telling of epic makes its people and passions and places and artifacts at once more distant and more particularizingly vivid. Epic delight is at once more serene and more sensory than tragic pleasure and thus just a little less questionable than tragic pleasure—perhaps.

The word delight fits that pleasure because it carries in itself two meanings, lightness and deliciousness. They may not seem to apply altogether to the *Iliad*—though they surely do to everything in that poem that is not battle—but they do catch what seems to me the most characteristic feel of reading Homer, the one the postulate of pleasure in the poems specifically intends: the delight given by the lightness of being, manifest above all in the gods, who are light to the point of levity (1), as well as the piquancy of appearance incarnate in the singer whose blindness betokens a heightened acuity of imaginative vision.

READING AND INTERPRETATION

Besides telling some of the delightful discoveries any well-disposed reader can make in the epics, I would like, really incidentally, to demonstrate a way of reading the epics that will, I think, make more such things reveal themselves. "A way of reading" is not quite the same as what critics call "a reading," that is, a total interpretative hypothesis, but rather the aforementioned mood of trusting expectation, a receptivity to the poet's signals, and a reliance on all our own life and learning. Although these words are being written in mid-winter the mood is exactly this:

> The house was quiet and the world was calm.
> The reader became the book; and the summer night
>
> Was like the conscious being of the book.
> The house was quiet and the world was calm.
>
> The words were spoken as if there was no book,
> Except that the reader leaned above the pages,
>
> Wanted to lean, wanted much most to be
> The scholar to whom his book is true, . . .

The axiom behind such reading, the rather minimal, though by no means uncontroversial working hypothesis, is that the poet made a world that we are authorized to enter and enabled to inhabit by the mere title of our humanity; for all the lands of the imagination live in a territorial union that imposes no passport checks or import duties on the traveler. Less fancifully: If you're human, Homer is home territory.

That could be said of all poetry of stature, but it holds with special force for the Homeric epics. Homer is the most interactive poet imaginable, who nonetheless requires of his readers—it used to be listeners—nothing more than that they be all there. I am about to give a list of obstacles, of distractions in the way of mere attention that, invented with the best of intentions, prevent access to the poetry. Not everyone will be interested in this sorry disquisition, so skipping is encouraged.

Before being caught up in Homeric ways, some readers will be put off by the occasional cumbrous stateliness of Homeric diction. A hero will say: "What word has escaped the fence of your teeth?" where we would say "Why didn't you keep your mouth shut?" Or the poet will say "When they had put from themselves the desire for food and drink . . ." (usually after a meal of shish kebab, bread, and wine, prepared in front of our eyes by the heroes themselves), where we would say: "When they were full . . ." One gets used to these graphic and noble formulas, however, and ends up wondering why we can't talk like that. But then it may be that no one ever did say these things, for Homer's language is an art language, like Milton's —the natural language of his imaginative realm: "Heroic spoken here." In any case, these heroes have no difficulty in descending to ordinary fishwifery; they are splendid pilers-on of insult: "You sodden with wine, who have the face of a dog and the heart of a deer, . . . you people-eating king who lords it over nobodies," says Achilles to his commander in chief. They can produce the most irreverent hilarity; the singer Demodocus—his name means "People-Enchanter"—tells a tale Homer himself might be above repeating, which gives a graphic account of one of the funniest mishaps ever to befall a pair of adulterous divinities, who are quite literally caught in the act (8). Homer is, to be sure, constrained by the stately tread of his heroic meter, but this constraint makes for a wonderfully throwaway deadpan humor, as when old Nestor, that inveterate giver of superfluous advice, instructs his young son in the tricks of chariot racing "as one knowing to one who well knows it." This heroic hexameter is also capable of presenting a slice of purely ordinary life, as when the great Achilles is reminded in dactyls by his godfather of how as a toddler he used to dribble wine on the old man's shirt.

Winckelmann, who founded the study of Greek art and with it esthetic philhellenism, coined a famous capsule characterization of Greek masterworks of sculpture and writing: "noble naiveté, silent grandeur." It is one of those delineations that are very true from afar and begin to fade close up: Homer *is* simple and grand at a certain distance, but get into the detail and he becomes very sophisticated and *very* human; those heroes are anything but stiff exemplars of splendid idiocy and glorious infantilism.

As Homer's stateliness should not stand in the way of our engagement, neither should a certain stuffiness in his interpreters. It has a very respectable origin and is very old. Readers have evidently always had the sense of Homeric wisdom and have tried to turn Homer into a crypto-philosopher and the poems into theological allegory.

For those who prefer to get something *out* of Homer to reading things *into* him, another course seems better to me: to acknowledge what was anciently called "that old quarrel between philosophy and poetry" first openly articulated by Socrates, but first engaged in, implicitly though unmistakably, by Parmenides. As Homer of infinite variety is the first poet for us, so single-minded Parmenides is the first philosopher, the first annunciator of the one and only Being that is the chief preoccupation of philosophy. He wrote perhaps two and a half centuries after Homer but in his style: a poem in dactylic hexameter, brief where the epics are long, having as its hero the writer, where the Homeric epics are anonymous. And he is in almost every way the intended opposite of Odysseus. Like Odysseus' Return, Parmenides' Way is guided by female divinities, but there the two diverge; while Odysseus, a mature man of many thoughts and many stories, meanders home collecting experience and material treasures on his way, Parmenides is a youth who takes a wild ride right into the heart and house of Truth where one thought overwhelms all multiplicity and ends all speech, and it is this unspeakable treasure,

Being, that he is bidden to take back with him. It is the opposition between the poet's scintillating sensory particulars and the philosopher's illuminated intelligible oneness that these poems exemplify.

It seems to me quite natural that people passionately devoted to philosophy, to a unifying intelligibility beyond and its reflected wisdom within the world, should try to capture Homer for this august enterprise by finding philosophemes and political proto-theory in the poems. I have no doubt that they do contain them, but embodied and contingent, as life contains them, so that we are as welcome to construe Homer as we do the world. But that he meant his poems to contain covert systematic lessons to be laboriously inferred and pedantically formulated—that I doubt: sufficient unto the lay is the subtlety thereof.

Of course there is wisdom to be gathered from the epics, for Homer makes a world for us to enter which is a condensed, heightened, extreme, ideal version of our own and made to yield meaning in ours. Homer's world contains the encampments of war and their strains, civil communities and their crimes, gods and their fateful antics, demigods and their entangling spells, and above all men and women and their antagonistic mutualities. Moreover, the beings of the epics, divine or human, are exuberantly judgmental; they have a large vocabulary, both abstract and adjectival, for virtues and vices, for example: gentlemindedness, thoughtfulness, presence of mind, soundmindedness, kindliness, and their opposites.

So it does seem to me that each of the two epics contains an overarching wisdom for meditation, and why not state it here? The *Iliad* shows a harsh truth about human wishing and willing as expressed in the prayer of Achilles and the plan of Zeus (13), the human intention and the divine realization that are the supporting arcs of the *Iliad*'s incidents: The god grants the prayer and inflects the wish through his own impenetrable purpose. Achilles learns that we may accomplish our will and get what we least wished. The *Odyssey* raises looser meditations on the enigma of Return: how the ardently focussed wish to come home is nevertheless deflected by a diverting desire to wander, gathering goods material and immaterial, and how Home tries and rewards the circuitous Returner.

Both Homer's stateliness and the occasional interpreter's stuffiness are hindrances easily overcome, even turned to good account. But there is a veritable Cerberus, that triple-headed guard dog of the underworld, set over the epics to make them inaccessible—a notional threesome that may go by the names "mentality," "formulaicism," and "intratextuality." Let me explain these ungainly terms and how they function.

1 *Mentality*. Homer's heroes are said to have a "mentality." I would not wish to have a mentality, a mind-set, imputed to me, and I imagine you too as having not a mind-set but thoughts, thoughts spontaneous enough so that I can never second-guess them. No more can we second-guess those vividly ambivalent heroes of Homer. To be sure, since their sayings and deeds are written out, by the second reading we know what they in fact will say and do, but that's just the trivial fact of the fixed past; Homer shows often that he thinks they could have done otherwise, that the characters of epic can act spectacularly out of character or from a deeper nature. I might go so far in riddling speech as to say that it is in their character to go out of character: Aging Helen, for example, still has surprises up her sleeve (24).

There are, of course, good reasons to speak of a Homeric mentality, often an "archaic," that is, an early, not to say primitive one. The Homeric world is considerably different in its circumstances from ours, and introductions to the poems tend to make heavy weather of these differences: The gods mingle with humans, some men are kings and others serfs, women belong to men, all the appurtenances of culture are handmade, and glory is on every hero's mind. But since readers could not possibly miss these facts of Homer's world, they need help not in dwelling on its differences but in entering into it.

And that is an entirely achievable goal: The Athenians, who first established and introduced into their ceremonies a canonical text of the epics, regarded Homer as the universal educator of Greece even when the age of kings was long gone, their politics were democratic, chivalry was a distant memory, and the gods were no longer seen among humans. And Homer himself was twice as far away in time from the world of the Trojan War—a world that he brings to a more brilliant life than it may ever have had in fact—as these Athenians were from his time. You really have to be temporally parochial to feel that we in turn are so very distant from those Athenians who gave us the two words that govern our lives: democracy and technology.

But all those grave cogitations would not count for much were it not that on closer reading almost all the social and personal relations some scholars are so bent on finding alien did not grow more and more familiar: Odysseus is, to be sure, a king, and what we might call a conservative, who despises that ill-favored and low-bred incendiary Thersites (5). But he repossesses his island realm with the aid of a swineherd and a ranch hand, whom he regards, out of gratitude and plain feeling, as sons; his relations with women could not be more complex were they the invention of a contemporary novelist, and his wife is his one and only mortal equal (42). Primitive!

Even the gear that forms life's background is not so much beyond our ken: a fully suited-up fullback breaking through the line of scrimmage, ball in hand, to run into a tackle is surely no less weird to the equitable eye than a fully armed Greek forefighter in front of the line of battle leaping off his chariot to fight a duel with spear and sword (19). Nor are we less attached to the giving and getting of proudly possessable objects of beautiful craftsmanship; witness the gift counter of any department store.

The gods are *the* enigmas in reading Homer (1), but glory- and prize-seeking (28) are immediately comprehensible. Almost invariably freshmen discussing Homer are fixated particularly on Achilles—whom they tend to think of as much younger than he actually is (7)—and what mystifies them is only this: what they themselves are required to mask, their thirst for recognition, this hero of heroes is allowed to make the center of a terrific personal drama. As for the prize seeking, let a few years pass for these youngsters, and that too will become perfectly comprehensible. Then again, to complicate the matter, there is, once more, Odysseus, who announces himself as one whose fame reaches heaven, but who willingly goes into a secluded realm where he is out of sight and out of hearing for a decade (29).

All this would hardly need saying were it not a serious theoretical claim that other societies and eras do have different mentalities, mind-sets ultimately incommensurable with ours. These inaccessible worldviews are not to be contradicted by flamboyant examples of empathy such as I have given, for these might be illusory superficialities (though it is a source of comfort that the proponents of ultimate otherness often supply a vivid description of the "inarticulable" differences).

This "mentality," an archaic mentality for instance, descends to individuals from their time and their society. (How time and society come by such a mentality, if not from individual human beings thinking, is a yet-higher-order problem.)

It is therefore presented as inescapable for them and inaccessible to us, radically so. Since this is a dismal theory under whose aegis to read an ancient text, I offer this modest resolution: Let it be granted that the Homeric world is full of conditions and objects very different from those of our world. It would follow that Homer's people *think about different things, not that they think differently.* A leisured teenager in America might think about a souped up hotrod, and a young prince of Ithaca might care about a well-wrought chariot, and the differences between car and chariot carry a myriad of implications, but if we have some empathy for the dreams of the one, we will understand the hopes of the other. They do not think differently, if by that we mean "think in an alien mode." Truth to tell, since it is in principle impossible for me to ascertain what the object of such thinking might be, because the matter of thought becomes indeterminate when the mode is incommensurable with mine, there couldn't be much profit in reading anything that wasn't in time and space right next to me. So the hypothesis of "mentality" will be avoided in the chapters to come, and every Homeric being will be expected to display the spontaneity proper to an individual and the intelligibility expected of a human being.

2 *Formulaicism.* The most widely accepted interpretative theory for several generations has been this: A good proportion of the epics is composed of building blocks, the memory stock of oral poets. These blocks may be whole passages or single lines that are repeated, but more often they are epithets, descriptive tags attached to names such as "Achilles, swift of foot" (. . . pŏ- dăs | ō- kўs Ă- | chīl- lēus) and "Odysseus of many designs" (. ‾ . pŏ- lў- | mē- tĭs Ŏ- | dŷs- sēus). They can be seen to fit neatly into the last part of the dactylic hexameter and can be used routinely with others that fit elsewhere to

ease the strain on the orally composing poet. To be a professional singer would be to have a large supply of such tags
handy and not to scruple to repeat passages just to get twice
the run for the honorarium.

There is no denying that there is repetition in the epics,
though not enough to produce a sense of hearing the same
thing over and over. Some of the long, repeated passages are
repetitions of messages. We hear the original message and its
delivery. The point is that the delivered message usually contains some minute but poignantly significant alteration. Whoever listens will hear something wonderfully new. For example, our Odysseus, the universal ambassador, delivers to an
angry Achilles a not-altogether-well-conceived message from
his commander in chief, Agamemnon, who has deprived him
quite gracelessly of his prize and its glory. Odysseus repeats the
message accurately as given—with a tiny graceful courtesy
stuck in at a particularly delicate part: "my lord," delivered
no doubt with a courtly obeisance. Greek audiences into classical times, the era of Athenian drama, seem to have had a phe-
nomenally fine ear; if I can see it, surely they could hear it.

The nametags, called epithets (21), are undeniably sometimes routine. In particular there is an epithet that occurs over
a hundred times in the *Odyssey*; it is translated anywhere
from "divine" through "brilliant" to "goodly," and applied to
anyone and everything because it is so usable a metric frag-
ment. Right in the beginning, Aegisthus, the hobgoblin of the
Odyssey, is unfavorably recalled by Zeus, but given the epithet "blameless," which not even my ready trust in Homer's
acuteness can bring itself to read as irony; it's just a metrically
convenient, denotatively inept adjective.

But far more often, apparent inappropriateness—howlers
evidently born of Homeric nodding—turns out to be subtly
perfect. Here is an example from a great scene in the *Iliad,* the

above-mentioned embassy to Achilles, who is sitting before his tent, sullenly *hors de combat,* out of the public eye but face-to-face with the friend he will soon send to his death, singing to the lyre of mortal fame. The delegation arrives; Achilles, surprised by their coming, jumps up, lyre in hand, to greet them. So doing, he is called "swift-footed"—surely not for his gesture of amazement. The proponents of formulaic composition might cite this as a case of ineptitude, but in fact it is Homer at his most adept.

Let me again call Aristotle to aid. He invented a term for that culminating completion in which a being is what it was meant to be: "Held-in [the timeless moment of its own] fulfillment": *entelecheia.* The usual translation is "actuality." He distinguished a first and a second such actuality. Feet may be actually swiftly moving, but this runner's actuality is only second to a primary one: whether sitting, lyre in hand, or rising in greeting, Achilles *is* a swift-footed runner; it is his very nature to be swift, swift footed and swift fated, whatever he might "actually" be doing (7).

So as an interpretative theory, formulaicism is a hindrance to attentive reading. It has had this effect on some translations that omit epithets at will, so readers cannot even judge whether they are missing something delightful.

3 *Intratextuality.* This formidable term belongs to literary theory and means that compositions of words are not about the world but about themselves, that words refer only to other words of the text, so that the text is its own world and is the only world of poetry—the poet's characters cannot cast loose from his words. Thus a responsible reading should not reach beyond the words to any actual being denoted by them and displaying occasionally a certain independent originating power and solidity, the kind called "subsistence" by philosophers: a determinate, consistent, stable way of being. In other words, the reader is to stay within the text and not to speculate that the author *meant* to be talking *about* that person or that place, and not to round out the text by the auditory and visual imagination. In consequence of this theory fictions are "radically incomplete," a logical phrase which means merely that you can't answer most questions about the characters of the fiction because the author doesn't give the information and there is no being beyond the words to appeal to. Thus, if you ask the text what is the color of Odysseus' hair, the answer is auburn, tawny, reddish gold, because the text says so in a word, but if you ask the color of his eyes, there is no answer; we know only that they were beautiful. And yet I have a sense, amounting to conviction, that I do know the color of his eyes. Similarly, the ancients and their modern successors have liked to think that they might ask just what song the Sirens sang to passing sailors that would be so dangerous for Odysseus to hear. But that would, on the intratextual hypothesis, be a proscribed question, and yet the very one to which an engaged reader might have a plausible answer (33).

Such readings of the word without a world—denatured readings one might call them—often lead, oddly enough, to irresponsibly inventive, witty word construals, at odds with the postulate of trust that a great poem should be in at least one respect treated as sacred text: insofar as the reader tries to be no more than the faithful servitor of the poem, the eager discoverer of the poet's intention rather than the proud inventor of unintended linguistic windfalls. Reference to a coherently imaginable "extratextual" world seems to be both a better warrant for the feasibility and a better control on the plausibility of an interpretation than staying within the verbal texture. I don't deny that there are works whose fictional beings are woven into a background tapestry of scenes and situations, beings that take their character from the web of relations which delineate them—flat creatures intended to be serviceable to a plot and so well bonded into the texture of the text that they have no independent life. But Homer, though he may well have inherited story lines, takes his departure from the people, who spin their tale out of their natures—the scenes, settings, even the artifacts, emanate *from them*. In the *Odyssey* this description becomes spectacularly true when Odysseus becomes the weaver of a fairyland that is an externalization of his own soul (39).

There is a fact specific to the epic against such a self-confining approach of reading words without their world. Homer *himself* thinks that he is telling the tales *of* a passion, the anger of Achilles, and *of* a man, the wanderer Odysseus, and that these come to him through the Muse who sings for him of the people and of the events known among the gods (16). Thence comes the fact that Alexander, who wanted to reincarnate Achilles but lacked a Homeric Muse, merely conquered the world for a moment, while his avatar Achilles captivated the ages (7).

Hence I shall write of the epics as of a finite number of words telling of an indefinitely large world.

ODYSSEY AND ILIAD

Early death and a young warrior's baneful attempt to deflect it is the theme of the *Iliad* (10), and battle deaths have a grim grandeur that makes the intervening moments of life all the more poignant. Long life, its multiplicitous experiences, and its single-minded purpose are the theme of the *Odyssey*. The brief life of deathbound young heroes is more glorious than the extended life span of aging survivors, but the latter is a lot more interesting. To me, at least, the vicissitudes of the *Odyssey* are more involving than the grandeur of the *Iliad*. To put it another way: The *Odyssey* more reliably rewards the noticing attention, and noticing is the working mode of trustful reading.

Longinus, after Aristotle the best-known critic in antiquity, thought that Homer composed the *Odyssey* in his old age, not just because it is an epilogue to the *Iliad*, but because it is in old age that poets become lovers of confabulation, the telling of fantasies and myths (*to philomython*). What he says is borne out by Shakespeare, whose late plays, for example *Cymbeline, The Winter's Tale,* and *The Tempest,* are works of sophisticated fancy. It is also true that *Iliad* and *Odyssey* belong together as War and Peace: Ten years of war before the Trojan gates has hatched in the young warrior Achilles the anger that bursts out in the *Iliad;* ten years of voyaging home have prepared for the returning veteran Odysseus the situation he meets in Ithaca. The first circumstance might account for the far more straightforward telling of the *Iliad*, compared to the complex composition of the *Odyssey* (25, 36); the second means that the *Iliad* and its aftermath are, so to speak, contained in the *Odyssey*. Not only is the memory of the great and costly expedition, launched for so unworthy a cause and concluded with so trifling a gain, on the minds of the humans and divinities of the *Odyssey;* the soul-stirring events that occurred between the *Iliad* and the Return of Odysseus are artfully insinuated into the *Odyssey:* the death and funeral of Achilles (31), the capture of Troy by means of the Trojan Horse (35), the suicide of Ajax (6), the fatal Return of Agamemnon (30). (These events are expanded on in the post-Homeric poems called the "Epic Cycle.") Aristotle thought that Homer was "divinely inspired" in not attempting to make the *Iliad* into a poem of the whole war, for the multitude of incidents would have robbed the poem of its monumental unity. But he could not say that of the *Odyssey*, which is the compensating catchall, a tightly woven container of the whole war as it is relived in the memories of wives, veterans, and singers.

Moreover, while the *Iliad* is Achilles' poem, the record of a terrific tantrum and its fatalities, and the *Odyssey* is in name and fact Odysseus' poem, relating the veteran's circuitous and perilous Return, the figure of dead Achilles is an animating principle, a latent presence, and, so to speak, the hidden armature of the *Odyssey;* he appears implicitly in its first lines (14), overtly at its dead center and gloriously at its end (31), and, again, implicitly everywhere as Odysseus' opposite (7). We might well read the *Iliad* without knowing the *Odyssey*, but to read the *Odyssey* without reference to the *Iliad* would be to read under a handicap, for one defining aspect of the second poem's protagonist, the tardy homecomer, is that he is the incarnate antithesis of the prematurely culminating young warrior. Where Achilles is short lived, swift-fated, and swift-footed, Odysseus will grow old, endure heavy vicissitudes, see his runner's legs go through wear and tear, and reach his great moment in late middle age; Achilles has one man as bosom friend while Odysseus is befriended by a series of women, young and not young, human and divine; Achilles is, in his own estimation, a man of truth while Odysseus is a proudly accomplished liar (10, 38). All in all, Achilles is a blazingly prodigious being while Odysseus is just an interesting man—though perhaps the most interesting man ever to get into a poem.

The epics surely mirror their protagonists' nature, the one marching forward over a few weeks, grandly, simply, and inexorably (5) to Hector's death and Achilles' end, the other meandering slowly and expansively, over ten years of artfully involuted time toward Odysseus' recovery of Ithaca and Penelope.

The *Odyssey* is therefore a work complex in its very conception: at once a self-contained poem *and* a complement to
its predecessor. For that and all the reasons given above, I concentrate on the *Odyssey* but refer continually to the *Iliad*.

Aristotle says:

> In drama episodes are abbreviated, but it is through them that
> epic poetry gains its length. The story (*logos*) of the *Odyssey* is
> not long. A certain man has been away from home for many
> years, he is stalked by Poseidon and is alone. Furthermore the sit-
> uation in his house is that his wealth is being spent by wooers and
> his son is plotted against. After being storm-tossed he arrives, re-
> veals who he is and, attacking his enemies, saves himself and de-
> stroys them. That, then, is the story proper, the rest is episodes.

In the chapters to follow, I will recall just enough of the
"story," the plainsong, as it were, of the *Odyssey*, as is needed
to sustain the contrapuntal voices, those "episodes," the Homeric moments.

1

THE GODS

I HAVE TO BEGIN WITH THE GODS because *they* are the apparently insuperable bar to entering the Homeric world. Did the gods once mingle with humankind, or is Homer a visionary madman, or, what is worse, a mere poet, a maker-up of beautiful falsities, an elegant liar? I shall grapple with that perplexity, only to emerge as I went in, in a cloud of unknowing, if perhaps a little the wiser.

In all matters requiring merely human ingenuity we and the inhabitants of the epic world are similarly endowed with "skill" (*techne*) and with devices—Odysseus, particularly, is the man "of many devices" (*polymechanos*); you will recognize in the ancestral Greek our "technique" and "machine." But in one respect they appear to have had an advantage over us. They had the gods to help and harass them. The reader of the epics may come away believing that to be so stalked—in Aristotle's term—from on high, as Odysseus was by Poseidon, is a grander and more bearable lot than to be left severely alone to cope with mere misfortune. I am taking it as given here that in our world the gods are gone from the scene—to the relief of the rationalists and the sorrow of the poets:

> But, o Friend, we come too late. True, the gods are alive
> But over our heads, beyond in another world.

. . . .
For not always may so weak a vessel contain them,
Only from time to time can a human bear the divine
repleteness.
. . . . . . Meanwhile I often surmise
That it is better to sleep than to be so without companions,
So to wait; and what to do meanwhile and to say
I know not, nor to what purpose a poet in indigent times?

Hölderlin's lament seems to me straight and genuine, and I too
do not mean to engage in bad faith romanticism when I reject
two current ways of dealing with the Homeric embarrassment: either to consider the gods as the superseded objects of
the simple-minded heroes' archaic faith or as the sophisticat-
edly agnostic Homer's poetic devices. Both of these evasions
require that famous "willing suspension of disbelief for the
moment, which constitutes poetic faith," whereas my postulate of trust demands a frame of mind not of studiedly can-
celled skepticism but of spontaneous initial receptivity.

The mode of belief or disbelief is in fact quite misapplied
here. The Homeric gods are not "believed in." The single God
of the other Western tradition is, as his Book says, indeed the
object of a strenuous and difficult faith: He is wroth with Is-
rael "because they believed not in God and trusted not in his
salvation," and in particular because they slip from the belief
and knowledge "that I am He: before me there was no God
formed, neither shall there be after me." And this faith is "the
substance of things hoped for, the evidence of things not seen."
Faith in a God who exists, is one, alone saves, and is invisible
to the eye is a task to be achieved and a test to be passed.

No one in the Homeric epics ever evinces the slightest interest in urging the existence of the gods, in insisting that one
god is *the* god, or in claiming that there is an inherently in-
visible deity. No one shows any inclination to disbelieve in the

gods because no one believes *in* them. They are simply presences, whose absence is a felt lack.

There is a hierarchy, to be sure. There are the three great brothers who have by lot divided the domain of the world. Zeus holds the heaven and rules the house of Olympus. He could, if he would, bind all the earth and sea by a golden chain to a peak of Olympus, so much, he says, "am I beyond gods and am I beyond men." Hades holds the House of Hades, the murky darkness at the margins and also beneath earth. Poseidon, who has won the sea, claims that earth and Olympus are common domain; he is a resentful god whose persecution of Odysseus is an obscure reflection of his resentment against Zeus.

Just below the chief gods are the other Olympians, independent to the point of insurrection, but always finally obedient to Father Zeus. Closest to him is his daughter Athena; his wife (and sister) Hera lives with him in perpetual marital tension broken by episodes of Olympian lovemaking. Beneath the Olympians rank the divinely born ancestors of the epic heroes, and lower yet there is an unruly fairy realm of demidivinities, among whom Odysseus will get lost. The cosmic polity is uneasily yet quite stably patriarchal. Paternalistic Zeus on Olympus has troubles mirrored by feudal Agamemnon at Troy.

The matter of visibility is similarly unfixed. The gods do not appear clearly to all; it is only at their will that they become manifest to human eyes. Thus Odysseus recognizes the goddess where his son Telemachus doesn't; the son, however, soon suspects, though he does not see, the goddess in the two older men in whose physically unlikely likeness Athena comes to him —though both are "Minders," Mentes, the Taphian stranger, who first rouses Telemachus to action, and Mentor, Odysseus' vice regent. And mindfulness is what occurs in the presence of

Athena, who does not seem to be particular about gender in the shapes she takes over. I might mention here, as an example of the tight knit of Homer's tale, that the Taphians, a real tribe whose name means "Burial People," live up north in the vicinity of the legendary entrance to Hades, and that is where Odysseus is at just about the time Mentes appears at the court of Ithaca.

To return to the varieties of divine visibility: Sometimes when walking the earth they show only the back parts of feet and their calves; sometimes only their tracks, their footsteps, appear—several times Odysseus or his son "follow the footsteps of the god." Sometimes they make dim phantoms do their work, as when Athena sends Penelope's sister Iphthime to alert and encourage Penelope about Odysseus' return. Gods themselves don't appear in dreams; it seems to be below the dignity of their actuality. Thus humans see traces, though some see not even that; it is unimaginable that Thersites, the stoop-shouldered, warped-headed, ill-conditioned rabble-rouser camped before Troy, ever saw so much as the heel of a divinity.

So gods have *two* kinds of visibility. Among themselves they have their proper face and form and appurtenances known to themselves and to those, like the Phaeacians, who are close to them and to whom they are manifest in their own shape. As gods they are imaged (the best proof of being visible) by the craftsman-god Hephaestus who represents them on Achilles' shield as larger than men "and the folk at their feet were smaller." Just so are they later shown on the frieze of the Parthenon, Athena's temple in Athens. Gods have special non-blood to shed, *ichor,* and they drink their own divine *nectar* and eat their own *ambrosia,* the food of the immortals or of the blood*less* (for *brotós* means mortal and *brótos* gore). That they eat and drink and inhale the appetizingly savory smoke of sacrifices betokens that they have nonetheless more physicality than would belong to mere phantasms. Once in a while they tangle with mortals in battle and receive real, though inconsequential, wounds; Aphrodite's mother, Dione, recites a whole inventory of such incidents in the *Iliad,* taken lightly by the divine combatant, but surely for the human antagonist an unforgettable singling-out. And to Homer himself it seems to have been granted to see directly the beautiful robes of the goddesses and the embroidered belts they borrow from each other and how they dress their hair and the magnificent chariot, "a wonder to behold," they have at their command and what grows in the meadow where they carry on their amours: soft young grass, dewy lotus, thick soft clover, and hyacinth. That they appear to each other betokens that appearance is of their essence; that they evidently made themselves manifest in their own forms to Homer bespeaks their good sense.

Their second visibility is then, as I have said, not to each other and to the poets but to mere humans, and that might happen in any shape, animal or human, though usually human: a wise old man or a charming maiden; gender is no object at least to Athena. Indeed all the goddesses are addressed by Zeus as "female he-gods." There are fleeting moments when their manifestation seems to oscillate. The princely young shepherd in whose guise Athena receives her Odysseus home to his island quite suddenly and shimmeringly turns into a tall, beautiful woman who seems to *be* the goddess to whom Odysseus then says: "It is hard, goddess, for a mortal to know you when he faces you, however knowledgeable he may be, for you make yourself resemble anything." That is Odysseus to a tee: He is secure enough in his goddess to expect to come face-to-face with her. And she complies—I think (37).

And of course, similarity being reciprocal, as the gods appear as humans, so are humans given the epithet "godlike" (*theoeides*); both likely and unlikely customers bear it: seers, women, Odysseus' boy, but oddly enough not Odysseus himself, though his looks are indeed gloriously transformable (2).

Are Athena, say, and Poseidon projections of human properties and personifications of natural forces? Athena, to be sure, is always there when people stop to think for their lives, and Poseidon ever harasses sailors who ever fear for their lives. So do they "stand for" the ready wisdom that saves or the resentful element that drowns? I think Homer would have silently turned his back on that sort of reductionist talk. A human being, Achilles, say, may contract himself for a week or so into *one* passion, but no god is reducible to a trait—a Roman god, perhaps, but not the Homeric gods. They are too vivid to stand for anything else: beautiful and able, childish and ageless, cruel and kind, deadly and saving, elegant and on occasion quite vulgar. The fixity of an emblem is not in them, for though they have eons of duration, they are far less steadfast than your average hero.

That being how the gods appear and what they are not, we are head-on with the question: What then *are* they? Or perhaps before that, what do they *do?* How do they impinge on the human world?

They impinge in four ways I am able to discern: 1. They give gravity to mortals by the contrast of their own lightness of being; 2. They shed grace on human life by the spectacle of the elegant flamboyance of their freedom; 3. They bestow dignity on human actions by their avid interest in them; 4. They confer complexity on human affairs by being involved in them.

1 "Living lightly" is the god's way; it is their most revealing descriptive tag: *thĕ-* | *oī reī-* | *ā zō-* | *ōn- tēs-*. Note the irony of the heavy line, as of gravity countermanded, expressed in the long syllables even in that normally dactylic fifth foot! The gods are ever at leisure; they have all the time in the world to accomplish their aims, for they are deathless—not eternal but immortal. Yet though they live *in* time, they do not live *through* time as a span, for they are ageless, and though they remember, their memories are not attached to the phases of a passing life as are ours. Since almost nothing they do has serious consequences for them, they give themselves over completely to the present: They break into wild hilarity as they drink, that divine "unquenchable laughter," while worthy humans laugh rarely, and Odysseus, who despises drunken laughter, never at all, though he has both a grim and a sweet smile. Only the guilty and overexcited break into uncontrolled guffaws; so the wooers, sensing the coming catastrophe, "are like to die" from hysterical laughter (44). The gods fight with a relish never seen in humans, belabor each other with vulgar insults and absurd beatings: "Dog-fly," Hera calls Aphrodite as she leads her lover Ares by the hand out of the battle—Ares, the god of war, whom Athena has just savaged. And the *ichor* is stemmed, and all the wounds are healed immediately, and death is not a prospect. The gods fight parody battles, battles parallel to the human fighting; for their most futile free-for-all they choose exactly the moment when Achilles is seeking deadly combat with Hector. But the gods' face-off effects nothing; at least nothing happens that could not happen without them. And so it is always; Zeus himself disclaims responsibility for human fate right at the beginning of the *Odyssey*: "Oh dear, oh dear," he says, "how readily do the mortals blame the gods," but it is not from us that their pains come but from their own folly.

So the gods are weightless, and their lightness of being is akin to levity. Seen against them, as dark shadows against a scene of light, human mortals gain their gravity. The ability to lose one's life is magnified by the divine inability. Even a bloodless flitting shade in dark Hades has weight compared to the sunlit airiness of the Olympians. And one might almost say, conversely, that the weightiness of mortal life is the counterpoise that raises the immortals on high.

2 Yet the parallel world of these bright Olympians is a world incorruptibly beautiful, full of hilarity, exquisite artifacts, ever-fresh lovemaking, a world in which distance is not laboriously conquered and time is not inescapable. The gods fly through the sky and skim over the earth, assume whatever look suits them, and what is more, females become males, while all are untrammeled by the social decencies of the human world: They offer the spectacle of wittily wordy brawling females exuberantly fighting in close combat and held harmless, of scandalous amours merely rousing laughter, of sex solicited by the queen goddess for ulterior motives yet idyllically executed, of rank favoritism freely admitted. Yet all is done with such perfect grace and unfailing elegance that the mortals, both men and women, who have singers to tell them what "the gods living easily" are up to, take a sheer delight, even a proud delight in their divinities. For the mortals who are constrained by the powerful proprieties enjoined by their customs and ever anxious about breaches of decency, especially where women are concerned, here have before their minds' eye a realm of beauty incorruptible by license, a parallel world that by its mere being sheds a grace over their laborious, constrained and consequence-laden lives. "Men who eat grain on the earth" move under a sky full of ambrosially ethereal presences, and their lives are lightened.

3 These gods, who have time on their hands and sacrifices on their minds, are also inveterate onlookers, watchers of hu-

manity and eager interferers. No hero or heroine is ever so un-
companioned as Hölderlin felt himself to be. To be sure, as I
said above, *nothing* is ever done that could not have been done
by the humans themselves: Their sudden wisdoms, spiritings-
away, accesses of strength, transformations in looks—these are
all things that come to people even when there are no gods
about, and nothing much would change in brute effect if it was
a good arm rather than a helpful god who guided the spear to
the enemy's bowels. But everything would change in significance if all these effects were not achieved under the watchful
eye and eager regard of some god. "Regard"—that means
"respect." The heroes live under the regard of their observing
gods, and it gives them dignity. Where we moderns at our best
rely on self-respect to give us our worth, the Homeric heroes
have the blessing of being regarded by their gods, gods who
do not watch *over* mortals so much as they just *watch* them.

4 Yet these interventions also throw human merit in
doubt. For though all that happens in the epics *could* be attributed to human action, much is in fact attributed to divine
intervention. Hector might finally have stopped running and
faced Achilles after three dreamlike laps around Troy, but in
epic fact it is Athena in the likeness of Hector's brother who
persuades him to stand and turn (19). So when Achilles finally
thrusts his spear into Hector's gullet it is only incompletely *his*
deed. And so the presence of an aiding god seems to impinge
on the purity of people's responsibility; every human accomplishment or failure has a divine signature on it. But the converse is also true: Every divine intervention duplicates a human
intention and its execution. At crucial moments, the god helps
that hero who helps himself, and the hero can help himself because a god comes to his aid (37). Such reciprocity, or circu-

larity, makes the origin of every human deed questionable, and Homer's moral frame as ambivalent as any modern sensibility might require.

BUT NOW THAT THE GODS' indispensable function in human life has been delineated, there is still the residual question of their existence to be faced in all seriousness. Yet perhaps seriousness is the wrong frame of mind in which to approach the being of the gods. Perhaps what is wanted is a certain light-mindedness, a receptivity to Olympian grandeur and Olympian mischief, which is not a suspension of some prior rational disbelief, but a withdrawal from questions of belief in existence that force a yes or no answer, when existence—with its connotation of hard fact on earth and demonstrable necessity in the realm above—seems dissonant with the way of being attributable to Homer's gods.

Homer's humanity encompasses flea-bitten dogs, dribbling toddlers, one-eyed monsters, dreaming girls, noble servants, hysterical usurpers, aging wives—and gods. Are they "real" to Homer's people? Surely, for no one ever surmises that they might be mere extrusions of individual imaginations. Did they "exist" for Homer himself? Yes, since he sings of them with same unaffected sense of presence with which he tells of his heroes and heroines who are to him, I am persuaded, no mere inventions. Can they be actual to us?

There is a capacity that seems to be peculiarly human:

> Talkative, anxious,
> Man can picture the Absent
> and Non-Existent.

But we ought not falsely to infer a converse: that whatever we see only in the imagination is therefore nonexistent. Suppose then that the gods are indeed just beings of the imagination; there is nevertheless nothing merely imaginary and so inactual about them. For Homer, I hope to have shown, has woven them so inextricably into human life that without them it would be a sceneless life, unilluminated and unaccommodated, a life of brute success and bare misery. The beings who alleviate this condition are highly actual in Homer's world, and so they might be in ours. Consider that often in human affairs what is most necessary is least missed.

2

ODYSSEUS: HIS LOOKS AND TRANSFORMATIONS

OUR FIRST BUSINESS IN THE HUMAN REALM is to bring onto the scene the man, the man for whom the epic is named. I think we are meant to and we are able to see him. He emerges in our inner sight; his features are to be collected from the nooks and crannies of the poem.

He is not ordinarily handsome, this man, but attractive to the nth degree. Athena tells us that his hair is auburn, reddish gold—or once was. Now, at the time of his Return, it is silver and sparse. In fact he is close to bald. We know this because the greediest of those wooers of his wife Penelope who have been beleaguering and infesting his house during his tardy returning, makes fun of him as he sits there, unrecognized, in the guise of a ragged beggar: "Not godlessly has this man come to Odysseus' house; anyhow, there is, it seems to me, a gleam of torches from his head, since there are no hairs there, not even the least." Odysseus himself picks up on the joke. He is incognito and must give himself a name when he first faces his wife and tells her a false story (38). He says his "famous name" —it is in fact the name of a horse in the *Iliad* and otherwise unknown—is Aethon, which means "Ruddy-Blaze."

His upper torso is large, his chest is deep, and his neck powerful; his thighs are great. But he is somewhat short in the leg, even bandy-legged. The old Trojan Antenor, who was his host

46

when he came into Troy together with Menelaus on one of those negotiating missions for the return of Helen, seems to have inspected his "physical shape" closely. He was overtopped head and shoulders by Helen's husband when both were standing, but when they were seated, Odysseus was the more impressive of the two Greeks. When ready to speak, he held himself stiffly, eyes fixed on the ground, almost stupidly, but once he uttered with his great voice, the words were "like winter-snowflakes"; no one could match him and all marveled at his looks. In our language, he snowed his audience.

Priam, the king of Troy, points him out as being a head shorter than Agamemnon, the Greek commander in chief, but somehow "like a thickfleeced ram that goes through a great flock of white ewes"—clearly a somewhat ungainly but very distinctive presence. What is wonderful here is that both these Trojan elders tell all this to Helen, who is visiting them as they sit on the wall of Troy—to Helen, who, it turns out, knows Odysseus' physical aspect very well indeed (24). But she discreetly identifies him to the dim-sighted ancients as a man of all sorts of wiles and dense plans.

This shrewdness of his, and the wear and tear of his ordeals, has taken its toll ten years later. To an elegant young Phaeacian, one of those princely sailor boys who people that fairyland, he looks like the skipper of a merchantman, and the youngster who tells him so gets a tongue-lashing: This whippersnapper, named Euryalos, "Wide Sea," is told that his case is that of one whose looks are outstanding but whose mind is vacant—one would not like to be in his sandals. He has also taunted Odysseus with not being a sportsman. In fact Odysseus is an all-round athlete, not quite as good as Heracles to whose labors his own ordeals (*aethla*) are implicitly compared (30). He is, he says, second with the bow only to Philoctetes, the greatest Greek archer, a crucial fact in his Return. At Troy he could win a footrace, especially when his little-loved opponent—the "lesser" Ajax, not the great one (6)—slips on a cowpat, with Athena's help. But now, ten years later, after his recent shipwreck, he cannot compete as a runner, though he can outthrow the slighter Phaeacians with the heaviest discus. The well-bred youngster apologizes handsomely.

His face? Nothing is so hard to capture in words as a face because nothing is so particularly particular, so ultimately individual, and the most exhaustively piled-up words cannot at their common intersection bring up a facial look. But this is for sure: no more than his figure is it classically handsome. We can imagine that it is dark tanned, weather-beaten, and expressive, above all expressive: charming, dangerous, brooding, sardonic, wickedly comical, kind, controlled, cruel, and always shrewdly intelligent. We do know that he has beautiful eyes, "surpassingly beautiful" says Athena as she conspires to dim their luster to aid his impersonation of a beggar. I imagine them as brown, sometimes large and gleaming like chestnuts, sometimes small slits, shrewdly and amusedly peering.

For Odysseus is a man of transformations, planned by him and bestowed by the goddess. In the first line of his poem he is called "many-turned," versatile (14), and he is that not only in mind but in body. He plans and executes that impersonation on which depends his plot to regain his palace. He is helped by his own gift of observant mimicry. As a beggar he picks up his swineherd's rustic servant's sayings: "I know, I get it; you are giving orders to one who has a mind." He also has that greater gift, one bestowed by his goddess and yet totally his own: His looks are transformable in a moment. For Princess Nausicaa, Athena changes him from a wrinkled, briny, waterlogged castaway into a larger, smoother man with flowing hair. She works on him as does a skillful metalworker, onetime apprentice of Hephaestus that she is—she overlays silver with gold to make his gray hair auburn again, shedding grace on his head and shoulders. As he sits, gleaming with oil, in a new tunic Nausicaa has given him, she has thoughts of a husband. Once arrived in Ithaca, Athena again touches him with her wand, and he wrinkles, shrivels, and withers, his beautiful eyes are dimmed, his hair looks thin, and she puts rags on him for safety. He and his son converge at the cottage of Eumaeus the faithful swineherd, their refuge, and once again she touches him to make him presentable, youthful, and dark skinned for the first meeting with the young man whom he left as a baby. This transformation is momentously successful: "No, I am not some god," Odysseus has to say soothingly to his awed son. Another touch and he is again the ragged beggar for Eumaeus, and in this shape he enters the wooer-infested palace, a woebegone, aged beggar leaning on a stick. He has a knockdown-dragout fight with the real, the endemic beggar and bully Irus, for which Athena returns his powerful physique, but he remains in rags—even for his first face-to-face meeting with his wife, even to the great moment of his self-disclosure. Still in his rags, he effortlessly in one smooth motion strings his own great bow, deftly shoots—sitting—through the shaft holes of the twelve axe heads Telemachus has set up, leaps to the doorway, strips off his rags, and for one moment youthfully naked, shoots his chief enemy clean through the throat as that one is about to drink Odysseus' wine out of Odysseus' cup. Not much later he and his little band put on the armor they have cached nearby.

Only when he goes to his first fully declared meeting with Penelope, after a bath, an oiling, and a change of clothes, does Athena once again make him beautiful—he *can* be beautiful, as can we all at our own moments—by combining all the magic of all the moments. He is now in physical form like an immortal, and husband and wife address each other with restrained, deliberately estranged formality using an untranslatable term of address meaning something like "You god-possessed, you amazing one!" (*daimonie*). But more of that later (46).

Such transformations happen to others too, never to the young who don't need them, but to middle-aged Penelope and old Laertes, her father-in-law. Athena beautifies Penelope by the aid of sleep and ambrosial cosmetics. As Odysseus' complexion is darkened, so hers becomes "whiter than sewn ivory" before she descends where—she knows (45)—her husband is this minute awaiting her.

Decrepit old Laertes too is made tall and strong by Athena for the final battle to reclaim Ithaca for the Laertidae. In these remarkable two days even the palace glows; "a wonder for the eyes," Telemachus exclaims as he and his father prepare the hall for the next morning's battle. "Be silent! Contain your thought and ask no questions," commands his father, "this, I tell you, is the custom (*dike*) of the gods who hold Olympus."

What is this custom, the usage, the right of the gods? What are these transformations, instigated from on high but realized in a susceptible nature, in Odysseus almost scintillatingly? Odysseus is in both poems too mature to develop as might the hero of some novel; if anything he oscillates between ways of being. Whenever his goddess is upon him he is most himself, at times decrepit and miserable, at times powerful and splendid. Nothing happens to him that does not happen to us all; we too glow and crumble and have our alternating moments. What is wonderful about that? Or rather when is it ever less than a wonder? Even in our world, where the gods are not asserting their custom and their right to enhance the scenery of human action by making the looks of people and places adequate to their inner nature, these transformations are wonderful. But when *gods* are at work—that is a Homeric moment.

3

ODYSSEUS: HIS NATURE

IT'S ALL RIGHT TO DESCRIBE who Odysseus is up front because he really does not change between the *Iliad* and the *Odyssey* or between the first and the last day of his odyssey. He is a grown-up, a man who is what he is, when he leaves for Troy, and he is the same when he comes back home twenty years later. Of course he learns a great deal—the first lines of his own poem proclaim it—and of course he meets his many vicissitudes in different ways—he is not called "versatile" for nothing—but he is the embodiment of a truth obscured in our infantilistic age: Learning begins when development ends, for growing into oneself absorbs all the cognitive energies which, once "identity" is achieved, are free to turn to the world. For how can we learn if it is not *we* who are there to learn? We either change or grow wiser, but not both. A man who has visited Hades and is thus "twice-dead when other men die once" will see things in a new light. A man who has dealt with crafty, experienced witches *and* virginal princesses will have shown adaptability, "flexibility" as we say, and the attendant features of wiliness, tact, ingeniousness, ready charm, and occasional formidableness. For these are all traits for managing circumstances so as to protect the essential Odysseus, a man whose harmoniously two-faced soul confronts the outer world of ordeals with steadfast daring and returns to the inner world of

the imagination with poetic vision. Of this essentially unbudgeable man, sanguine in his depths through all catastrophes, a
contemporary poet will rightly say: "What better antidote to
the perils of the present, self-intoxicated for its unexampled capacity for change?"

Poly and polla, the Greek words for "much, multi-, many,"
are clustered about him. Listen to the first four lines of the
proem of his epic:

Andra moi ennepe, Mousa, polytropon, hos mala polla
The man relate to me, Muse, the many-turned, who so much

plangthe, epei Troies hieron ptoliethron epersen.
Wandered since he sacked the sacred city of Troy.

pollon d'anthropon iden astea kai noon egno,
Of many men he saw the towns and knew the mind,

polla d'o g'en pontoi pathen algea hon kata thymon
Many pains he suffered on the sea in his spirit.

You can hear the plosive agitation of the sea where Poseidon
persecutes him, as you are told of the multitude of pains and
pleasures to which he proved receptive as well as of the multiplicity of his modes—among which duplicity will not be the
least. His epithets, the adjectives regularly modifying his name
throughout the epic (21), are polymetis "much-designing"
(over five dozen times) and polymechanos "much-devising"
(well over a dozen). His own goddess, who herself loves the
crafts, lovingly uses this word of him at a memorable moment:
poikilometis "dapple-designing," "pied-planning." Poikilos is
used of complicatedly crafted artifacts; Sappho (who is to lyric
poetry what Homer is to epic) speaks of Aphrodite as poikilo-

thronos "she of the parti-colored throne." There is, wonderfully, an epithet reserved only for Odysseus and Hephaestus, the artificer god (8), Homer's favorite: *polyphron,* "veryingenious," with no hint of trickery but betokening pure sagacity; *poly* can also mean just "very," "intensely"—Odysseus is nothing if not intense. But with all his daring, devising, designing, he is, as I said, solidly steadfast, daring in the sustaining sense: *polytlas* "much-enduring," "much-bearing," in sum, "much-daring" (three dozen times). "If again some one of the gods should shatter me," he says,

> on the wine-tinted sea,
> I will bear it in my breast, for I have a pain-enduring spirit,
> Having already suffered so much and labored so much
> In waves and war. So let this come on top of those.

> *eni oinopi pontoi,*
> *tlesomai en stethessin echon talapenthea thymon;*
> *ede gar mala polla pathon kai polla mogesa*
> *kymasi kai polemoi; meta kai tode toisi genestho.*

Again the poetry sputters in *p* and *th* (pronounced as aspirated *t*).

So with his endurance goes enormous self-control, the character theme of his adventures (29) and the undergirding of his wild imagination. It is at no time more in evidence than at the feeling-fraught moment when he catches his first glimpse of his palace, his house and home, and hears the untimely music from the depredatory feast within. He catches hold of the swineherd's hand and almost gives himself away to his supposed guide as he bursts out: "Eumaeus, surely this is Odysseus' beautiful house!"—and then catches himself: "It is easily known, though seen by just anyone."

...nd as he is steadfast in conduct so he is in his attach-
...nts. Though he is with several women in the fairyland of
his odyssey, he is not polygynous: he has one wife, who is his
goal.

Like many resolute, imagination-ridden men he can be curiously passive, surrendering himself to the dangerous element: "From Ilium a wind bore me. . . ." At crucial moments
he can sleep (26). And the three years of rampages and incursions at the beginning of his Return are followed by seven
years of lassitude with the "Concealer" Calypso (34).

And for all his proprietary stake in the imaginative world,
maybe even because of it, he is the most acquisitive of men in
the real one. He'd stay away from his by now anxiously sought
house for another year, he suggestively tells his Phaeacian host,
so as to get some treasure together.

And, of course, as he is a weaver of long plans, so he is a
conniver for the moment. In the evening he tells Eumaeus a
trickster tale of which one Odysseus, Eumaeus' lost master, is
the hero. On a chilly night patrol at Troy, he, Eumaeus' guest,
had forgotten his cloak. As he lies freezing and complaining
on the ground, Odysseus devises a trick. He sends an eager
young runner (felicitously called Thoas, "Fast," a real Greek
at Troy) with a message to Agamemnon; Thoas jumps up, leaving his coat, and the teller sleeps warmly. Of course, Eumaeus
responds by giving him a thick cloak for the night.

But full though he is of humor, even fun, he never laughs,
as I said; he only smiles a very sweet smile, as when that
youngster of his tries to teach his mother how to receive his
father (46)—and once grimly, sardonically, at the suitors.

He is a man of delicacy, not always uncalculated. For example, Eumaeus (*Eumaios*), a gifted breeder of pigs, is named
after Hermes' mother, Maia, "Midwife," and prays to Hermes
specially; Odysseus picks that up and gracefully names Her-

mes as his own god, "who endows with grace and glory the works of *all* men"—surely the most modern words ever spoken by a supposedly feudal king. Of course, the swineherd is deeply moved and instantly devoted to the man who is in fact his much-missed master.

The kindness of King Odysseus is much remembered by the faithful subjects, but this man of control can go cruelly out of control. He is, after all, the grandson on his maternal side of Autolycus, "Wolf-Himself," and on his paternal side of Arceisius, "Bear-Man." One beastly night in the *Iliad* he and the young hero Diomedes go on a cruel rampage, ostensibly a reconnaissance mission (5). To be sure, it is a night of universal desperation, for Achilles has just refused to rejoin the coming battle in which, without him, the Greeks are doomed to die or be driven into the sea. Still, this excursion has a crafty savagery very different in feel from the blazing fury with which Achilles is about to rage over the battlefield. It gained Odysseus in later days a reputation for deceitful brutality. He is so portrayed in Sophocles' play *Philoctetes,* where he cajoles Achilles' young son into a nasty betrayal of Philoctetes, the greatest among Greek archers; he has been quarantined on a desert island because of a smelly, suppurating wound, but the Greeks now need to get his bow to take Troy. Young Neoptolemus in the end keeps faith with Philoctetes, in contrast to deceitfully cruel Odysseus.

As war veteran in his epic, however, though he can be cruel, he is never again so brutal. The carnage in his house is unavoidable, and the real brutality is carried out by his deeply and protractedly offended son (22); he himself wants no triumphal cries over these executed youths: "In your own heart rejoice," he says to the faithful nurse Eurycleia, "but hold it in and don't be loudly jubilant; it is not holy to triumph over slain men."

Those near and dear to him think of him as gentle. His mother in Hades tells him that she died of longing for his tenderheartedness; his serf Eumaeus tells of his love for a master more gentle to him than could be even his own family from which he had as a baby been kidnapped and sold into serfdom.

Not only within the family, but as king, too, he is kind and just in a fatherly way. Athena complains to Zeus of Odysseus' continuing confinement on Ogygia by the nymph Calypso while his palace is occupied. She grows artfully alliterative in her indignant plea as well as subtly exhorting; she intimates to him that a lord of men is the image of the king of gods in his fatherliness:

> *Father* Zeus, and all the blessed gods that are forever,
> Let no one henceforth be forthcoming, kind, and gentle—
> No sceptered king, nor let him evermore in his breast know
>   equity (*aisima*),
> But ever let him be harsh and wreak iniquity (*aisyla*)
> Since no one remembers divine Odysseus
> Of those whose lord he was; and he was gentle as a *father*.

And Penelope, talking across the customary herald directly to the wooers, berates them: You couldn't have been listening as children when you were told "what kind of a man Odysseus used to be among your parents, / How he never wreaked or said anything iniquitous / Among the people—as is the usage of divine kings." It seems to speak to the wisdom of his kingship that the island realm has, under Odysseus' own generation of men, managed stability although all political activities such as public assemblies are in abeyance; their own sons have become rambunctious only in the last years (43). And there is this to be said for them: Where are most of their fathers who went out under Odysseus' command? Why is Odysseus gone so long, and where is the old king? (46) It is a kingless island with an underage crown prince, a retired royal father, a dead queen mother, a struggling queen. Why isn't Odysseus there to govern his island realm, Ithaca, and, in Homer's recurrent phrase, "Dulichium and Same and wooded Zakynthos"? The answer is that he is Odysseus, to whose nature it belongs to have an odyssey (39), a ten-year sabbatical from the realities of war and of home.

At any rate, he returns to be just and gentle in time to come (48), but first to resume the rule. His manner of doing it is colored by his character: Like many men of extreme imagination and extreme self-control he is an utter conservative (5), and a change of polity does not enter his head; he was king of the islands twenty years ago, and he will be their king again. Accordingly, he can assume, on occasion, the mantle of royal dignity: In Phaeacia he has, so far still incognito, covered his head to weep unseen as the tale of his Troy is told. But now the time has come to uncover and reveal himself. He does it in kingly style, with flair and dignity:

> I am Odysseus, son of Laertes, who plies all manner of wiles
> Among men, and my fame reaches heaven.

Imagine the effect of this great moment on the appreciative Phaeacian court!

4
HEROES

ONLY ONCE IS ODYSSEUS called a hero in his own poem, when the witch Circe sends him off to Hades with instructions: When you come to the place where the three underworld rivers roar into one, "then, hero, approach very near. . . ." Young Telemachus, who has done nothing heroic so far, *is* given the title "hero" by Homer and again by his host Menelaus, for this is a great moment in his young and confined life: He is for the first time acknowledged as a young noble among noblemen.

But under the walls of Troy Odysseus *is* a hero among heroes. What is a hero? Preeminently a hero is a warrior with acknowledged victories, a perpetrator of killings, and a garnerer of spoils. It is a title for men: "hero-men." The women are known instead as the wives and daughters of the best; there are no "heroines."

Sometimes it is a term of respectful address; the unfortunate Dolon, who to save himself keeps frantically repeating that he will tell everything, calls Odysseus, the senior of the spy team, "hero." Sometimes it means no more than "milords," as when the wooers are called "Greek heroes" by Athena. But usually it is a title of respect for accomplishments—Homer calls Demodocus, the gifted blind Phaeacian singer, "hero"; or for age —in abdication old Laertes is still "hero" to Penelope as she weaves his shroud.

But the throng of heroes is at Troy and in Hades. These are the true "Achaean heroes" (I have called them by the latter-day name of "Greeks," derived from an old designation for a small tribe known to Homer as Hellenes who live in Achilles' domain). The *Iliad* opens with the mention of the many *Greek* heroes who are sent to Hades through Achilles' anger (32).

So "hero" in the epic vocabulary has almost as wide a meaning as it does for us: Homer has favorites and we can almost hear him refer to one—though of course he doesn't—in the style of a writer of novels, as "our hero." But above all, a hero is one who is acknowledged as belonging to the band of the best, comrades who deserve fame and prizes.

Odysseus is a hero under the walls of Troy because he is known to all. In the *Odyssey* he is largely lost to sight and hearing—below herohood in celebrity and way beyond it in audacity.

5

ODYSSEUS AT TROY

ASK FIRST-TIME READERS of the *Iliad,* especially young ones, who are the great Greek heroes of the poem and they are likely to mention Achilles first, then Diomedes, Antilochus, Ajax, and perhaps, and with wrinkled nose, the Atreidae, Agamemnon and Menelaus. Finally they might remember Odysseus. But if you asked the heroes themselves they would, I imagine, name Odysseus among the top ones, pretty close to the hero of heroes, Achilles. For as Achilles casts his shadow over Odysseus' poem, so Odysseus plays a central role in Achilles' poem.

Odysseus is not the greatest fighter at Troy, but he is the most ubiquitous presence there. Homer intimates who is who by the position he assigns them. Achilles' ships are beached at one extreme end of the Greek line in the plain of Troy, Ajax's at the other. But Odysseus, who is captain of one of the tiniest contingents at Troy, a fleet of twelve ships, each probably with a crew of fifty, and so the chieftain over a mere six hundred men—Odysseus is stationed in the middle of the line, next to the commander in chief and the place of assembly and adjudication. He is within shouting distance of the two extreme heroes, at the command center of the expedition.

Here is a calendar of events for the *Iliad* which shows how central Odysseus' role is in the poem and also reveals the artful structure of the *Iliad.* My dates may be off by a day or so, because it is easy to miscount the nights, but I think the pattern itself is right:

PRELUDE

Nine days: Plague in the Greek camp (I 53).*

Day 10:   Achilles calls fatal assembly; he withdraws from battle because Agamemnon has taken Achilles' woman in compensation for giving up his own, Chriseis, to stop the plague (I 54ff.).

Day 11:   Odysseus returns from delivering Chriseis to her father (I 478).

FIRST OLYMPIAN ASSEMBLY

Day 12:   Zeus grants Achilles' prayer to give the Trojans the advantage (I 523).

ACTION

Days 13–15:   Indecisive duels: Greeks build wall; Trojans advance (II–VIII).

Day 16:   Odysseus' failed embassy to Achilles (IX).

Night 16:   Odysseus' rampaging reconnaissance (X).

Day 17:   Ships afire; Hector kills Patroclus; Achilles returns to field and shouts (XI–XVIII).

Day 18:   Achilles rages in battle and kills Hector (XIX–XXII).

Days 19–20:   Patroclus' Funeral and Games (XXIII).

---

* See the notes on references to the *Iliad* and the *Odyssey* on page 305.

Nine days: Gods debate Achilles' desecration of Hector's corpse (XXIV 107).

LAST OLYMPIAN ASSEMBLY

Day 30:   Twelfth day after Hector's death; Thetis is sent to order release of the body (XXIV 31, 112).

Night 30:   Achilles returns Hector's body to Priam (XXIV).

POSTLUDE

Nine Days: Suspension of hostilities; preparation of Hector's funeral (XXIV 784).

Day 40:   Funeral of Trojan Hector (XXIV end).

After admiring the artful time frame, notice that just before the event-center of the poem, the two days in which Hector kills Patroclus and Achilles kills Hector, Odysseus is at work. By day he is the leader of that famous embassy sent to persuade Achilles, with prizes and suave words, to return to battle. He fails, and that night he is chosen by Diomedes—he is the most trusted of the older generation by the young warriors—to go out on that desperate and shameful reconnaissance that yields no useful information but some loot. Even Athena is debased that night and bears, this once, the epithet "Looter," in empathy, it seems, with her best-loved hero. They catch and cruelly play with and then murder that poor idiot Dolon (misnamed "Wily"), who frantically repeats that he will recite to them every detail he knows. This poor specimen—ugly, only brother among five sisters, fast but not fast enough—has come as an eager volunteer on a night mission, for which he equips himself with a bow! (Truth to tell, someone gives Odysseus, as well, a bow to take along, which he puts to use as a whip when they rustle some fine Thracian horses.) For this beastly exploit they all wear animal appurtenances, Odysseus a boar-tooth cap his grandfather Autolycus had stolen, Diomedes a bull-skin helmet, Dolon a wolf-skin and a ferret cap. There is a view that the "Doloneia" is a later interpolation, but whenever it got there, it is Homeric, a humanly convincing postlude to a strained and ominously failed day.

The reason that a man like Odysseus must be front and center in the Greek encampment is easy to find: Agamemnon. He is king over all the minor kings, commander of a hundred ships, and so of about five thousand men, his Argives, "the most and the best." His sister-in-law's alleged abduction by a Trojan prince is the cause of the expedition. This king is a pathetic personage, pathetic in two senses: a sorry figure and a pitiful one, for he provides the great tragedy of the Returns (15). He and his brother, the probably cuckolded Menelaus, are the sons of Atreus—called by their patronymic "the Atreidae," as Odysseus and his son are the Laertidae—and their family has an old doom on it. But as always in these histories, the men are driven by their natures to make the doom work itself out: gentle, even feeble Menelaus and Agamemnon the magnificent hollow man. This good-looking younger brother, for whom Agamemnon has gone to war, is as stately as Agamemnon himself but by his own admission slack and without initiative in war and evidently equally so as a husband. He is in want of constant protection from his older and grander brother, whose care for Menelaus is his most likable trait; thus he keeps him surreptitiously out of that infamous night expedition. Menelaus at home—or rather his recaptured wife —will play an important part in the *Odyssey* (24).

The fact is that Agamemnon is simply incompetent—why else have they been sitting before Troy for ten years? If you want to see Agamemnon's magnificence full blown and shading into blind pompousness, read Aeschylus' tragedy *Agamem-*

non, which dramatizes the event that is the backdrop to Odysseus' Return, the returning king's murder (or execution—the play allows either understanding) by his wife and her lover. It is the same man.

Agamemnon has poor intuitions and balefully misleading dreams. He is stubborn where he ought to yield generously, self-assertive where he ought to forget self, extravagant where tact is wanted. Above all, this "lord of men" has ever-failing judgment; given a decision to make, he'll make a wrong one.

Odysseus always saves him. He collects and calms the troops whom Agamemnon's false visions have sent fleeing to the ships—always under Athena's orders, for she loves him, as his young admirer, Diomedes, observes. Agamemnon repeats this panicky maneuver, half hoping that no one will comply, and this time Diomedes steps in. He does it a third time and Odysseus prevents it again. Agamemnon gratuitously insults Diomedes, his best fighter in the absence of Achilles, and even his savior Odysseus. The epitome of his blindness is his seizure of Briseis, Achilles' prize of war—a girl he really loves—having first threatened to go after Odysseus or Ajax. It is, of course, this fatal error that Odysseus and Ajax are sent to set right with Achilles.

Odysseus is thus the universal ambassador, the natural diplomat. In his own, correct, estimation thoughtful planning is his great excellence, and he candidly concedes that Achilles is far better with a spear. He is a good but not an outstanding warrior, certainly a hero but not one who has his own moment of glory, as do other warriors who take advantage of Achilles' absence to shine, above all Diomedes. Once he runs away, but he is also honorably wounded, led from the battle by kind Menelaus.

One notable fact about Odysseus as warrior is that he, an outstanding archer, has left at home his great weapon, the bow with which he will regain his kingdom. At Troy he is no bow-man, and in fact, these distance fighters, who shoot from cover, are despised here. Thus Teucer runs under his mighty brother Ajax's great shield as a child to its mother's skirts; Philoctetes, the greatest archer, is absent with a stinking wound; and most tellingly, that skirt chaser and cause of all the agony, Paris (also called Alexander), is insulted by Diomedes: "Bowman, No-account, Exulter-in-a-hairdo, Girl-peeker . . ."

I might observe here that the death of Achilles, which takes place soon after the conclusion of the *Iliad,* is fraught with poignant irony because he is shot from behind by a man he despises and with a weapon that is dishonorable except for hunting. It is another of those grim fulfillments of a divine promise, for Thetis had promised her son a death by Apollo's darts.

Odysseus' missions, however, are remarkable. He is chosen to return Chriseis to her priest-father who has called down the plague on them. Several times in the past decade he has been inside Troy to negotiate for Helen's return (24). Before the war he had gone with Nestor to recruit Achilles in his home, Phthia —quite a task because none of them, least of all Odysseus himself, *wants* to fight this futile war. Now he is sent to Achilles on that difficult mission, and this conveyor of messages does better than Iris, the gods' courier, who simply repeats by rote what she is told. Odysseus delivers the gist: "I'll do all this for you if you'll give up your grudge (*cholos*)," to which Agamemnon had added: "[Only] Hades is so unsoothable and unmanageable, and that is why he is the most hated of gods among mortals"; and he adds something about his being more kingly and older. That part of the message Odysseus wisely represses and reinvents: "If you hate Agamemnon too much, him and his gifts, at least pity the Greeks as a whole. . . ." In the house of the short-lived, one does not speak of Hades, and to his human incarnation one does not denigrate him—these things are true of Achilles, I hope to show (13). Instead Odysseus appeals to his larger "friend-mindedness" (*philophrosyne*). It is because Achilles cannot hear that general appeal to friendship now that he loses his one intimate friend later.

In sum, Odysseus is the statesman of the *Iliad,* the man in the middle, keeping what balance he can among the parties. He shows himself at Troy, as later on Ithaca, as a firm conservative, in the sense that he props up the status quo—in this case, his insufficient chief. In his own poem a complementary side to his law-and-order propensity will show itself: a wide and deep imagination. The man of order, balance, and tradition, the centrist par excellence in public life, is a vividly imagining free spirit in his inner life.

In the Greek camp there is an impudent demagogue, Thersites (possibly meaning "Nervy"). He is misshapen, pointy headed, stoop-shouldered, and lame. It is not Homer's way to make ugliness a sign of inferiority and beauty of excellence: Paris is beautiful and Hephaestus, his best-loved god, is crippled (8). But in this brawler "of unmeasured wordage," shape and nature coincide, though he too can attract a small share of sympathy: He speaks for the otherwise nameless troops.

I have not dwelt much on or even thought much about the "historicity" of Homer's people: Were they once among the mundanely living? The reasons are three: 1. Unless their names and titles turn up in force in the Mycenaean palace records, there is no knowing. (These records consist of clay tablets incised with "Linear B," as the script of the period is called, the pioneer in whose identification as Greek and subsequent decipherment in the forties of the last century was my college teacher Alice Kober, in whose class I first read the Homeric epics.) 2. It would not matter much to our reading of the epics if they did so turn up, though it would give us the nice twinge of satisfaction which a proof that the ancients knew whereof they spoke always induces. 3. There is, in any case, no question in my mind that these people once lived, under whatever names and circumstances—after all they live now, too. That there was a Thersites at Troy, if there was a Trojan war, is then a foregone conclusion; there always is, and he always has some right on his side.

This unattractive embodiment of—justifiable—discontent, then, stands up in the assembly held after the impounding of Achilles' girl and, taking advantage of Agamemnon's misjudgment, incites the Greeks to leave, calling them She-Greeks for staying on, and insolently presuming to take up Achilles' cause. For he has it in particularly for Achilles and Odysseus. The latter loses his temper at the rabble-rouser and beats Thersites about the shoulders until he is bloody and a big tear falls from his eye—clearly Homer sympathizes even with this unlovely man. Moreover he gets the masses (*plethos*) to laugh and applaud this humiliation, which he had preceded with a speech containing what I take to be his politics: "No way will all the Greeks rule as kings here / Multi-rulership (*polykoiranie*) is not a good thing. Let one be ruler, / One king, to whom the son of crooked-counseling Cronos [Zeus] has given / The scepter and the adjudications, so that he may do the planning for the people." I think I can detect here an undertext, saying: "This king is not the best choice Zeus might have made, but the god-given order is to be conserved in any case."

Shakespeare has the same intuition about Odysseus: a conservative, a preserver of hierarchy. He has Ulysses give a great rousing speech in defense of "degree":

> The heavens themselves, the planets, and this center,
> Observe degree, priority, and place, . . .

If these distinctions of rule were lost, "so should justice too" be lost:

> Then everything includes itself in power,
> Power into will, will into appetite;
> And appetite, a universal wolf,
> So doubly seconded with will and power,
> Must make itself a universal prey . . .

This is the very wisdom of the grandson of Autolycus, "Wolf-Himself." It is the conviction he brings to his reassumption of authority in Ithaca. It fits with this dynastic bent that Odysseus thinks of himself even at Troy above all as Telemachus' father: "May I no longer be called the father of Telemachus," he says to Thersites, if I'll put up with you. And later he says the same to his chief who is insulting him.

His thought of Telemachus, however, is not merely dynastic; he is the Greek who most candidly misses married life: "For he who stays away even one month from his wife in his many-benched ships, frets." But he continues: "Yet even so, it is shameful to stay so long and to sail back empty," and that *partly* explains his lingering Return (15).

And his insistence on "degree" is combined in the *Iliad* with a care for the men; he insists to Achilles, who is now raring to go to battle to avenge dead Patroclus, that the men must eat: "Let the Greeks not ever mourn a corpse with their belly."

The *Iliad* and *Odyssey* are both mindful of generational friendships and conflicts. At Troy, Odysseus is already among the elders: "I was born first and know more things" he says on this occasion to Achilles, who does not disagree. But the young can be resistant. One Sthenelaus angrily tells Agamemnon "We proclaim that we are better by far than our fathers; *we* took the seat of seven-gated Thebes," while "they perished by their own blindness." This is a dig at his father, Capaneus, of the generation of superheroes, who perished in that siege of Thebes (the legendary clash between the sons of Oedipus) because he boasted that he was unstoppable. Homer punishes Sthenelaus for this impiety by referring to him twice merely as "the son of Capaneus." Diomedes rebukes him gently; he himself takes respectful pride in being the youngest among the great ones. Actually Nestor's Antilochus, who falls at Troy and is still mourned in the *Odyssey* ten years later, is the youngest boy before Ilium; that charming wiseacre calls Odysseus "a well-preserved senior," clearly with affection. At Troy there are somewhat oppressive older dignitaries, such as Nestor and Agamemnon, but Odysseus is friendly across the generations. At home this generational question will become more urgent.

Odysseus is profiled in yet another way at Troy: against the two men at the extremes but in shouting distance. Insofar as they are comparable, Achilles is Odysseus' antithesis (7). But there is a day, the day of Patroclus' death, after which Achilles is no longer comparable to anyone, is no longer part of the human polity at Troy, but is as a god among men and a law unto himself—to cite Aristotle, writing about an incomparably distinguished man. When Achilles returns to the human community it will not be by anyone's persuasion but through a death-anticipating burnout (13). And that is a way of being beyond Odysseus.

At the other extreme is Ajax, in his way as far out on an equally fatal extreme; he too casts a somber shadow on Odysseus' being.

6
AJAX THE SILENT

AJAX IS THE ODD MAN OUT at Troy, not pathetic as is Agamemnon but genuinely tragic, perhaps the only tragic figure of the war. In the House of Hades he comes to look at the living visitor Odysseus. But Ajax will not speak to him or respond to Odysseus' soothing words, though he beckons to him, addresses him as "Lord" and apologetically brings up the "baleful equipment."

Here is what has happened between the end of the *Iliad* and Odysseus' descent: After the sack of Troy and the death of Achilles, his armor, which includes the most marvelous shield ever made (8), was set out as a prize by his goddess-mother Thetis. Athena and the "sons of the Trojans," the young survivors of the sack, were the judges. It must have been a curiously fraught moment: the boys of Troy adjudicating a prize in honor of the man who sacrificed twelve of their like on his friend's funeral pyre and whose own son hurled from the walls Hector's baby son—as Priam had so grimly foretold—whom the Trojans fondly used to call Astyanax, "Lord of the Town."

Neither Odysseus nor Ajax, the two survivors of the great trio, has ever had armor as exquisite as Achilles' shield. Odysseus' arms are undistinguished; Ajax carries a shield to fit his stature: huge, solid, heavy, inelegant, like a turreted wall—as he himself is called the "bulwark" of the Greeks. It is made of seven layers of bull's hide and one of bronze and is impenetrable. Hector's spear simply cannot pass through it in that abortive duel that might have saved Troy and made Hector *the* hero of another sort of *Iliad*.

Odysseus wins the armor by Athena's favor, that is to say, for his acuity, even craftiness. Ajax cannot bear the loss; after all, the contest is for the succession to Achilles' distinction. Like many a physically outsized man, he is emotionally fragile, excessively sensitive to slight, and thus too readily embarrassed into madness and self-extinction. He kills himself.

What has Ajax been like at Troy? Helen, with her eye for manly looks, describes him as enormous, a hulk of a man. In battle he is formidable, unbudgeable, like a lazy ass that gets into a field of grain, and boys break many a cudgel trying to drive it out; in retreat he is like a beast that keeps turning and turning around as it slowly gives way. He is stubborn, stormy, and vulnerable.

These two, Ajax and Odysseus, have been good comrades during the siege; Agamemnon mentions them in one breath. One bond is that they are both chieftains of tiny fleets, a mere twelve ships. Ajax, the man of few but straight words, comes along on that embassy to Achilles, and his impatient warrior's plea comes closer to touching Achilles than Agamemnon's promises: Show some grace toward us who want to be close to you and be your friends, he says. All this for one girl, when you're being offered seven! And it is Ajax whom Menelaus, who never goes alone, calls on to help save Odysseus when he is wounded. At the funeral games for Patroclus he and Odysseus fight to a draw—at wrestling, bulk against the canny hold, until Achilles calls the match and gives them equal prizes.

Odysseus, then, has won the Shield—and it is, irony of ironies, never again heard of. He must have lost it, along with everything and everyone else, on the way home. He is no more the man to inherit Achilles' world than is Ajax; moreover, its unsung loss signifies his disentanglement from the war and his descent into an ever deeper and more revealing privacy (33).

The story of this fatal contest is reported by Odysseus in Hades, but the madness and suicide of Ajax are only alluded to. These later became the subject of several tragedies of which only Sophocles' *Ajax* survives. It is an unusually affecting play of personal suffering, though the death itself, as is the custom, is not shown onstage. This death is, so to speak, a missing Homeric moment.

This deficiency is made good by a pot painting. Here, in a minor medium, we find a monumental moment. I include it as an interlude because the painter, whose name we know—Exekias—has achieved exactly what I mean by a Homeric moment. For just as the flowing Homeric narrative can produce in the attentive reader as a cumulative result a detailed mental image, so, reciprocally, a painted picture can be developed verbally into a *tableau vivant,* a living image containing the gist of a whole story, a still, fraught, vibrating stasis.

Death of Ajax

This poignant painting is situated on the shoulder of an amphora, a two-handled jar of the later sixth century B.C. It is in the archaic Black-figure style, in which the figures loom as silhouettes of black glaze against

the orange back-
ground of the Attic
clay. Details are in-
cised or painted on
in purple or white.
Soon after pot paint-
ers will reverse the
scheme so that in
the Red-figure style
of classical pottery
the figures are "re-
served." Rather than

Detail

black bulks blocking the light, they will appear as sunlit open-
ings in the lustrous black glaze that circumscribes them and is
also used to inscribe details.

The earlier grand Black-figure style seems made to depict a
Hades-bound soul, a prospective shade, Ajax, at the moment
before he enters the House of Hades. This painting truly is a
supplement to Homer, though Homer in reverse: a story in
a still.

First the setting: To the left Exekias has put a palm tree;
palms have eastern provenance, so read: foreign parts, away
from home. On the right is Ajax's mighty spear and his huge
shield; the "figure eight" shield betokens "Homeric" in the visual vocabulary of these pot painters. The shield has a boss, a
Gorgoneion, a picture of Gorgo the Medusa, who could turn
those who looked at her to stone. Such a figure was not on
Ajax's but on Agamemnon's shield, but never mind; the meaning is: *not* Achilles' shield. For this is Ajax who has lost the
contest.

He looms in the middle, huge, with hamlike haunches and
curiously delicate feet, squatting. He is fixing his sword in a
little mound that calls to mind a funeral mound, a miniature

of the one on which Odysseus fixed Elpenor's oar (48). Everything about the crouching, furrow-browed figure betokens furious, fanatical concentration, as he carefully pats the earth around the sword on which he is about to impale himself. His staring eye belongs to the archaic style, but it fits the mood perfectly. He is caught in a bare, contracted world, muscle-bound and delicate, too silently single-minded to be viable, a victim, perhaps the first among many, of multiminded Odysseus' know-how. Of the great trio, Achilles and Ajax are dead now, but Odysseus survives.

7

BRIEF ACHILLES AND
ENDURING ODYSSEUS

HOMER ATTENDS TO AGE. Achilles is not actually a youth at the time of the *Iliad*, the tenth year of the siege of Troy. He has a son old enough to take his place after his death and to participate in the sack of Troy, which probably takes place within the year but is not related in the *Iliad*. This son, Neoptolemus, need not be more than sixteen at his father's death; after all, Alexander the Great had his first command at that age. If Achilles himself were, say, seventeen when his boy was born and went to Troy at twenty-three, he would be about thirty-three when he killed Hector and sealed his own fate—to die within the year, the tenth or eleventh of the Trojan war. Alexander, whom Hegel called Achilles' "antitype" or avatar, made a solemn ceremonious stop at Troy upon entering Asia Minor on his way to conquer the world. He took the shield said to have been Achilles' (it couldn't have been) from Athena's temple at Ilium. That was in 334 B.C., 850 years after the traditional date of Troy's fall. He too died at thirty-three, about eleven years after. This *jeu d'esprit* of history has significance: both the hero and his antitype embody the spirit of youth, and with it, of a fatal brevity.

Achilles even at a mature thirty-three or four is in his essence a youth, indefeasibly though counterfactually youthful. What is young is his passionate pride, his all-concentrat-

rath, the *menis,* that deeply mindful, minding, remembering anger at an insult and an injustice to which his poem is devoted:

$\bar{Me}$- *nĭn ă-* | $\bar{ei}$- *dĕ thĕ-* | $\bar{a}$ *Pē-* | $l\bar{e}$- *ĭ- ă-* | *dēo Ă- chĭ-* | $l\bar{e}$- *ŏs.*
The anger, sing, Goddess, of Peleus' son Achilles.

Odysseus, his antithesis, is, on the other hand, an elder at Troy, mature more by nature than by age (3), since he must be less than ten years older than Achilles. As Achilles is taken over by *menis,* Odysseus is the man of *metis,* of measured, calculating planning. The term of deepest opprobrium he has for Thersites is that he is "unmeasured in verbiage" (*ametroepes*). Recall that it is Odysseus who is normally sent when calculatedly tactful diplomacy is needed. Only once, significantly, is someone else sent. It is Ajax—Ajax the delicate—who thinks of sending Nestor's Antilochus, the youngest Greek in the expedition and Achilles' second-best friend, to tell Achilles of Patroclus' death—the comradeship of the young.

Even before they arrived at Troy these two, Achilles and Odysseus, embodied a special contrariety, that between extreme and mean, as their positions in camp signify (3). At a feast they had a famous quarrel, mentioned in the *Odyssey.* The two "best of the Greeks"—so called by Agamemnon—argued about the right way to take Troy, Achilles being for simple force, Odysseus, of course, for guile. We know that Odysseus' way finally worked, for it took a "fifth column," the Trojan horse, his idea and his command, to penetrate the city. But Achilles, dead by then, had opened the way by killing Hector, the "Holder" of Troy (11).

Of course, the two have much in common, above all their acknowledged superlativeness; they are each the best (*aristos*) in their modes. And their excellence is their own, for both are minor chieftains with fairly small fleets.

For the rest one might say that even what is comparable about them distinguishes them. Each is a ranger within his domain; Odysseus is all over the encampment, as mission leader, mediator, morale builder, while Achilles, when he is not sulking in his tent, charges all over the battlefield. Both sing in their way, Achilles of the "fame of men," Odysseus of his Return (28, 27). Each knows friendship in his way: Achilles is good comrades with young Antilochus, but he is passionately focused on Patroclus, though there is no hint that they are lovers, as has been claimed. Each of the two goes to bed with a woman at night, and it is clear that Achilles loves Briseis—with Patroclus' approval. His affection for her is one cause of his fury when Agamemnon seizes her. We came to get back his brother's Helen, he says, and now he's taken away her "whom I love from my heart." Are the Atreidae the only ones who love their wives? Clearly he regards "the captive of his spear" as a wife. But still, his friend is dearer to him than father and son, he cries in his grief. The Greeks are pleased to think that he has cast aside his wrath and "chosen friendship" for them when he returns to battle, but in truth it is only that his anger, his *menis,* has assumed a new complexion; it is now *cholos,* a more centered fury, pointed at killing Hector, his friend's killer.

Odysseus too has a wife, a real, legitimate wife, though far away, to whom he is true in his heart, even in the world of women he enters during his Return. He too is a good friend to his chief and is well liked in camp, especially by the younger warriors, but he is no man's bosom friend. Essentially he is Telemachus' father and Penelope's husband; he was also a kind son to his mother who has died of missing him has an immortal mother of whom he requires conti

...ss from the beginning of his calamitous course; in fact, he is a mama's boy.

Both men know suffering, and so both their names signify (21), though one is temperamental and the other enduring. And both, in their way, are twice-dead: Achilles lives in a virtual Hades, and Odysseus visits the real one (13, 30).

But Achilles really dies and Odysseus returns alive from the abode of the dead, and that is the crux of the antithesis about which the two poems pivot.

In Achilles youthful passion and early death are intertwined. So described he might seem like a modern romantic hero, a Tristan for whom love and death melt into one. Not so; there is no sentimental yearning for death in Achilles. He hates the House of Hades, but the terms of his being lead him there. This hero is as "swift-fated" (*okymoros*) as he is "swift-footed" (*podos okys*); his assigned life span is "minute" (*minyntha*); he expends himself youthfully, lives, even withdrawn from action, the intense, concentrated, single-minded, abbreviated life of the death-bound. And there is another aspect about Achilles to be remembered: Many heroes boast of divine ancestry; Achilles is the closely tracked child of a minor but attentive deity, the nymph Thetis. He has thus a touch of immortality about him which might well give his consecration to death a special injuriousness in his own eyes—and a special gravity in ours.

But everything about Odysseus is extended; he is a mortal man of infinite variety, a man of many talents and many travails—a far-traveling, long-suffering, long-enduring, long-lived survivor, all human. For Homer these figures of brevity and of duration come in tandem.

8

HEPHAESTUS' WORLD: THE SHIELD

THE SHIELD THAT HEPHAESTUS MAKES for Achilles represents a world, the world of the god who makes it but just as much the world of the man who bears it.

This shield, over which Ajax kills himself and which Odysseus loses, is like no other thing ever owned by a human being. It is not imaginable as a mere trophy for display, but neither could either of the two contestants have borne it into battle, not Ajax because his enormous stature demands more massive equipment, not Odysseus because he would simply have tripped over it; we know that Achilles' old armor had to be shrunk by the god to fit Hector, whom we may imagine as a big solid man.

There is a phrase Homer uses in both poems to express his admiration for beautifully wrought artifacts, chariots, garments, and shields: "a wonder to behold." But the shield Hephaestus makes for Achilles is, it seems, even beyond that. Instead Homer devotes 130 lines to the depiction of the images within the confines of the five-layered shell, beginning with: "First he wrought the earth, the star-studded heaven and the sea," and ending with "and in it he placed the great might of the River Ocean, around the outermost rim of the solidly-made shield." The word for "solidly" can also mean "wisely." The shield is at once a sound piece of defensive equipment and a work of Hephaestean wisdom.

To get a replacement for the armor that Achilles lent Patroclus when sending him into battle as his surrogate, the old armor which Hector stripped from Patroclus and donned himself, Thetis goes to Hephaestus, a god like no other. This is, I think, the only god who has weight, human weight, for Homer. He is the god who achieves in his divine smithy in pictures what Homer does on earth: He makes a world. Recall that the other gods are not creator-gods; they make nothing of consequence—all but this one, who is lame as Homer is blind.

He is the most physically vivid of the gods. He is severely crippled; his epithet is "Crook-foot." He is the only god whose deeds have had physical consequences: Zeus had hurled him from Olympus for helping his wife Hera in one of their continual quarrels. She threw her lamed son down, and Thetis took him into her home beneath the sea and nursed him for nine years, while he made fine jewelry for her. On Olympus he is a buffoon, huffing and puffing about as a wine server, arousing the gods' friendly-cruel "unquenchable laughter." He has been married to Aphrodite (of all divinities)—the goddess whose domain is sexual attraction, but who is for Homer a slightly ignoble female, laughable in battle and faithless in bed. She tries to deceive him with Ares, the brawny god of war, and on this occasion the artificer-god is the cause and not the butt of the gods' laughter, as he devises a net with which he entangles them in uninterruptible congress.

To him in his star-decked, bronze-built house, comes silver-footed Thetis to call in a favor. Here, in the house he himself has built, Hephaestus looms large and distinguished. He is weary from moving fast about his bellows; he is making—believe it or not—robots (*automatoi*), tripods that will roll in and out of the gods' assembly by themselves, presumably saving him further humiliation; there are twenty of them, "a wonder to behold."

Here in the *Iliad* he has for a wife a more fitting goddess, Charis, "Grace," who receives Thetis courteously and calls her husband. He, himself the soul of courtliness, rises from his anvil, huge, panting, yet moving his slender atrophied shanks nimbly, supported by two crutches in the shape of golden girl automata. The god—who would not prefer an hour in his workshop to an eon on Olympus?—is indeed blind Homer's counterpart in the world of visible art, a god of "cunning skill." But here is a wonder to contemplate: Homer will now best the god by being himself the author of Hephaestus' masterpiece, the maker of a word-picture of a piece of visual art. Homer has started a long tradition of so-called "iconic poetry"; probably the best known modern instance is Keats' "Ode on a Grecian Urn."

Before the god sets to work, he and Thetis have a confidential talk; this once unhappily married god has a sympathetic ear for her griefs: Her aging mortal husband, Peleus, Achilles' father, is impotent. More important, her son is to die young.

Then Hephaestus, the ambidextrous, sets to work. Onto the Shield's disk-shaped mound he works the world, the image of the world that Homer sees in his mind's eye and that Achilles will lose, a wonder to behold. In it are two cities. One is at peace, celebrating marriages with processions, music, and dance, while the women stand at their doors marveling; there is also a case being adjudicated by elders and cheering onlookers. In peace, gawking is a joyful recreation.

The other is, like Troy, a city beleaguered, and two plans are being considered within: to be destroyed or to hand over half the possessions of the lovely city—Hector will make this proposal to the Trojans. On the city wall old men and the wives and children watch. Just so the Trojan elders sat chattering on the wall of Troy where Helen visited them and where

Andromache brought little Astyanax to look for Hector in the most poignant scene of this bloody poem: They finally meet at the Scaean, the "Left" (or "Sinister") Gate, and Hector's crested, mask-faced helmet frightens the little boy. This encounter is relived down the ages:

> How long ago Hector took off his plume,
> Not wanting that his little son should cry,
> Then kissed his sad Andromache good-by—
> And now we three in Euston waiting-room.

The gods too take part in the battle by a river, and the elemental forces join in—just as in Achilles' final battle with Hector. And presaging the terrific aftermath, Hephaestus' shield shows a corpse being dragged around by the feet (13). This is Troy, to a tee.

There is also the country: a fallow farm and plowing, and at each turn of the oxen the plowman is served a cup of honey-and-wine; there are reapers, binders, a king watching—no action is complete until it is contemplated by those at leisure. There is a vineyard with a ditch of blueglass paste, a fence of tin, a grape harvest accompanied by lyre-playing boys, cattle wrought in gold and tin, and two terrific lions seizing a bull and devouring its entrails.

Finally there is a dancing floor with golden youths and maidens whirling back and forth, as when a potter sits at his wheel and tries it out, spinning it this way and that. It is all encompassed by River Ocean. Hence there is nothing beyond, which means that on this shield are earth, heaven, and sea, the common and separate domains of Zeus and Poseidon, but no House of Hades, the murky realm of the third brother, whose poetic Greek name, *Aides,* was commonly understood as *A-ides,* the "In-visible," and his location as being beyond Ocean and the visible world (12). Yet he too is there—not in the armor but in its wearer.

Not only is most of the brilliant, loving detail missing from my summary description, but even more the vivid grace and fierceness, the rhythm and violence of the motion in (Homer always says "in") this shield-world. Hephaestus, the maker of self-moving tripods, knows how to make moving pictures within his round frame. I have the sense—it is sheer speculation—that Homer imputes to this god the power of bringing stasis to life because he has it himself; what Hephaestus can work in metal Homer can work in words, and it is no less a "wonder to behold," this miracle of the movement-conveying word texture. Think of it soberly: Homer speaks and a sounding vision arises, always the same because the words have been the same through millennia, like a painting in its momentousness, yet always vibrant to the eye and ear:

> Ah, happy, happy boughs! that cannot shed
> > Your leaves, nor ever bid the spring adieu;
> And happy melodist, unwearied,
> > For ever piping songs for ever new.

Here is a more specific similarity between Homer's war poem and Hephaestus' shield: They both encompass a complete world, with all its opposition and variety, war and peace, city and country, cultivation and wilderness. In the space of the shield these oppositions are depicted as *contiguous,* here the city at peace, there the city at war, here the harvest, there the lion. In the realm of the poem they are *simultaneous;* they may even be the same city: Troy once at peace and now at war. Homer brings this superposition about through the double vision of the simile, whose effect it is to project over the endless incidents of intentional human violence a recollection of innocently terrifying wild nature, and over the fiercely bloody works of war remembrances of the satisfyingly sweaty labors of peace (20). Thus the contiguities of space and the sequences of time are collected into one instantaneous sight.

When, however, we have had our fill of looking at Hephaestus' handiwork, we have to recall that this shield is made for Achilles and that he bears it into the final battle of the *Iliad*, when he is nearly berserk, a raging elemental force assaulting the elements. This is the man behind and under, "covered," by this sturdy five-layered shield with its beautiful but presumably fragile surface. Spears smash it; Aeneas drives his spear nearly through it, and one cannot help wondering what he hits—perhaps the golden dancing youths and maidens? Once the shield is all but drowned in River Scamander, and when Achilles finally rushes at Hector, whose spear has rebounded, Homer thinks to say, "from the fair and artfully made shield." This is what Hector last sees in the minutes before death: a world that has repelled his thrust.

To speculate on the meaning of Achilles' shield is irresistible but also somewhat superfluous. While I feel sure such meanings are there to be apprehended (just as they are in any world), it does not follow that an explicit symbolic exegesis helps Homer's poetry. Besides, some truths tarnish when exposed, especially so shimmering a wealth of meaning as this shield of shields gives off. Still, here is a tentative try, and it won't be the first one. In 1955, and so still within the age of totalitarianism, Auden wrote "The Shield of Achilles." Thetis is watching Hephaestus at work:

> She looked over his shoulder
> > For vines and olive trees,
> Marble well-governed cities
> > And ships upon untamed seas,

But there on the shining metal
        His hands had put instead
An artificial wilderness
        Aňd ă sky līke lēad.

[Note the inversion of the Homeric line ending.]

A plain without a feature, bare and brown,
No blade of grass, no sign of neighborhood,
Nothing to eat and nowhere to sit down,
Yet, congregated on its blankness, stood
An unintelligible multitude,
A million eyes, a million boots in line,
Without expression, waiting for a sign.

Out of the air a voice without a face
Proved by statistics that some cause was just
In tones as dry and level as the place:
No one was cheered and nothing was discussed;

.   .   .   .

There follows the most succinctly accurate account of life in a modern totalitarian state I know. He goes on:

The mass and majesty of this world, all
That carries weight and always weighs the same
Lay in the hands of others; they were small
And could not hope for help and no help came:
What their foes liked to do was done, their shame
Was all the worst could wish; they lost their pride
And died as men before their bodies died.

It ends some stanzas later:

The thin-lipped armorer,
Hephaestos, hobbled away.

Thetis of the shining breasts
Cried out in dismay
At what the god had wrought
To please her son, the strong
Iron-hearted, man-slaying Achilles
Whŏ wŏuld nōt līve lōng.

I have found the poets to be good exegetes of Homer, and so
is Auden, but by opposition. The modern space of his shield
is everything antithetical to Homer's world. There the land is
green and communities flourish; there the wilderness is natural, and the troops are allowed to eat; there statistics are unknown, and all the faces are fully expressive; there the visible
gods come to help and *everything* is debated. Perhaps one
thing still holds: Achilles is one who dies before his body dies
(13)—but not for shame.

What Auden's great revision of Hephaestus' shield teaches
by contrast through its godless and heroless space (which is no
world, just a level expanse) is this: The Homeric world, the
poet's and artisan's world, is in its visible surface indefeasibly
beautiful, no matter what happens within it. Dancing youths
and devouring lions, wine-refreshed plowmen and brutal am-
bushes are all equally golden. This is, after all, the truth about
the *Iliad* itself: a blood-and-guts poem of unfailing beauty
which, through its similes and storied recollections draws all
the ordained labors and graceful recreations of the peaceful
world into itself.

It is this world, whole and hale and soberly glorified by the
artist, that Achilles carries into the last battle. He bears it; it
shields him. He exposes it; it covers him. He exposes it to the
thrust of spears under which it is punctured and staved in but
never completely penetrated (as any world is reparable after
war), while during battle it insulates the warrior—but barely—

from totally berserk dissociation. Achilles carries the shield into battle as a real enough defense against mortal wounding, but he also bears it about—earth, star-studded heaven, seas, cities, land—as if he were the power behind the cosmos. I surmise, I imagine, that Homer thinks of swift-footed, swift-fated Achilles as the being who makes possible the poetry that makes the full world visible. It's not the clearest thought, but I think it approaches some truth.

9
PATROCLUS THE FRIEND

IF WE CAN TELL PEOPLE by their friends, Achilles is not just a passion incarnate or a magnificent savage or the iron-hearted manslayer of Auden's poem. His dearest friend is simply the most lovable man in the *Iliad*. Achilles loves him unreservedly, and his grief at losing him is unassuagable. But so do they all love him. For he is gentle and softhearted; he cries like a little girl at the plight of the Greeks—Achilles makes gentle fun of him for it. He is universally courteous. He is a physician, having learned the healing art from Achilles; in fact, "the beginning of evil" is a mission of mercy he undertakes. Homer does him, more often than anyone else, the rare honor of the intimacy of addressing him directly. Only a few others are similarly distinguished: the kindly Menelaus when he stands his man in battle; the noble swineherd of the *Odyssey,* Eumaeus; and once even we, the readers—to alert us to a critical moment when things have come full circle: Hector has just reached the first Greek ship, the very one from which the first Greek leaped onto Trojan soil to be also the first to die. To Patroclus, Homer says in foreboding that, as a lion devastates a farm and his bravery is his destruction, "so you, Patroclus, furiously leaped on" a Trojan. Clearly he has a soft spot for the good and the gentle, somewhat like Jane Austen who once calls her all *too* gentle heroine "My Fanny."

It is my impression that when Patroclus puts on Achilles' armor to represent him on the battlefield something happens to him. He has been told not to storm out ahead, but—for the first time in his life, I imagine—he bursts through his own bounds and feels himself no longer as Achilles' alter ego but as Achilles himself. He forgets that he is a placeholder and becomes an actor in his own behalf. And so, Achilles unwittingly colluding, he gets himself killed in an access of blindness—"the helpless fool." It is with him as it will be with Hector who strips him of it: The wearing of Achilles' armor changes him and makes him foolhardy. Soon it will make Hector think that he has a chance against this force of nature.

The whole earth weeps for dead Patroclus: Antilochus cries; the captive girls weep—Briseis, newly restored, with real sorrow for the man who comforted her in her captivity; Thetis and her watery sisters come to mourn with Achilles. Most marvelously, Achilles' immortal horses shed hot tears, and Zeus pities them; Cavafy imagines his thoughts:

> When they saw that Patroclus was slain,
> who had been so stalwart, strong, and young,
> the horses of Achilles started to weep;
> their immortal nature was indignant
> at the sight of this work of death.
> . . . .
> Zeus saw the tears of the immortal horses
> and grew sad. . . .
> > You for whom neither death nor old age lie in wait,
> You are harassed by transitory calamities.

This Patroclus is the man who has pressed a question on Achilles, just before leaving, that only an intimate can ask. It elicits something from Achilles that is out of kilter with his image as a straight arrow, a single-minded Phthian from the simple North. Achilles, Patroclus has divined, is not without duplicitous depth.

10
ACHILLES THE UNWITTING LIAR

ACHILLES, THEN, THE LORD OF PHTHIA, thinks of himself—and the world agrees—as a straight arrow.

> For hateful to me as the gates of Hades
> Is he who hides one thing in his breast, and says another.

He makes this declaration of candor to Odysseus, of all people, that Olympic-class liar (37). As so often, these two seem to be antithetical. But not quite.

Achilles' proclamation is quoted in a strange Platonic dialogue on lying that Socrates carries on with the Sophist Hippias. Together they consider the different reputations of the two Homeric heroes. Before long the philosopher has discombobulated the Sophist by proving to him in general that to lie well one must know much and that the accomplished liar is the better man (a *jeu d'esprit* not entirely false in the case at hand, I think). In particular, Socrates shows by careful consideration of the text that Achilles, in fact, speaks falsehoods in a vital matter. In his anger at Agamemnon he says early in the epic that he will go home, so that

> On the third day I would come to deep-soiled Phthia

and again,

Now I shall go to Phthia.

Yet he makes no preparations at all to sail. Hippias, who hasn't
got the point, objects that Achilles lies unintentionally, while
Odysseus always intends his falsehoods. And so they argue on,
Socrates defending the subversive notion that the ultimate excellence is to know what you're saying.

Socrates makes the Phthia line his own; he thinks of himself in half-jest as in certain respects the Achilles of Athens. In
prison, shortly before his execution, a beautiful woman beckons to him in a dream and says: "Socrates, on the third day
you would come to deep-soiled Phthia."

This is what "coming to Phthia" signifies to Socrates: There
is a Greek verb, *pthio,* which means "I perish," "I die." So too
Achilles' destination, "deep-soiled Phthia," is unwittingly and
unknowingly death, and his true native land is the land of
death. Late in the poem his mother Thetis puts Phthia and
Troy together when she mourns that fact that he "is to perish
in deep-soiled Troy." She has always known it, and by now her
son too acknowledges his fate.

Here is the course by which Achilles first lies to himself and
later learns to accept his fate. I cannot say outright that Socrates in his conversation with Hippias was intimating what I
am about to develop, but I have my suspicions.

Between mother and son, Achilles' early death seems to be
acknowledged: "Mother, since you bore me as one who is brief-
spanned (*minynthadios*)," surely the Olympian owes me honor,
he says. "My child, why did I nurse you, who now has so brief
a lot and has so little duration and is so swift-fated," she says.
Others too are "minute-spanned," especially Hector. But for

him it is a fact, not a fate; the fact is called Achilles, whom he can hope to outlive. For one may hope to circumvent a *mere* fact as one can never elude one's proper fate.

Achilles is born to die young, but now he unveils his own, more bearable version of his lot. He refuses the offers of restitution and compensation brought from Agamemnon by Odysseus. He passionately rejects all the wealth of Egyptian Thebes and all the treasures of Delphi as measured against his soul, which, once it has passed the barrier of his teeth, no sacking and no seizing will bring back. Then he says:

> For Mother, the goddess, silver-featured Thetis, says
> That two-fold fates bear me toward the end of death.

I have a chance, he claims; I can stay here and lose my Return, but my fame will be imperishable *(a-phthiton)*. Or I can return home and lose great fame, but my life span will have duration. And that is when he says for the second time that he'll leave for Phthia tomorrow, going, we may think, from the devil to the deep blue sea.

If she has told him any such thing it was not in our hearing. But she hasn't—it is Achilles looking for a way out.

On the next day, Patroclus, full of sorrow for the hard-pressed Greeks and begging to be sent into battle, asks Achilles outright that so pertinent question. To be sure, it is old Nestor who has suggested it to him (for we may imagine the lovable Patroclus as not being overly acute). Ask him, says Nestor, "if he is evading some oracle in his breast and his lady-mother has declared something to him from Zeus." It seems to hit home with the friend, the only one who may put this question outright. And as he begs that he and Achilles' Myrmidons (as his followers from Phthia are called) might be sent out so that "I may be a light to the Greeks" (that too comes from Nestor), he does ask. Achilles gets very excited. "Zeus-born Patroclus, what have you said! I care nothing for any oracle that I know nor has my lady-mother declared any to me from Zeus"; I am just full of grief (*achos,* playing on his name), he goes on, at being treated by Agamemnon as some alien without rights who can be dishonored at will. From this outburst no one can tell whether he *has* heard something and doesn't care, or whether, as far as he knows, there is no oracle. He had, in fact, claimed the day before to have heard just such an oracle about his choice of fates. Where is the heroic candor?

In our latter-day language, Achilles is in denial. This is self-deception, self-ignorance, unwitting lying—though lying to oneself can never be witless deep down. It is a poignant moment Patroclus has elicited, this unintentional confession of the hero's fear of death; he has brought out the wily sub-soul of an unwily hero. Achilles *says* that he hates lying as he hates the gates of Hades, but it is, after all, the gates of Hades he hates more. They are most appalling to him because they open into his destined realm, for which he, part immortal, all youth, is yet least fitted. An elemental vitality is his immortal essence.

Patroclus is dead, and now is the moment of truth. Achilles' grief is boundless, and out of it he speaks perhaps yet unacknowledged truth to his mother. He cries in his agony: "Him have I lost! (*ton apolesa!*)" It makes one's hair stand on end because once again his words have a second meaning: "Him have I *killed,*" for the verb he uses means both "to be deprived of, to lose" and "to destroy, to kill." Odysseus, who loses all his comrades on his Return, will occasion the same wordplay.

And who can doubt that foolishly eager Patroclus' death is Achilles' responsibility? No, more: It turns out on attentive reading that he must have known from his mother of Patroclus' imminent death, for it is in Zeus' plan, of which she tells him (12), and he is actually troubled by this knowledge just as his young friend Antilochus arrives with the devastating news.

It increases the fury of his grief that Hector has taken and donned Achilles' huge old armor, which we now learn belonged to his father Peleus; it too was "a wonder to behold"; it was given him when, as Achilles says to his mother, they "threw you into bed with a mortal man," that is, on the day of his conception. He speaks of himself as "your son, already perished" (*apopthimenoio*); Antilochus fears that Achilles may cut his own throat. Later, facing Hector, he says to him bluntly: "Be dead! I will accept my fate." He is now utterly plain about it. He says it repeatedly, even to his horse that pities him: "Xanthus, why are you prophesying my death? You don't need to. Even I now know it well." And he gives a lock of his golden hair into Patroclus' dead hand to precede him into Hades, since he himself will now never sail to the land of his fathers. Thetis, sent after an interminable divine assembly to peremptorily order Achilles to return Hector's body, which he has been dragging about, uses strong language: "You won't be long in life, but death and mighty fate stand close by." And she bids him to eat, drink, and "mingle in love with a woman," presumably Briseis, newly restored and untouched by Agamemnon.

Achilles has heard, denied, obfuscated, and finally accepted his fate. What does fate, "lot" (*ker*), mean here? As ever, two things: "Destiny spun her thread for him at birth," *and* his own being confirms his fate. For is it thinkable that, had he in fact a choice, he would have sailed home to Phthia, there to perish without fame and glory? Can one imagine for him a life without imperishable fame but of respectable duration—old, gray, impotent as Peleus, a domesticated half-god?

11

HECTOR THE HOLDER

THE TARGET OF ACHILLES' concentrated, baleful fury is Hector, Hector the foursquare, the unwilling warrior. He has the most straightforwardly tender relations to his noble wife Andromache and his baby son, conceived during the siege and affectionately called by the townsfolk Astyanax, "Lord of the Town." The father's name too speaks of the city: Hector means "Holder," "Stay" of Troy. He is always thinking of the women and the families. He is saddled with the responsibility of Troy's defense in the face of an aging royal father, pusillanimous elders, and an irresponsible fop of a brother who is the cause of all the troubles for Ilium. For all that, Hector is realistically modest about himself as a warrior, especially as compared to Achilles.

He is an altogether solid though very human being. He refuses to drink on duty, stays to save his men, is kind to Helen —and wisely keeps his distance; he is solicitous even of his morally slight brother's feelings. Like Achilles' other victim, Patroclus, he has in him a strain of gentle civility. He is in Chaucer's words the "verray, parfit, gentil knyght."

He knows his fate and how it will all end. He has accesses of fear, and like all who deal with Achilles, he is seized by an uncharacteristic folly in the face of this force; he becomes reckless. But normally his chief thought is for Andromache, just as her mind—she is not named "Battle of Men" for nothing—is always on his whereabouts. He thinks of her lost freedom and his boy's suffering should Troy fall; she thinks of him as taking the place of her father and mother, whom Achilles has killed. When she hears of his death she faints and loses her veil, Aphrodite's gift: in a reserved and respect-demanding woman, a sure sign of being undone and exposed. Helen, in contrast, seems to go about unveiled (24).

This stolid fighter for a lost cause is not lucky in war. He is thwarted in his one chance to save Troy in single combat against his inferior in fighting, the wronged husband Menelaus. He is even, irony of ironies, deprived of the glory of killing the man for whose death he dies: He is only third in the group-killing of Patroclus, as Achilles well knows. Hector nonetheless remains the foremost focus of Achilles' hatred, being the Trojan most worthy of it.

It is Hector who utters, modestly and soberly, the most famous of soldiers' credos: "It is not an unseemly thing for one to die in the defense of his country"—as long as wife and child are safely left behind. This brave, unflashy fighter, the soul of decency, the perfect Trojan (14), undergoes as a corpse what has escaped him in life, a kind of apotheosis. Aphrodite—a goddess friendly to the Trojans through that connoisseur of female beauty, Paris (24)—anoints him with ambrosial oil so that Achilles does not succeed in desecrating his corpse. But for all that, neither he nor any Trojan attains the immortality accorded by Homer to those heroes who are commemorated in the House of Hades. If Hector's soul does not reach Hades it is not because no soul whose body is unburied can enter, as Patroclus urgently tells Achilles, but for a less remediable cause (32). The later poet Edwin Muir will, as if in compensation, write of "Hector in Hades," a sad hero who, together with the lifting of his earthly burdens, feels the withdrawal from all caring:

The race is ended. Far away
I hang and do not care
While round bright Troy Achilles whirls
A corpse with streaming hair.

In the *Iliad,* Hector's body lies unburied in Achilles' compound. It is the one corpse on which Achilles cannot wreak his anger in the way, as Homer tells in the beginning of the poem, he has done to so many heroes and as he, using Homer's very words, threatens to do to Hector: to make his remains a "spoil for the dogs and a feast for the birds." From this indignity, which Achilles brings on his own Greeks, Trojan Hector is exempt.

12
THE PLAN OF ZEUS

"AND THE PLAN OF ZEUS WAS FULFILLED," says the fifth line of the *Iliad,* but it does not say what it was. There is a long-range plan, the fall of Troy, accomplished beyond the *Iliad,* a grand Olympian marital concordat, by which Zeus gives up Troy to Hera for the option of destroying her three cities: "Argos and Sparta, and broadwayed Mycenae." *We* know that in Homer's time Zeus had taken up the option (or history had been at work, an equally elusive agency) and that the great Argive palaces were in ruins and the kingships gone.

But Zeus also devises and fulfills a plan *within* the poem, and it is a truly Homeric plan: We cannot definitively assign responsibility for its accomplishment. When Agamemnon had seized Briseis, Achilles appealed to his mother for redress from Olympus. In that assembly on the twelfth day of Achilles' withdrawal (5) Zeus, having heard Thetis, pauses to ponder—an ominous, time-stopping silence—and then nods in confirmation of the wish of Achilles, the swift-fated. Zeus will show him honor by giving the Trojans victory until the Greeks honor and magnify him properly. This seems to be the plan of Zeus that is fulfilled, but at what a price! It is Zeus' specific "ordinance," enacted early in the poem, that Hector will press the Greeks into retreat until Achilles returns, and Achilles will return when Patroclus has died.

The survivor will be burned out, and though Troy will then be without Hector, its stay, Achilles will die soon after without having taken the city. "It is not destiny that by your spear the city of the brave Trojans be sacked, nor by Achilles," Apollo tells Patroclus during battle.

What Achilles had not taken in or reckoned with in his deep fear of his own early death is that the human being he loves best will die even sooner than he, and by his agency. As he waits and prays for Patroclus to return to him, he does recall that Thetis has said that neither of them would live to sack Troy. But his prayer is too late and not part of the plan of Zeus. What he hadn't heard was that Patroclus would die first; he hadn't heard it because Thetis hadn't named his friend but only said that the best of his people would die. He *could* have known, but that knowledge he has suppressed along with that of his own impending death (10).

After Patroclus' death, Achilles understands that Zeus has given him what he asked for in both senses of the phrase: This calamity is the natural issue of Zeus' promise that the Greeks would be pushed to the ships, together with his own ungenerous half-measure, to let Patroclus frighten the Trojans into retreat by going out in his guise and his stead. Zeus has all too completely fulfilled his prayer, "but what is the pleasure for me in all this?" So both Achilles' unyielding pitilessness for his own comrades and his relenting half-measures are the human enabling acts for the plan of Zeus. "But Zeus does not fulfill for men all they have in mind; we two are destined to redden the same earth in Troy," he says to all and none. But, we may conjecture, Zeus *has* fulfilled it all, only in its fulfillment it no longer resembles what Achilles had in mind. Here is the archetypal unintended consequence!

13

ACHILLES **AS** HADES
AND ACHILLES **IN** HADES

ACHILLES AS HADES

SOME TIME BEFORE ACHILLES GOES to the House of Hades, the House of Hades has come to Achilles' tent: A strong sense comes upon the reader that Achilles is, in a somberly vital way, a dead man after Patroclus' death—a dead man, but not in the way of human mortality, a man who has figuratively killed himself (19). Zeus orders him, who will not eat or drink, to be fed the divine diet of nectar and ambrosia. He won't eat because his heart is set on nothing but "killing and blood and the terrible groaning of humans."

When after his friend's death he first shows himself in the field unarmored, he is ablaze with a gleaming fire and turbaned with a golden cloud. The next day, in his new Hephaestean armor, he rages about the battlefield, outwardly in a blaze of bronze, inwardly in a blaze of fury, eyes terribly aflame, an incandescent being beyond mortal humanity and loose in a world of elements let loose.

Xanthus, one of his divine horses, suddenly achieves speech and tells of the near day of Achilles' death. The gods come down in opposing array to watch and whip up the battle. Achilles leaps into River Scamander, which, choked with corpses, leaves its banks and rushes after him as he emerges. The other rivers become torrential. Then, Hephaestus sets fire against River Xanthus, the Ruddy River, as Achilles wreaks carnage among the Trojans: "A man in no way sweet-spirited or gentle-minded was he," comments Homer in appalled understatement.

He kills Hector; the corpse is now in Achilles' compound. Patroclus is finally incinerated, in a savage and somber nocturnal ceremony that first threatens to be a macabre miscarriage, but concludes when only ashes and white bones are left to collect.

Then everyone scatters and an eerie, desolate silence of nine days descends on Achilles. When he can't sleep he gets up to roam around and once more to drag Hector's body about by the feet in a futile attempt to desecrate it—it has become inviolable (11). Then again Achilles is prostrate; he lies majestically in the dust "great in his greatness"; the same phrase will be used of him as a dead man in the *Odyssey* (31). He talks to dead Patroclus all night, conducts him to Hades, and corrects Hades' work: Even if in Hades they forget the dead, *he* will remember Patroclus. But Achilles is not just recently death-directed and Hades-bound. Early on, he had sworn his resentful oath of withdrawal by a staff stripped of its green foliage with the bronze knife and for evermore dead. Agamemnon, in the part of his message suppressed by Odysseus, likens him to Hades who is not to be soothed (5).

Zeus on Olympus rules in intermittent impartiality over all the Greeks; ever-resentful Poseidon will persecute Odysseus on the seas; but Hades, the lord of the dead below, is preeminently Achilles' god. At Patroclus' funeral the hero labors one last time in the *Iliad* to fill the House of Hades, as he butchers twelve Trojan boys, as well as horses and dogs, until the blood flows in cupfuls, creeping around the pyre that won't burn until a high wind finally whips it to life. "He had made up his mind to bad work," Homer says in sober condemnation.

And then, with the unaccountable suddenness of a divinity, he is another being: the courtly, peace-keeping, tactful, and generous host at Patroclus' funeral games, who saves his now-reconciled chief from the embarrassment of competition by presenting him with a courtesy—or booby—prize. It is an interlude of light, charming gentilesse, psychologically sophisticated and civilized in its material amenities—though even here there is a dark undertone: Achilles gives away his valuables as one might whose life is finished. Again the Greeks scatter to their tents and Achilles is alone—and savage once more to Hector's body.

For nine days the agitated gods debate whether to end the unseemliness by just letting Hermes Argeïphontes, the thieving god, steal Hector's body. Finally an angry Zeus issues an order by Thetis to cease and desist. To Troy goes the messenger goddess Iris to tell Priam that he is to go—alone—to retrieve his son's body; Achilles will no longer be "mindless, unregardful, wicked" (*aphron, askopos, alitemon*), a whole litany of divine condemnation.

Hermes will be Priam's conveyer. He is not only the god of thieves but, above all, the conductor of dead souls into Hades.

In Troy there is rage. Hecabe, Hector's mother, too is savage with grief; she could eat Achilles' liver raw, just as he is savaging her son, and she is angry with Priam for risking the trip: "You have a heart of iron." He is furiously ill-tempered with the multitude of lesser sons, who hang around as he scours the palace for gifts of ransom, for not realizing what this death means to Troy. He has said earlier that sharp grief for Hector would bring him to Hades, and so he says now: "But for me, before I see the city sacked and wasted with my eyes, may I go down to the House of Hades." He will.

He drives out of Troy in a mule wagon loaded with presents, among them white mantles: white is the color of death, and they will be shrouds. Hermes, carrying his sleeping wand, meets him by the River—one might almost say River Ocean, though it is in fact Xanthus—disguised as one of Achilles' attendants, offering protection and comfort: Hector's corpse is still dewy fresh. A Homeric touch: Priam offers him a goblet as a tip, which Hermes refuses to accept—for verisimilitude—without his master's knowledge. He guides the wagon to the trench dug not long ago to protect the camp from Hector's Trojans, and having put the guards to sleep, he opens the gate to Achilles' compound, where stands his tent, really a solidly built thatched hall. Here he unloads and reveals himself to Priam, but he won't go within sight of Achilles; this god is not for being welcomed in this mortal's house.

Priam enters unseen. He finds Achilles sitting alone after a meal (attended by only two servants) and beholds him with awe. The old father begins awkwardly, for he tries to appeal to Achilles through *his* father Peleus, who hopes to see his son return from Troy. He, Priam, is the more pitiable, because he must endure what no mortal on earth has endured, to "stretch forth my hand toward the mouth of a child-slaying man." Achilles gently pushes the old man off as he falls at his feet, then leaps up to raise him and repeats Hecabe's words: "You have a heart of iron to come here." And he utters a desolate wisdom: Zeus has two urns, one of evils, one of blessings. Some receive a mingled lot, some only dire things. Achilles omits the third possibility—no one receives unmixed blessings. And he gently corrects Priam: Priam has fifty sons where Peleus has but one, who will die an untimely death. Priam has spoken of life to a man all but dead.

Priam is impatient to retrieve the body and be gone, and Achilles nearly loses his temper but restrains himself. He leaps out of his hut like a lion to order the preparation of the body—out of Priam's sight because he worries lest Priam then in turn lose his temper and cause Achilles to commit an offense; it is a strained, jumpy situation.

Once more Achilles leaps up to prepare a meal for Priam, the first for him after his son's death. After partaking, these two, the old king and the young warrior, both bound for death, sit and marvel at each other. Achilles, now still at last, sits in somber majesty, like a god in aspect—a living Hades in his house of death, a somatic shade presiding over an embodied hell. The epic world abounds in gods assuming the guise of men; here a man appears as a god, a nameable god, not just godlike. It is a great Homeric moment.

They sleep, Priam outside the hut, lest he be seen by visitors—of which there are none. Achilles has promised ten days' suspension of hostilities to prepare and accomplish Hector's funeral. Before dawn Hermes awakens Priam, conducts him back to River Xanthus, and is off to Olympus. The mules carry Priam and Hector's body toward the gates of Troy, unseen by any but Cassandra, the seeress.

So ends the terrestrial enactment of a descent to Hades, a Herculean labor of retrieval for the old king—Herculean because so far only Heracles has gone down to Hades to bring back a creature and returned. In the *Odyssey* there will be another such descent, this time to the real Hades, in which Achilles will appear once more as the lord among shades; in the *Odyssey* too we will see Hermes conducting souls to a Hades whose first-seen inhabitant will again be Achilles (30, 31).

ACHILLES IN HADES

The Achilles who appears *as* Hades is to be recognized by the aspect he presents to imaginative sight; the Achilles who appears *in* Hades becomes memorable through his words.

At the center of Odysseus' own poem is his descent to Hades (30). He finds there no figure more dominating among the dead, no soul more shadelike, no being less approachable than Achilles, to whom the House of Hades is hateful with all the passion a dead soul can summon; no one else speaks so rebelliously and irreconcilably of death:

> Do not extenuate death to me, glorious Odysseus.
> I would rather wish just to *be* as a field serf in service to another,
> Even to a man without allotment who had not much to live on,
> Than to *be lord* over all the dead that have utterly perished (*kataphthimenoisin*).

Achilles approaches with large strides in the company of his friends in life, Patroclus and young Antilochus, clearly holding aloof from the crowd of gibbering shades. Ajax is with him, so that in the House of Hades the great trio of Troy is reunited, but not in equal friendship—Ajax, we know, won't speak at all (6), and Achilles speaks angrily at Odysseus' unwarranted presence: "How did you dare to come down to Hades, where dwell the witless dead, the phantoms of worn-out mortals?" Odysseus explains his mission and tries to soothe Achilles: You are the most blessed of men for all time, "For before, when you lived, we honored you equally with the gods, and now, *being* here, you rule mightily over the dead. So don't let being dead grieve you, Achilles." He uses Achilles' word *akachizeu* for "grieve"; we can hear in it a part of his name: *Achi-* (21). It is then that Achilles, indignant and dignified, utters the famous words quoted above.

It is the same soul that spoke out of Achilles in the *Iliad* quoted before: "Not all the wealth that, they say, Troy used to possess in time of peace, nor the treasures of Delphi are worth to me my life (*psyche*)." He doesn't want Agamemnon's daughter for a wife, and as for the rest, "by rustlings can cattle be got and fat sheep, and tripods and heads of sorrel horses can be had for the taking, but that the soul of a man might come back, for that there is no rustling nor seizing, once it has passed the fence of the teeth." This grim knowledge of the finality of death makes Achilles who he is in life: resistant to offers of material compensation and fixed on his fame.

But it is equally because he is desperately averse to shade-like oblivion that it is not in him to choose—and it is this that is called "fate"—a life of normal duration. And so, since those who cannot stay out life cannot find rest in death, he is scarcely consolable in Hades—though Odysseus, the conciliator, will find words even for him (30).

Homer's magnificently irreconcilable pagan in Hades is the very opposite of Milton's rebellious Satan in hell who has borrowed a heroic shape but who says, in deliberate distinction from Achilles:

Better to reign in Hell, than serve in Heaven.

14

BEGINNINGS AND ENDINGS

THERE IS, AT EACH HEARING, something awe inspiring about the first lines of both epics. It is not only that for the 110 or so generations that separate us from Homer (counting four generations to the century and placing him in the middle of the eighth century B.C.) someone or other must always have known them by heart, but that their *incipits,* the commencements of fifteen and of twelve thousand lines of heroic hexameter respectively, have kept all their signifying solemnity without losing any of their fresh vividness. As always, the delight is in the details: Both beginnings are precisely fitting keys to their epics, as they are carefully keyed to each other. These beginnings *are* beginnings, of the kind the Greeks called *archai,* the principles that come first in order and govern the whole.

The endings too are the essence of epic, but to opposite effect. They are less completions than expirations, less finales than fadings away. One might say that it is by its ending that drama differs from epic. Drama has a denouement which occurs after some hours of viewing. (The Greek verb for such viewing is *theorein,* whence our "theater," and *theoria,* "contemplation"; thence, by one of those devolutions and evolutions of connotation that encapsulate the way of the West, we get our "theory.") You go home purified or titillated—these are the different views of the "tragic pleasure"—but in any case with a sense of a drama, an action, concluded. The epics, on the other hand, simply end when the poet judges they should, and if nothing is concluded, yet something is perfected.

BEGINNINGS

Both epics begin with the key word:

> *Iliad*: The *Anger,* sing, Goddess, of Peleus' son Achilles . . .
> *Odyssey*: The *Man,* relate to me, Muse, the multifarious, who very much . . .

So the poems announce, in the most general way, different themes; the *Iliad* is concerned with an aspect of a man who is contracted into one angry purpose, while the *Odyssey* is about a whole man who has multifarious ways. The single-minded man is named in the first line: the hero Achilles. We wait twenty-one lines for the man of many deceits to be revealed: Odysseus. The *Iliad* takes about a month of linear time for the man's passion to begin and work itself out at Ilium, while the *Odyssey* appears to take about a fortnight of time running concurrently in Ithaca, Argos, and some magical islands, but contains in that span flashbacks covering a decade during which the man accomplishes the multifarious stations of his Return (5, 25, 41). This fierce concentration of the one poem is expressed in the—apparent—completeness of the first line, as the expansive dilatoriness of the other is signified in its incompleteness. Yet the *Iliad* is longer by nearly a fourth than the *Odyssey* because in the *Odyssey*'s dead time, seven years, Odysseus is lost to the world and it to him, while in the seven days of Achilles' withdrawal the much-suffering camp has him well in focus and he it; in fact the first three-fourths of the poem takes place in Achilles' absence from battle (5). The *Il-iad* is *sung to the world* by the divinity, but the *Odyssey* is *related to the poet* by his Muse, and this distinction signifies that Achilles' poem is a public song of war, death, and glory, while Odysseus' poem is a private tale of adventure, survival, and obscurity (29).

The preludes continue; first the *Iliad*:

> The baneful anger, that put ten thousand pains upon the
>   Greeks,
> And sent forth many mighty souls to Hades—
> Souls of heroes, but made them themselves prey for the dogs
> And a meal to the birds. And the Plan of Zeus was fulfilled
> From the time that first these two stood apart, quarreling,
> The son of Atreus, lord of men, and divine Achilles.

In translating, one must always sacrifice something, so here as below, straightforwardness is given up to preserve Homer's order of telling. All the tale is there in all its implications for those who know the poem—and epic, if ever there was a genre, is meant for the second and subsequent readings. First the *Iliad*: The here-anonymous souls Achilles will send to Hades will be, to begin with, those of his own Greek comrades, and above all that of his dearest friend; his worst enemy cannot be made a prey for the dogs (11); the plan of Zeus is indeed to grant Achilles' wish, only with a terrible twist; Agamemnon, however, here named only by his doomed lineage, will have to surrender the rights of his lordship to the need of the Greeks. Achilles has now been twice named.

Of Odysseus, as yet unnamed in his poem, it is said that he "very much"

> Wandered since he sacked the sacred city of Troy.
> And of many men the towns and mind he knew,

d in the sea he suffered many pains in his spirit,
  iving for his own soul and the Return of his comrades.
But he could not rescue his comrades, though he was eager,
For by their own wantonness they were destroyed.—
Fools! who the cattle of the Sun On-high
Ate up. And so their Returning-day was taken away.
From anywhere, Goddess, daughter of Zeus, begin and speak
  to us, too.

The *Iliad* did not include the fall of Ilium, which happened between the epics; we now learn that Odysseus is the acknowledged sacker of the city—for he devised the stratagem of infiltration, the Trojan horse (35). As Hades is the warrior's home, Poseidon is the seafarer's element and the sailor's persecutor; so Odysseus' wanderings bring not death but multifarious knowledge "in the sea," meaning "on its islands." The wanderer suffers much to save his own *soul* and his comrades' *return;* it is a different thing, evidently, just to come home and to come home as Odysseus. We are told precipitously that he does not succeed in half his intention and also where—as *he* will say—the blame lies, and the story will show how he too sends heroes to Hades (26).

"Begin anywhere," the poet of the *Odyssey* asks the goddess again, using the word "Speak!," *eipe* (whence comes our term "epic"), at least a drier word, a word more of relating than celebrating, than the "Sing, Goddess" of the *Iliad*. Though both epics are intoned words, recited to the accompaniment of the lyre by the poet who "sings words taught by the gods and lovely to mortals," the *Odyssey* is by far the more sober of the two— sober *and* fantastic, where the *Iliad* is somber *and* passionate.

Of course, the Muse knows exactly where to begin: not just anywhere. Where has Odysseus been while all the heroes have returned? With Calypso, whose name means "I will cover" or

"I will conceal," and also with Poseidon, Odysseus' particular persecutor—it is in Athena's telling of Poseidon's anger against him that Odysseus' name is first mentioned, with an epithet meaning "god-comparable," in which it is hard not to hear a second meaning: "god-opposed" (*anti-theos*). Poseidon, as luck would have it, has gone to visit far-off friends while all the other gods are assembled on Olympus. And there the Muse takes us second, while Zeus is expatiating on the way mortals blame the gods for troubles that are their own fault. Thus enters the great scandal of all the Returns and the event that shadows Odysseus' homecoming: the murder of Agamemnon by the usurper Aegisthus and Agamemnon's own wife Clytemnestra. Zeus mentions right away that their son Orestes has already avenged the murder by killing Aegisthus. That he also killed Clytemnestra we only learn later, from Nestor; Clytemnestra seems to be taboo on Olympus. Then the sons of the Returners are brought on the scene and the stage is set for Telemachus' role in his father's retaking of Ithaca. And, of course, Penelope is tacitly present from the beginning on. The Muse does not begin just anywhere but indeed everywhere.

Poseidon's absence gives Athena a chance to complain to her father of Odysseus' virtual imprisonment by Calypso on her island, Ogygia. She asks him to dispatch Hermes to order the nymph to end the detention while she herself darts from Olympus to the palace gate in Ithaca. Well over two thousand lines but only a few days later Zeus fulfills his daughter's request—but that must be on non-linear divine time, for Odysseus has in fact been free more than three weeks before Athena returns from Ithaca to Olympus to urge Zeus finally to do it (41).

One thing more is revealed in that scene on Olympus that begins the action proper, the meaning of Odysseus' "speaking name": "Why do you now hate (*odysao*) him so much, Zeus?" she asks her father, associating his name with the assonant verb. Once more: Achilles and Odysseus have in common names marked by suffering (21), though their epics are as different as single-minded passion (*menis*) and many-faceted planning (*metis*).

ENDINGS

Neither ending is a culmination or a climax; both are more like a fading away. Dramas end dramatically, in "reversal and recognition." The *Iliad might* have ended with Achilles' blazing reentrance into battle, his climactic killing of Hector, his awesome Hades-like interview with Priam. But it goes on for ten days of inaction to end with Hector's funeral, the pyre, the bones, the mound over them: "And then they held the burial of horse-taming Hector." These are the last words of the *Iliad*.

Now this is strange: Hector is not the hero of the *Iliad*, and he tames no horses in it. Yet someone early on, perhaps Homer himself, did name it the "*Iliad*" rather than, say, the "Achilleis," and Hector is the "Stay" of the poem's city. In peace the Trojans were indeed horse tamers and so, presumably, was he. "Horse-tamers" is the ethnic epithet of the Trojans; "horse-taming Hector" means "Hector the Trojan par excellence." Hector himself is compared to a high-spirited horse. It is a horse that is finally Ilium's undoing, the famous Trojan Horse told of in the *Odyssey*. So it is horses that make and break Troy, though not within the *Iliad*.

Yet whoever named the epic did right, and not only because it culminates in an exemplary Trojan's death. Aristotle regards it as one more perfection of Homer that he excludes the end of Ilium from the *Iliad*, and so maintains its unity and concentration. The last line, however, intimates that end, for the man who had the fine sense, backed by power, to tame flesh-

and-blood horses, might have been the breaker of the wooden horse, and he is dead. But it is only an intimation, for the essence of epic is to be always *in medias res*.

The ending of the *Odyssey* is even more a fade-out. It has multiple opportunities to end: the stringing of the bow and the first few fatal shots, Odysseus' first night with his wife, the wooers' descent to Hades. But it keeps going, until the three generations, grandfather, father, son—the Laertidae: Laertes, Odysseus, and Telemachus—face nearly half of surviving Ithaca in revolt. In assembly some of the older men have been persuaded of their own responsibility for the massacre; the usurping youngsters have been consigned to Hades; the middle generation is largely lost at sea; the rest are out in force, fathers facing fathers. Eupeithes, father of the worst wooer, is slain by Laertes—and that is enough. Athena darts from Olympus to be present at the final battle, not under orders but yet with advice from her Father: Let us bring about "a deep forgetting" (*eklesis*) of the killing of these sons and brothers; "Let them love one another as before and let there be peace and plenty in abundance." Athena, in the guise of Mentor, encourages this one killing, which brings Laertes back among the man-slaying heroes. Then, when Odysseus and Telemachus follow Laertes' lead, she shouts loudly: "Stand apart right away and without bloodshed!" Here there is, at the end of the second epic, a reminiscence from the beginning of the first. There: "They two stood apart quarreling," here: "Stand apart without bloodshed" (*diasteten, diakrinthete*). Odysseus shouts too and tries to disobey; a flaming thunderball from Zeus falling in front of Athena reminds her of his advice. She speaks to Odysseus in all formality: "Zeus-born son of Laertes, Odysseus of many devices, hold and stop . . . !" lest you incur the wrath of Zeus. He comes to and "rejoices in his spirit." Oaths are administered to both sides for all time to come by

> Pallas Athena, the daughter of Aegis-bearing Zeus,
> Looking like Mentor in body and voice.

So the poem ends as it began, with Athena the helper of much-enduring Odysseus of Ithaca. She is in the shape of Mentor, the "Minder" (1), as the poet reiterates, so how does Odysseus know her? Does the bodily shape and voice of a human that has been assumed by a divinity change? Or does the initiate see *through* the guise to the Olympian shape of the Olympian goddess? It is possible, for three times in the last thirty-odd lines of the *Odyssey* Athena is called *glaukopis,* a word of uncertain meaning—"gray-eyed," "gleaming-eyed," even "owl-eyed"—but her very own. Does he see her in that oscillating way to which the secular analogues are those spontaneous optical reversals in which students of vision are so interested, like that famous Necker cube whose front face suddenly appears as a back plane? It is possible, but we do not know; the poem ends with the Homeric marvel and mystery: the divinity among humans.

Anyhow, it is over—and yet not quite. We know that Odysseus has one more trip to make, a token death to die (48). And then peace, plenty, mutual love, and a long life do indeed ensue. The real, the Homeric Odysseus is no perpetual wanderer who "cannot rest from travel," who is

> Made weak by time and fate, but strong in will
> To strive, to seek, to find, and not to yield.

The Homeric Odysseus comes home for good to rule his island, guide its promising crown prince, and live to a ripe old age with his peerless wife, his partner.

15

THE RETURNS

"RETURN" (NOSTOS), RETURNERS, RETURN DAY—these are re-current key words of the *Odyssey*. It is the poem of one Re-turn, that of Odysseus. "You ask about honey-sweet Return, splendid Odysseus, but the god will make it hard for you," says the seer Teiresias to him in Hades; he means Poseidon, but Odysseus' own palace will make it even harder.

"Return" is almost a technical term: It applies to the dis-charged war veterans coming home from Troy, each in his own way. It is not just Homeric; for example, in Aeschylus' nobly empathetic play *The Persians*, the Persian ancients bewail the reduced Return of their defeated expedition after the battle of Salamis in 480 B.C.: This time Asia invaded Greece, but once more lost. The word *nostos* is familiar to us in "nostalgia," "return-ache," a word coined in a medical treatise of 1688 for the debilitating sadness affecting mercenaries long away from home.

All the Greek chieftains except Odysseus have completed the story of their homecomings; some were normal though sad because a father came back without a son (23); some were dreary because the price has been too great (24); one was ter-rible because a wife had been faithless and helped to kill her returning husband (14); some, indeed, will never take place.

There is sweet Return, honeyed Return, lost Return, grim Return.

For most it must have been no different from what it always is—disorienting:

> Reading the wall of Troy
> Ten years without a change
> Was such intense employ
> (Just out of the arrows' range),
> All the world was strange
> After ten years of Troy.

Odysseus' Return, however, is distinct from the others. Not only is he late by ten years, but so very much has happened that Troy itself is a distant memory—almost as distant as Ithaca—and no longer the hated and missed cocoon of the encampment.

Everything about Odysseus' Return is prolonged by a sort of purposeful procrastination. As Augustine prayed, "Lord, make me chaste, but not just yet," so Odysseus seems to pray, "Zeus, speed my Return, but make it slow." On his circuitous and obscure route home it has been his purpose to gain "the Return of his comrades"—we will see just why that fails (33)—and of "his own soul." To be sure, in the epics "soul" (*psyche*) means the breath of life in the body on earth and the shade in Hades after death, not evidently a human spirit in need of salvation. Yet the poet makes so marked a distinction between Odysseus' ambition for himself and for his comrades that I want to ask: What is it in his purpose for himself that is different from his plan for his comrades? We will see what in fact he gains, and that in fact he fails for them (39).

At any rate, his Return is all prolongation, orchestrated in careful stages, even once he is out of Poseidon's inimical sea:

his convergence with his son who is returning fr
telemachy, his cautious, step-wise coping with th
the wonderfully choreographed postponement o
pair's mutual acknowledgment (41, 45).

Penelope will maintain, like a mantra and against all evidence, that "Odysseus far away has lost his Return to Greece,
and he himself is lost"—echoing Odysseus' own distinction
between himself and his return. It appears that Coming Home,
Return, is not so simple as surviving the sea and retaking a
palace; you may come home but not be there, you may return
but not be you. We will see how Homer's Penelope copes with
that truth (46).

16

THE POET OF THE ODYSSEY

THREE BEINGS HAVE A PART in the making of the *Odyssey,* the poem of Odysseus' Return. The first is the Muse; she has related the epic to the poet who invoked her. The second is the poet himself—call him Homer—who sings the composition that the Greeks heard and we read. The third is the teller of a tale of travel, the sort that we still call an "odyssey," and this is Odysseus himself (27).

Though she is the fountain and origin of the poetry, I cannot claim to know much about this Muse. She is a divinity, one of nine who sing for the gods on Olympus and sometimes on earth for mortals: Homer says "sing to us *too*" (31). This much the Muses' presence in the epics clearly betokens: It is not Homer who *creates* either the tale or its telling, the matter or most of the form; he *conveys* what they vouchsafe him to know—that is his claim. Poets evidently need to become creative only when the divinities recede.

About Homer as poet, Aristotle has this pertinent observation:

Homer deserves praise for many other things but especially because he alone of poets is not ignorant of what he himself ought to do as a poet. For the poet himself ought to say the least possible. For it is not in that respect that he is an imitator. Now the other poets are [themselves] in contention throughout the whole and imitate only a few things and rarely. But he, after a short prelude, straightway brings in a man or a woman or some other character, and nothing that is without character, but all have their own character.

The quality that Aristotle so admires in this epic poet, his personal reticence in favor of his proper work as an imitator of people and deeds, is even stronger in the *Odyssey* than in the *Iliad*. In the latter he does turn up a number of times after the prelude. For example, in the division of the *Iliad* made in antiquity the long manifest of the Greek naval contingents at Troy was known as the "Catalogue of Ships," and in beginning that section Homer especially calls for help: "Tell me now, Muses, who have your home on Olympus—for you are goddesses and you are ever-present and know all, while we hear only rumor and know just nothing . . ." Here the poet is asking for what we would call information, names of captains, places of origin, numbers of ships. And again, in that last confused battle when Achilles has returned to the field, he calls for help because he lacks the overview: "Difficult is it for me to proclaim all this as if I were a god." To make it absolutely clear that the poet knows himself to be beholden and inferior to the Muses, Homer adds into that same Catalogue of Ships, as if by the way, an account of the fate of Thamyris the Thracian, who boasted that he could conquer the Muses themselves, the daughters of Zeus, were they to sing against him. (Recall that Aristotle says that the less praiseworthy poets are forever contesting.) They, in their anger, maimed him and "took away his divine song and made him forget his lyre-playing." There seems to be some fear mixed into the grateful respect a poet has for his Muse.

Homer's poetic reticence is, as I said, even more noticeable in the *Odyssey*, where, as far as I know, the poet himself appears only in the prelude, unless we count the times Homer talks to his favorite, the swineherd Eumaeus, addressing him in the second person (43). But what he says in the prelude shows his trust: "Tell me, Muse, the Man . . ." he begins, and ends by turning the choice of starting point over to her: "Wherever" among the incidents befalling this man you want to begin, he says, "Goddess, daughter of Zeus, tell me *too*." I think he means: You sing to the gods, now let me hear.

With her help, then, he produces wonderfully inventive duplicities of poem making. He delivers a large part of the epic over to its "man"—I don't call him a hero because Homer never does (4). Yet although Odysseus by and large gets to relate his own adventures, there are exceptions: The two final adventures, Calypso's Ogygia (where Penelope begins to preoccupy him and from which he needs rescuing) and Alcinous' Phaeacia (where he requires hospitality and where he first tells his odyssey)—these two Homer reserves for himself to tell, so that he can anchor this Odyssean fantasy voyage in his own Homeric world (34).

Homer's Odysseus is the equal of his poet in artfulness as a teller of tales, a cunning mixer of truth and invention—I say "invention" because *Odysseus is not under the guidance of the Muses.* He never appeals to them. He experiences adventures, invents lies, tells truths on his own. His tales are as multifarious, as versatile as he is, and some of them will bring news of an Odysseus quite otherwise engaged than in fantasies (38).

This triplicity of authorship—Muse, Homer, Odysseus—together with the duplicity of the chief actor, makes the *Odyssey* the most complexly told tale I know. It is complicated though not bottomless, but rather clear and decodable. The abysmal infinities of romantic irony are not the Muses' way.

The singer to whom the Muses tell great things must be a master of the craft of poetry. That craftsmanship is separable from "the Muse who teaches, . . . or Apollo," we learn from Phemius, Odysseus' court poet, a man not overly courageous but loyal by his lights. Both Demodocus and Phemius have the divinity—it seems to be Apollo—within. Of the one Homer says that he is "moved by the god" to begin his song; the other speaks of the god who has planted in him all sorts of song. But Phemius in pleading—successfully—for his life also says proudly: "Self-taught am I"; he must mean that he has his Muse but no master who taught him the craft. He is, however, a minor minstrel; he orchestrates amusements and imagines that the gods listen. Homer casts a cool but humane light on him, for the poet of the *Odyssey* himself is no craven court entertainer, and his craft is not that of an amateur. Let me now give examples of the kinds of craftsmanship to be found in the poem (17–21).

17
NAÏVETÉ AND INSIGHT

THIS POET IS, THEN, SUPERBLY RETICENT, about his own feelings and even about his people's inner life—it seems. Inner states are reported in a fairly small, bold, semisomatic vocabulary. People feel and address their hearts, the seat of life and passion (*kardie, etor*), their "midriff" or chest (*stethos*), their spirit (*thymos*), their soul or breath of life (*psyche*); their organs of passion shrink, are rent, broken, encouraged, rebuked, are glad, rejoice, delight, take note. The affects, located in anatomical parts, don't seem to be very subtly differentiated.

There is a justly famous essay by Schiller, "On Sentimental and Naïve Poets." A sentimental poet is what we call "subjective"; sentimental poetry is primarily about the poet's own inner reactions, and his characters are reflected through these. The naïve poet himself is naïve and childlike to the point of apparent childishness. His world, however, is ingeniously crafted, and toward it he is severe, reserved, and above all, an observer:

> Being without any familiarity, he escapes the heart that seeks him, the longing that wants to embrace him. The dry truth with which he treats an object appears not rarely as insensitivity. The object possesses him totally; his heart does not lie, like an inferior metal, right under the surface, but wants to be captured like

gold in the depths. As the divinity behind the cosmos, so he stands behind his work; *he* is the work and the work is *he*.

This naïve poet is exemplified for Schiller by Homer among the ancients and Shakespeare among the moderns.

I am not sure that Schiller would agree with the meaning I am about to take from his words—though they certainly support it—because it all but erases the distinction between "naïve" and "sentimental." Nonetheless, it seems to me that the poet he is describing does not so much abstain from internality and subjectivity as make it external and objective. The *Odyssey* is the story of a soul in its progress, but its inner realm is shown as an outer world. Homer's naïveté is that form of poetic insight which makes the soul sensible to sight. I will be more explicit later (39).

18
BEAUTY AND CRAFT

THE MUSE CHOOSES TO BEGIN THE EPIC with Calypso, and from her island, bearing the primordial sounding name Ogygia, comes what seems to me the loveliest sounding line in the poem. Homer loves it too, for he repeats it, evidently from sheer pleasure, thrice, once in transposition. Calypso holds back Odysseus' Return, to keep him

ēn spēs- | sī glă- phў- | roī- sĭ lĭ- | lāī- ŏ- mĕ- | nē pŏ- sĭn |
eī- naī.

in hollow caves, longing for him to be her husband.

It is the Concealer's signature line, her longing expressed in bewitchingly gliding, slithering sounds, and with them goes a luxurious landscape surrounding the cavernous womb of Ogygia, which is the "navel of the sea." Hermes, irritated at this remote errand, lands there and sees something that "even an immortal who happened to come on it would wonder to behold and would delight in his heart" to see. The nymph dwells in a large cave:

A great fire was burning on the hearth and from afar the fragrance of cleft cedar and juniper were diffused over the island as they burned. And inside, singing in a beautiful voice, she went back and forth before the loom, weaving with a golden shuttle. And a wood had grown around the cave, luxuriant, of elder and poplar and scented cypress. And there long-winged birds were nesting, owls and falcons and long-tongued crows who ply sea-work. And there about the hollow cave ran a long stretch of grapevine in its prime, swelling with clusters. And four fountains, lined up, were flowing with white water, close to one another and turned one this way, one that. And round about bloomed soft meadows of violets and parsley.

No wonder this passage inspired painters, Breugel the Elder and Hendrick de Clerck, for example, whose *visualizations* show hundreds of details the words do not state but do intimate.

The words also convey the island *sounds,* as do Caliban's:

Be not afeard: the isle is full of noises,
Sounds and sweet airs that give delight and hurt not,

except that to the nymph's sweet singing there is on Ogygia the ominous counterpoint of the raptor bird's screeching and the crows' cawing. This is the place where all-enduring Odysseus finally goes into deep depression (34).

Homer, however, captures for his poem not only natural idylls but also well-crafted artifacts, not always as grand as Achilles' Shield (8), but delightful articles of daily use: weavings, goblets, furniture, a rustic wine bowl of ivy wood. "A wonder to behold" (*thauma idesthai*) is one of Homer's cherished phrases, one that rings in a reader's ear. It is used of all sorts of artifacts, from robes to chariot parts; sometimes the very house glows, as does Odysseus' palace at a great moment, so that Telemachus is overcome: "O Father, what a great wonder this is I am seeing with my eyes!" But no special magical glow is usually needed; everything shines and is a wonder to behold: a Phaeacian cityscape, Helen's souvenir-stuffed palace, a novelty baldric, a cunning key, a shish kebab deftly prepared, a silver-haired man rejuvenated by a divine goldsmith's overlay.

Homeric music is not always as slippery-smooth as Calypso's line. The beginning of the poem pops, crackles, and sputters with the pounding and spitting of the sea and its sailor's polymorphic ways and adventures, as well as his suffering (which you can recognize in the following transcription in *pathen algea*, as in our *path*ology, "study of suffering," and an*alge*sia, "painkiller").

> *Andra moi ennepe, Mousa, polytropon hos mala polla*
> *Plangthe, epei Troies hieron ptoliethron epersen;*
> *Pollon d'anthropon iden astea kai noon egno,*
> *Polla d'ho g'en pontoi pathen algea hon kata thymon . . .*

Besides suggestively smooth or plosive alliteration there is another kind of word music in Homer's craft: silent music. If "Heard melodies are sweet but those unheard / Are sweeter," yet most wonderful are those that silently suffuse a particular significance over a scene. When Telemachus enters Helen's house, he hears wedding music; these are her daughter's nuptial days, a somewhat melancholy moment surely for a woman who was nothing but beautiful. And when Penelope and Odysseus are about to go upstairs to their first night in twenty years, the house is sounding with the guileful music of a pretended wedding, a truly Odyssean accompaniment.

There is a third sound effect: the twice-heard sound, in which one meaning reverberates behind another. One is the double meaning of "I have lost" and "I have destroyed" already mentioned (10). Besides Achilles who speaks thus of Patroclus: "Him have I lost [or: destroyed]," Hector later says of his people "I have lost [or: destroyed] them in my folly" be-cause he insisted on engaging with Achilles. And of course, Athena says it of Odysseus when he appears on Ithaca all alone: "I never doubted in my heart that you would return, having lost [or: destroyed] all your comrades."

So also, when Odysseus is asked by the one-eyed monster Polyphemus for his name, he fools him by giving it as *Outis*, "Nobody" (29). *Ou* and *me* are Greek particles meaning "no" and "non-" respectively, and so both *outis* and *metis* mean "Nobody." A discerning listener (poor Polyphemus is partic-ularly word-deaf) will know that clever Odysseus has in fact told who he is: *metis,* "design," is his signature word; he is al-ways *polymetis,* "much-designing" Odysseus. And he makes his intention quite clear; he says, "My own heart laughed at how my name and my perfect design (*metis*) had fooled him."

To these wonderful devices of the poetic craft add the sub-tle metric variations already described, particularly the heavy fifth foot in a dactylic hexameter that expects a light one. Yet another example, of significance in judging Odysseus, occurs when they torture the impudently treasonous goatherd Melan-thius by racking and hoisting him to the roof beam; the lines go heavy on the word for binding; although possibly a justi-fied act, it is still an ugly one (43).

It will be a comfort and an incitement to the reader of this book that for every wonder to behold or to hear that I have found, I have, I am sure, missed several dozen, and the precise charm of Homer's language escapes all paraphrasing.

19
VISIBILITY AND VISUALITY

HOMER WAS PROBABLY BLIND. He composed epic poetry which, by its very name, is a work of the word, the uttered, verbal word, *epos*. The singer, who must often have been the maker of the poem, intoned the words and accompanied himself with plangent strokes of a small, hand-held lyre and perhaps occasional licks. It is hard to imagine that the musical aspects of the performance, the intricate sounding of length, pitch, and stress, would mean much to us now, for the pleasures of the ear are, generally, somewhat more time bound than the significations of language. But the music seems to have been an integral part of professional recitation; it made the poet a "singer," *aoidos*. Yet right within the epic people do also tell tales that hold the audience rapt, in meter of course, because they live in the poet's world, but without benefit of singsong or lyre—Odysseus above all. So epic is words first, music—and sometimes beat-setting dance—second.

Now I want to show that epic is, third, pictures, being the most brilliantly illustrated poetry imaginable, in which the eye (though of course the inner eye) is inextricably involved.

VISIBILITY

Homer's blindness, insofar as it is legendary, signifies this truth, and if it was a fact, might even account for it: Blindness after sighted life might well intensify the inner sight particularly desirable for the epic poet, as it evidently did for Milton. So, apparently, Homer thought, for Phemius, the "Fame-Singer," Odysseus' court singer, may be blind—it isn't quite certain—and of the attestedly blind Phaeacian Demodocus, the "People-Enchanter," whom the Muse loves best—and so does Homer—he says that she quenched the singer's sight but gave him the gift of sweet song. One might infer that she dimmed the sight in order to enhance the song:

Aye, on the shores of darkness there is light,
    And precipices show untrodden green;
There is a budding morrow in midnight;
    There is a triple sight in blindness keen.
Such seeing hadst thou, as it once befel
    To Dian, Queen of Earth, and Heaven, and Hell.

On the other hand, Odysseus, who does have the sailor's keen sight, has a phenomenal visual memory as well. He says to his wife: "My heart envisions . . . ," which is all but a formula for mental imaging; and he proceeds to describe in the clearest detail a brooch she had given him over twenty years before (46). Of course he is also capable of superlative visual fantasy.

I have spoken now of the gleaming visibility of the contents of Homer's world (18), of the Homeric singer's second sight, of Odysseus' visual capacities. It is not necessary to belabor the point further that visibility is the fact of Homeric facts. If further proof is needed, it is in the never-ceasing visual realizations of the Homeric text, beginning with the earliest figurative Greek pot painting, through Roman narrative wall painting, to the movies of our times.

Visibility is particularly but not exclusively characteristic of epic: It has been said of poetry in general that *ut pictura poesis,* "poetry is like a picture," and that "phanopoeia," "mental image-making," is one way poets charge words with meaning. How words can bring about images, how verbal articulations can leave visual residues, how language, which, no matter how highly specified, can never lose its generality, is able to induce something so densely particular as a spatial picture—that is the mystery of cognitive mysteries, *in principle* a mystery, and therefore bypassed here. But what Homeric visibility in effect asks of the receptive reader—that can be shown.

VISUALITY

The visibility of poetry demands visuality from the reader. Visuality is the readiness to form mental images. It is a well-known fact, already observed by Aristotle, that through clear and distinct visualization tragic and epic poets (and, for that matter, eyewitnesses) can save their verbal accounts from incongruities. But Homer goes much farther. He insinuates into his visualizable descriptions crucial elements not made explicit in his narrative. Hence the hypothesis here is that these images are not merely illustrative or even verificatory but actually independently revelatory; by seeing them in your mind's eye you learn something that was indeed implicit in the words but not stated and probably not previously present to you. Let me try to show how it works using the most spectacular exemplar of a Homeric moment I can think of. Its proper epiphany requires remembering and envisioning. As so often, Homer tells the tale; *you* make the connections.

We are on the next to last day of the final battle that is the climax of the *Iliad.* To see the heroes on the field, we must visualize Greek armor: It covers the whole man; certainly the helmet hides the whole head with its nose piece and cheek plates. Men in battle are recognized mainly by their distinctive armor, sometimes also by their size. Achilles and Ajax are huge, Odysseus is short, and Hector is mid-sized. Achilles counts on this full coverage when he sends Patroclus into battle with his own armor. The Trojans cannot make out whom they are facing; at first they think, as they are intended to, that Achilles has returned. Hector, not shamefully but wisely, it turns out, flees when he sees Achilles, and does not return to battle until Apollo, in the likeness of an ally, tells him that it is only Patroclus. Not until he strikes off his helmet does Hector know by sight whom he has helped to kill. He strips Achilles' armor—"a wonder to behold"—from Patroclus' body and puts it on; Zeus has to shrink it to fit him.

It is now the last day. Priam sees Achilles raging all over the field, monstrous in size and magnificent in his new Hephaestean armor. He pleads with Hector to retreat within the walls, for he foresees all that is to come if his best son falls: little Astyanax hurled from the walls, Troy sacked. (In fact, it will be Achilles' son Neoptolemus who kills Hector's boy, son slaughtering son as father killed father.)

Death of Astyanax: sherd from c. 750 B.C.,
and cartoon reconstruction.

Hector briefly considers surrender, but as in a dream he knows it is hopeless. Everything is now dreamlike: "Never now can I dally with him from an oak or a rock as a maiden dallies with a youth, as a youth and a maiden dally with one another," he drawls to himself in the dreamy, drawn-out, repetitive ritual language of an old folktale. He trembles and turns to run from Achilles. Three times they speed around Troy, while all the landmarks so familiar to besieged and besiegers are recalled in the nostalgic detail of places already gone. They run "as in a dream it is not possible to pursue the one who is fleeing; no, he is not able to escape him nor the other to pursue"—so Achilles, the swiftest of all, cannot catch Hector, the shorter and heavier man: "In front a good one fled, but there pursued him a far better one—speedily"—though not speedily enough. They run as in a dream and they run as if already shades: "It was not for a prize like a bull's hide that the contest was, but they ran for the soul of horse-taming Hector"—and of course with Hector's death, Achilles' soul too is doomed:

> And in that space our shadows run,
> His shadows there and mine,
> The little flower, the tiny mounds,
> The grasses frail and fine,
>
> But narrower still and narrower
> My course is shrunk and small,
> Yet vast as in a deadly dream
> And faint the Trojan wall.

Achilles is driving Hector in toward the wall. Now comes Athena in the guise of Hector's favorite brother, a false phantom promising false aid, a desperate hope. So Hector stops and turns to Achilles: "Now my spirit prompts me to stand and face you."

The sight enrages Achilles past all humanity; he becomes beastlike. He refuses Hector's plea that his body be returned: "There are no oaths among lions and men, and wolves and lambs have no like-minded spirit. . . . It is impossible for you and me to be in a friendship." And Achilles looks for an opening in "the beautiful bronze armor that covered all the rest of his skin," the armor that Hector had stripped from Patroclus. He finds one at the gullet and drives in his spear.

When Hector faces around to confront his pursuer what is it Achilles sees? It makes one's hair stand on end to re-envision it in the mind's eye. But it is up to us to summon the image, for Homer says not a word till the awesome moment is past, and even then he won't remind us that Patroclus was wearing Achilles' armor. It has been almost three thousand lines since Hector stripped and donned Patroclus' armor, but we are to remember and to see.

Achilles sees before him Patroclus as he looked when Achilles last bade him goodbye! But there is something more eerie: He is confronting himself, as he looked before his friend's death—Achilles, son of Peleus, dressed in his father's armor. As his spear finds its way into Hector's collarbone, it is not the hated other alone whom he transfixes, but two intimate beings besides: his dead friend and his old self.

20

SIMILE: THE DOUBLE VISION

THE GLORY OF HOMERIC ART, however, is the simile. Similes are superimposed likenesses made in words. Schematically, the formula for a Homeric simile looks like this:

Like an imported image of something remote,
So is a given representation of something at hand.

For example,

As a Carian or a Maeonian woman stains ivory with purple to be a cheek piece for horses, and it lies in the treasure chamber though many horsemen pray to wear it—it lies as a source of pride to the king, an ornament to his horse and a glory to its driver,
So were your thighs, Menelaus, stained with blood, your shapely shins and your ankles below.

In general, similes don't, of course, have to be in pictorial form; they can be comparisons of ideas, of an idea at hand to an idea sought out for the purpose:

As the novel is to prose,
So is the epic to poetry.

But not in Homeric epic, where the likenesses are always visualizable. Moreover, a Homeric simile usually—not always—puts the remoter picture, the one introduced to make the comparison, before the given event that is to be so enhanced. The effect on the listener thus obtained is what gives Homeric simile the poetic power of a gentle rapture that carries the listener away to another land and peaceful pursuits: As the Carian dyer stained the ivory purple, so Menelaus' thighs were stained with blood.

A metaphor, on the other hand, turns the comparison into an identity. It is a "semantic impertinence," an abruptly instant conjoining of not obviously similar things without benefit of the comparing "like." Metaphors therefore have the formal aspect of lies, for without the mitigating intervention of the comparison, they tell patent, though illuminating untruths: "What light through yonder window breaks? It is the East and Juliet is the sun"—a literally false but metaphorically meaningful assertion.

There are in fact some few metaphors in the epics: "Sweet sleep, limb-loosening, leaped upon him, slackening the cares of his spirit." But there are many more similes. In the epics people do lie copiously, but not the author insofar as he wields this particular poet's craft. He sticks with the more leisuredly plausible and more gently assertive figure—the one that gives time for a double vision to arise. That is how Homeric similes gather their power, as I hope to show.

The *Iliad* does not only have more, it has more beautiful similes than the *Odyssey,* which in fact specializes in splendidly ugly ones. The reason is plain: The *Iliad* is full of the real ugliness and brutality of war, close at hand and described in incessant detail: teeth knocked out, gullets pierced, nipples punctured, chests crushed, innards dropping, gore spattered, spears trailing from wounds—one reason this epic is not the better-loved by women. The horror needs the saving grace of the simile's distancing double vision. The most poignant simile I know graces the death of one Gorgythion, an obscure side-son of Priam, mentioned just once—in death, killed by Teucer the archer, who is trying to hit Hector—an accidental death for an incidental youth. Teucer's arrow finds instead Gorgythion's chest,

> And like a poppy he let fall his head to one side, a poppy that
>   is in a garden,
> Laden with fruit and the showers of spring,
> So he bowed to one side his head made heavy with helmet.

If you've ever seen a blowy Greek poppy whose crepe-thin red petals glow in the sun, and then the slender stem buckles under the weight of its pod, you will know the vision through which Homer sees the broken young warrior.

It would take many pages to set out and classify all the similes of the *Iliad,* mostly war-mitigating similes; I say "mitigating" because the likenesses are far off and have their beauty: lions leaping on fawns, fires raging in forests, hunters pursuing a boar, squalls coming in from all directions, women weighing out wool in a balance, mules dragging a ship's timber, a ridge holding the floodwaters and then breaking, a dense cloud of starlings shrieking at a falcon, women staining ivory—and a myriad more, especially in the long battle scenes where they come thick and fast, often piled up in clusters.

To me the loveliest of the war similes is the likeness made for the Trojan camp hopefully burning its fires all night because the Trojans have come out from behind their city wall, expecting to storm the Greek line and fire the invaders' ships in the morning:

As in heaven the sharp-clear stars shine around the gleaming moon, when the air is windless and all the peaks and high headlands and glens show up, and from heaven breaks forth the immeasurable ether, and the stars are seen, and the shepherd rejoices in his breast,

Such was the number of the fires kindled by the Trojans between the ships and the streams of the River Xanthus.

In contrast, here is a grotesque but apt likeness from the *Odyssey*. It is the anxious night before Odysseus will string his great bow, the test whose passing means the return of his kingship. Odysseus cannot sleep and tosses about:

As when a man before a great blazing fire turns this way and that a stomach filled with fat and blood, eager to have it roast quickly,

So he tossed this way and that, pondering how he would lay hands on the shameless wooers, since he was alone in the city.

It is of course worry that gives him insomnia, but there is—in the *Odyssey* comedy is always close to the surface—a contributory cause. Antinous, the chief miscreant, had presented disguised Odysseus that day with a prize for beating up the endemic beggar: just such a roasted stuffed paunch—indigestible beggar's food, evidently.

Uglier yet is the simile for Odysseus when the suitors have been slaughtered and his old nurse finds him among the bloody bodies, himself befouled with blood and filth. As a lion who comes from feeding on an ox in a farmstead, breast and cheeks stained with gore and "terrible to behold," "so Odysseus was befouled, feet and hands above."

Then there is, on the contrary, Penelope weeping in Odysseus' presence; his eyes stay fixed, as though of horn or iron, as he hides his tears with guile:

As the snow melts on high-peaked mountains, the snow that the east wind thaws when the west wind has shed it, and as it melts the rivers run full,

So her beautiful cheeks melted as she shed tears and wept for her husband—though he was sitting by her.

These figures can make you a little drunk with their poetry, but eventually the question arises: How do they work? One answer is in the fact that the *Odyssey* has and *needs* fewer similes than the *Iliad*. It needs them less because a large part of the *Odyssey* itself takes place in that realm to which the "as" part of the simile transports you, those homely, idyllic, wild, essentially peaceable scenes. That is the clue to the way a Homeric simile works its effect. It is usually—not always—a kind of brief *rapture;* the listener is seized from the dreadful or murky present, the situation at hand, and taken to a larger and more peaceful, ordinary, or natural world.

More precisely, when the poet begins with "As," an image, an inner vision, forms. The tempo of formation is leisurely for the image descriptions are often long. This image, remote from war or present grief, lingers and lays itself over, or is projected by the imagination on, the real situation; the noises of war recede and the vision rises up. As I said, it seems to me to matter here that the image part of the simile comes first: *It* forms the scene, the world that is laid over (or hung behind, it scarcely matters) the irrational and hardly bearable reality of life. For that lions hunt, fires rage, squalls romp, and women workers stain ivory is comfortingly in order.

Especially in the *Odyssey,* however, similes don't only mitigate, they often magnify, as a great snowmelt puts a natural grandeur behind the woman who dissolves in tears. Sometimes they make just another casualty of war unforgettable, as happens to poor Gorgythion, seen through a broken-stemmed poppy in the *Iliad*. Sometimes they work broad fun, as when a roasting stuffed pouch casts its figure over an insomniac man. Sometimes, rarely, they intensify the beastliness of a human being.

Sometimes they simply double the beauty, as when the stars in heaven are projected on the Trojan campfires. This ether-inundated figure is particularly apt for showing what is characteristic of Homeric simile. Consider a reversed rendering of the usual order: "The campfires shone like the stars in heaven." The fact leads off, the figure follows after. But by then it is too late; the given situation has entrenched itself, the imaginative companion is just an adjunct, a mere embellishment. Strictly speaking, of course, the factual circumstance always does precede, since the narrative prescribes the situation on which the simile projects its image: The Trojans must be camping—for the first time in ten years—outside their walls for the simile to have something to take hold of. But then the narrative stops and the moment of double vision occurs: The image is given room to form in the reader's imagination and then to encompass, frame, color the real event, to lift it out of its narrative bonds into another world. No matter that the narrative is itself already poetry; within the simile it is the factor of mundanity or brute reality. Simile is thus the poetry of poetry. The image seizes the event into another world, under whose aspect almost everything is significant and beautiful. It is the world of the poet's imagination, a world that unifies and signifies by similitude; it is the world which makes possible that double vision by which everything in human life is *like* something that mitigates or magnifies it.

Similes, it is said, "defamiliarize" the placidly normal world by reflecting it in estranging likenesses. Homeric similes, however, often do the reverse: They project the excruciating enormities of battle onto an integral world of peaceful and homely work as well as onto beautiful and boisterous nature, and so they transfigure the incessant abnormality of man-made war. In a flash they show the isolated siege world of Troy as not so hopelessly disconnected from the sound natural world of work and weather, but bonded to it by sudden visions of similarity.

Here is an additional observation: It makes strange but wonderful sense that similes do much the same work in Homeric epic as do the gods, who also beautify and magnify human existence (1); the poet and the gods are colleagues in the transfiguration of human life.

21
NAME TAGS AND SPEAKING NAMES

EVEN BEFORE WE SEE SCENES and imagine similes, however, we hear names, at a rough estimate a thousand in the *Iliad,* where two armies, each with its heroes, are contending in a small place. Thus the *Iliad* is like a memorial wall on which the warriors, living *and* dead, of *both* sides are inscribed. In the *Odyssey* there are only half that many names; though its world is larger, its population is sparser.

NAME TAGS

The names of Homer's entities—people, animals, artifacts, places—usually have a tag attached, an identifying adjective, the so-called epithet. It is quite often metric filler, put in to make the hexameter come out right. The best example is *dĭŏs,* meaning "divine," a word made pallid by routine use.

But at important junctures the epithets are clearly, almost provably, used with most conscious intention—especially where they seem to be most egregiously misapplied. Then they are a heads-up signal; they effect a name connotation that we are expected to notice. They make a point, often poignantly.

The case of swift-footed Achilles, sessile by his tent, yet essentially swift of foot and fate, has been mentioned, as has that of horse-taming Hector who, although taming no horses, embodies the spirit of Troy at peace (11). So too Odysseus, who has not in fact sacked a city in a decade, is given by Homer the epithet "city-sacker" just as a jeering young nonveteran, one of the wooers, offers him employment as a farm hand. The epithet reminds us that Odysseus is the victor of Troy, then and now, and intensifies the impertinence under which he has to labor and control himself. It happens again near the end, when the most decent of the wooers, an older man, arrives in Hades where he is recognized by Agamemnon as his host at the time when he and Menelaus had come to urge Odysseus—a reluctant warrior, as were they all—to join their expedition. Odysseus was even at that early moment "the sacker of cities," long before he contrived to find a way into Troy; long before he even went to that city, Odysseus was its sacker—as he would be ever after. It belongs to his being, it is who he is from the poem's second line on.

The most frequent of Odysseus' epithets are the *poly-* adjectives that fit him like a skin: "of many designs" (*polymetis*), "of many devices" (*polymechanos*), "much-enduring" (*polytlas*). But one of these, the one given him in the first line of the *Odyssey*, "of many turns" (*polytropos*), is used only once again, by Circe, the witch, the "Encircler." When she sees that she cannot turn him, the man of many turns, the multifarious, the versatile, into anything he chooses not to be, she exclaims: "Surely you are Odysseus the multifarious!" His steadfastness and his flexibility are two aspects of one nature.

SPEAKING NAMES

The names themselves often speak: *Nomen est omen.* Above all, Achilles and Odysseus, those antithetical human beings, share the lot of suffering as expressed in their names. In "Achilles," the ancients thought they heard *achos*, "ache, pain, grief." Homer speaks of the unbearable pain, *achos*, that is in Achilles' heart as he arms himself in Hephaestus' armor. And Odysseus, speaking to Achilles in Hades, says soothingly: "Don't let being dead make you ache, Achilles (ak*ach*izein, *Ach*illeu)"; and as Achilles' home is Hades (13), so Hades' chief river is called *Ach*eron.

In "Odysseus," "lamenting and grieving" (*odyromenos kai acheuon*) can several times be heard linked together. But Odysseus' name is explicitly as well as implicitly interpreted. Three words and meanings contribute to the name-nature. The first is sounded out by Athena to Zeus: "Why do you now hate (*odysao*) him so much, Zeus?" It is the meaning his grandfather Autolycus explicitly intended when he named the newborn. Because he himself was "hated by many"—as "Wolf-Himself," a thief and liar, might well be—he called his grandson the "Hated"—a curious legacy for a man who, though quite a liar himself (37), is blessed with a prosperous old age. To be sure, Odysseus is hunted for a while by Poseidon's hatred, so perhaps the naming was meant apotropaically, as a charm to turn away the very thing mentioned.

Second, the word for one who weeps and laments (*odyromenos*) is to be heard in Odysseus' name, as when Calypso finds Odysseus sitting by the shore weeping for his Return (*odyromenon noston*).

Third, *odyne* means, like *achos*, "pain or suffering," as in our "an-*odyne*," a pain-allayer. "He has gone out of sight and hearing and left me in pains (*odynas*) and groans," says Telemachus.

One who is hated, has grief, and gives pain; the man who attracts persecution, the man who feels deeply, who inflicts pain—here is the counterweight to another Odysseus: the crafty survivor, the insouciantly imaginative poet, the faithful family man.

The great trio at Troy includes Ajax, and his name too speaks of grief: *Aias,* in which can be heard the Greek wail *aiai.*

As Achilles and Odysseus come close in their names, so their sons are distinguished by theirs. Both children were conceived before the war, but Achilles' son was by enough the elder to have come to Troy to replace his dead father; he was in fact Odysseus' most effective companion in the Horse (13). He is called Neoptolemus, "New-to-War." Telemachus, "Far-from-Battle," was a baby when Odysseus left; he sees no combat until he recovers the palace at his father's side. What the two men want for and from their sons is expressed in these names.

I would guess that Homer inherited the names of the major people with the outline of their stories—for all we know, they were once real, though, as I've said, that hardly matters, because somewhere, sometime, some such people have surely walked the earth—and that he made the most of what he had. And then he invented the subsidiary names to fit the people who turn up in such situations: the two singers, Phaeacian Demodocus, "People-Enchanter," who holds the folk in his spell, and Phemius, "Fame-Singer" or just "Voice" (*feme*); the two witches: Calypso, named "I will Conceal," who hides Odysseus from sight and hearing, and Circe, "Encircler," named after the hawk that gyres as a man-raptor; the pair of bad servants: Melantho and Melanthius, the "Black Ones," named for their defiled souls. The serendipitous exploitations and inventions of omen-bearing names is all but inexhaustible.

22
TELEMACHUS AND
HIS TELEMACHY

AS ODYSSEUS HAS HIS ODYSSEY, so Telemachus will have his telemachy before father and son converge. At the very beginning (14), we learned of Odysseus' captivity on Ogygia and what Olympus is planning to do about it, but soon the Muse shifts the action of the *Odyssey,* the incidents that Aristotle thinks of as its plot, to Ithaca, where Athena arrives to stir the son to action.

TELEMACHUS

She comes in the shape of Mentes, a traveler from Taphos, way out at the margins, where Odysseus may in fact have visited. She presents herself as a trader in metals and arrives in a guise at once plausible and unfamiliar to the boy. She gets his full attention immediately.

Telemachus was evidently left behind by Odysseus as a very little baby, along with the other folk, the old, the draft dodgers, and the wives—among these last we hear only of Penelope and Odysseus' mother Anticleia. That baby is now on the brink of manhood, perhaps a little immature for his age, which cannot be less than twenty. An ineffective viceroy, a debilitated grandfather, a declining grandmother, an elderly doting nurse, two loyal ranch hands, unruly house servants, and a beleaguered though staunch mother—these have peopled the growing prince's home life. Such fatherless children tend to hang around the kitchen and courtyard and to get their up-bringing from the servants, for well or ill. Telemachus calls Eu-maeus, the excellent swineherd, "Dad." Eumaeus himself was reared by Anticleia together with Odysseus' sister Ktimene (otherwise unheard of). Clearly Eurycleia, Odysseus' nurse, figures in his life for good, but not the servant girls, some of whom have run wild and gone bad.

It is easy to imagine the effect these impudently lewd, jeer-ing girls must have had on the boy who, as far as we know, is inexperienced. And here I might as well report one bêtise that stains Telemachus. After the slaughter of his first battle he dis-regards his father's orders that these treasonous girls who have been carrying on with the wooers should die a normal death by the sword. Instead he devises for them "no clean" death, for they have tainted his house by sleeping openly with the wooers, betrayed his mother—very likely it was Melantho who reported the stratagem of the unraveled shroud to the wooers (42)—and probably treated him without kindness or respect when he was a boy looking for company. These out-of-control wretches he hoists up en masse by a cable and hangs them dangling from the roof. To be sure, his father, whom we know to be capable of brutality in moments of stress (5), has suggested extreme measures to his son. While still in the guise of a beggar he has threatened Melantho, reared by Penelope herself and so the most despicable of the lot, saying that Telem-achus would cut her limb from limb; during the battle he him-self orders Melanthius to be trussed and strung up. But ex-ample aside, Telemachus' concentrated fury, accumulated over two shaming decades, is at least understandable.

For otherwise he seems to be a lovable young man, in some ways finer than his inveterately lying father. For example, when he makes a pretty serious mistake during the battle, having left the armory door unlocked, he candidly admits it.

Of the three sons that figure largely in post-*Iliad* life, he is by far the most appealing. The generation of Trojan veterans' children has come of age. Among them Orestes of Mycenae, saddled with the most excruciating burden of matricide as his father's avenger, is not a figure even a tragedian can make very attractive; Neoptolemus of Phthia is a young savage, though decent. But both their deeds are only hinted at in Homer's epics, while Telemachus of Ithaca is a full figure. Will he be Odysseus' equal? Well, we know that Odysseus will reign for a long time (48), and the son has time to mature. "Few sons are equal to their fathers, most are worse, a few better," says Athena-Mentes to him. But, she goes on, there is hope for you, since "the design-making of Odysseus is not entirely absent in you." He makes a natural team with his father, and he stands his man in his first battle. A poet paints a portrait of the son as seen through the father's eyes that strikes me as just:

> This is my son, mine own Telemachus,
> To whom I leave the sceptre and the isle—
> Well-loved of me, discerning to fulfill
> This labor, by slow prudence to make mild
> A rugged people, and thro' soft degrees
> Subdue them to the useful and the good.
> Most blameless is he, centered in the sphere
> Of common duties . . .

This is Tennyson's Ulysses speaking as he gets ready to sail once more into unknown adventures, and so there is a hint of condescension for his homebound son. But the real Odysseus, who stays, might say the same in fully expectant approval.

TELEMACHY

To Athena-Mentes Telemachus confesses a secret fear, such as a boy who has never seen his father might harbor. He receives Mentes with boyish courtesy, apologizing for the conditions in his palace. The goddess reciprocates by observing that he is like his father in his head and beautiful eyes. But he is doubtful: "Mother says that I am his child, but I don't know—how ever would any one himself know his parent?"

Much later we will hear Penelope say it to Odysseus in no uncertain terms: Telemachus was born of us two. But it bespeaks a certain tension, the tension between a mother beset by wooers and her adolescent son, that he has real uncertainties.

Athena reminds him of Orestes who avenged his father; she instructs him to call an assembly—his first act as a crown prince and a signal that things are changing. He is to call the wooers to better conduct; then he is to fit out a ship to go on a trip of discovery, to find out his father's whereabouts and to present himself at the courts of Argos, that is, in the Peloponnesus. Athena herself has told him a suitable half-truth: Odysseus is alive but kept captive on a seagirt island by a harsh and savage man—some description of the luscious Calypso!

The first Ithacan assembly in twenty years ends in inconclusive chaos. Moreover, Telemachus makes the mistake of telling the wooers of his proposed trip. They plan to assassinate him on his return leg, supposing that he has gone out to get help from Sparta or to procure from Ephyra the deadly poison for his arrows that Athena had told him his father had got there. Odysseus hadn't, or at least he will make no use of it, but Telemachus must have let on. They are still considering his death in the last moments before their own—a bad lot.

Telemachus gets off efficiently. Odysseus, who speaks his mind very readily to his goddess, later asks why she couldn't just tell his son where his father was rather than send him off on a wild goose chase, for indeed he learns nothing pertinent of his whereabouts. "Was it perhaps that he too might suffer pains wandering on the unresting sea?" he asks, with the very words that describe his own travels at the beginning of the *Odyssey.* His question gets to the point of the Telemachean exercise: It's *not* to learn *about* his father, but to *parallel* his odyssey.

It is a sort of abbreviated year abroad. He will present himself at the courts of Argos. His life will achieve, as I said, a certain parallelism with his father's (41). But above all, he is to learn something about himself that he needs to know with full certainty before he can play his role in Odysseus' Return: whose son he is. The telemachy is a trip toward what we call "identity," as the odyssey may be understood as a voyage of self-projection (39). When Nestor asks the young prince whether his business on this trip is private or public, Telemachus answers confidently that it is very private: to seek news of his father. But when Menelaus a day later asks him the same question, he avoids answering, for by now it has evidently come to him that he is on an intensely personal quest with large public consequences. And a woman who hasn't done the world much good so far will be his saving and enabling grace (24).

23
NESTOR AT HOME

NESTOR'S NAME MEANS "RETURNER," from *nostos*, "return" (15). Nestor's Pylos is Telemachus' first stop in the Peloponnesus. Here he learns what a happy palace, ruled by a duly-returned, kindly father, looks like. It is probably a revelation, but also an irritation, to him—and comic relief to us, in its ceremonious leisureliness.

Telemachus had set off clandestinely in a borrowed ship. He had extracted a promise from Eurycleia not to tell his mother of his trip unless he fails to make a timely return. Athena, now as Mentor (Mentes the stranger is replaced by Mentor the old viceroy—both his "Minders") has expedited matters. Telemachus takes the tiller, and they have a lovely night sail. Such nocturnal sailing is unusual for a Greek sailor but wonderfully recognizable for anyone who has ever had the tiller of an open boat, skimming along on a moonlit midnight, with a light following night breeze—Athena has supplied the favorable zephyr: "And the wind filled the belly of the sail and the purple wave gurgled loudly about the stem of the ship as she went." Homer can never resist an idyllic interlude. After an overland journey they arrive in Pylos, where Telemachus, so far homebound and without worldly experience, is shy and embarrassed and needs encouragement from his mentor. There is a slyly comical moment when Nestor hands Athena a cup to pour a libation to Poseidon whose feast it is—a goddess making an offering to the god with whom she is angry because he is persecuting her favorite among men. She makes the best of it, avoids Odysseus' name, and prays for Telemachus. Homer says, smiling: "So she prayed and *herself* fulfilled all." Later in the evening, she will decline, as the gods always do, to sleep in a mortal's palace and will fly off. After this evening Telemachus is on his own.

He makes himself known and asks for news of his father. Nestor being always Nestor, he gives meaning to the word "epic"; his tales are leisurely and extensive. In the *Iliad* he had the epithet *agoretes*, "Speaker," "Holder-Forth," even "Ranter"; it is the term Odysseus applies to the infuriating Thersites: "the shrill Ranter" (5). Nestor soon launches into long reminiscences of Troy and the "Returns" (*nostoi*). We hear this new item: that the Atreidae quarreled after the fall of Troy; brother Menelaus was eager to leave, and brother Agamemnon was anxious to stay to placate Ilian Athena with sacrifices—the fool, she wouldn't have listened, Nestor says with Athena right there. Finally he reminds Telemachus once more of Orestes' avenging of his father's murder, but tactfully suppresses the mother's part in it; as if to sensitize Telemachus to his own mother's situation, Athena amends his story. Again Nestor blunders into a comical situation: He has told Telemachus how Athena loves Odysseus: "If she would be willing to love you similarly and to care for you in her heart," you could easily drive thoughts of marriage from the wooers' minds— Nestor has belatedly remembered the situation in Ithaca. Telemachus is skeptical: Even a god couldn't bring his father home. Athena-Mentor is annoyed: "Telemachus, what a word has escaped the barrier of your teeth"—a god could easily bring anyone home. Nestor's ambiance induces conversational pratfalls.

He really knows nothing to the point, but by now Telemachus is anxious to hear more of the great scandal of the Returns. Nestor gives details, including Homer's own touch: the good man in this terrible tale is the singer, to whom Agamemnon had given the regency. This minstrel is exposed on a desert island, while Aegisthus takes Clytemnestra home, "he willing, her willing"—in poignant contrast to Odysseus who sleeps with Calypso "he unwilling with her willing." (The murder of Agamemnon is, incidentally, a much starker crime in the *Odyssey* than in Aeschylus' tragedy *Agamemnon;* in the drama Clytemnestra can persuasively represent the killing as an execution because he has sacrificed one of their daughters to gain the Trojan expedition safe passage; in the *Iliad* this daughter is safely at home, one of the three the king offers to Achilles as compensation for Briseis.)

Orestes has returned from exile after eight years—hence fairly recently—to kill his mother and her lover. Nestor ends by advising Telemachus to go straight home, but first to visit Menelaus at Sparta who is "newly" returned from Troy after much travel—Menelaus has been home at least two years, for we learn that he arrived in Agamemnon's Mycenae on the day of the usurper's funeral. But such is old Nestor's sense of time.

Nestor is a venerable old man and has been for a long time; Telemachus is awed: "They say he has been lord for over three generations of men"—and perhaps also a little cheeky: "For me he figures as an immortal." We know a lot about him in the *Iliad*. He can be irritatingly interfering. He can counsel doubtful practices, making it necessary for his gallant young son to return the prize he has won unfairly at Patroclus' funeral games. He can give fatally bad advice. And of course, he tells long reminiscences of his far-off youth at inconvenient times. To Telemachus he is warmly hospitable if none too tactful. Odysseus took the crown in all kinds of tricks, he says to the son, "your father, if you are genuinely his offspring." It is not what the boy came to hear. Moreover he and Athena between them must be raising the son's anxiety about his mother's conduct to a fever pitch.

But Nestor also has flashes of insight, as when he guesses the secret of Achilles' prolonged withdrawal from battle (10). He is kind and moderate, and the three generations of Pylos seem to live in amity a life that is slow paced, fussy, peaceful, and handsome—surely an eye-opener to Telemachus who has grown up in a roiled, single-parent household.

Telemachus sleeps one night at the palace. The next morning brings endless ceremony, and then they are off to Sparta, overland by chariot. Telemachus has not quite won the recognition he needs but he has gained a friend, a young friend of his own age and station, evidently his first. It is Peisistratus, Nestor's youngest—Nestor had, it seems, other progeny even younger than Antilochus, who was the youngest fighter at Troy and was Achilles' second closest friend, whose death is still mourned in Pylos. Telemachus will not stop in Pylos on the way back from Sparta; he will call on his new friendship: "We can boast of being hereditary friends from way back through our fathers' friendship, and what is more, we are of the same age, and this trip will further confirm our like-mindedness." Therefore, don't drive past my ship on to your palace, but let me off, "so that the old man won't detain me against my will in his house, wanting to be friendly, when I need to hurry to get back." Peisistratos knows just what he means and complies.

So, on this comic note, delivered deadpan in heroic meter, ends Nestor's part in the *Odyssey*, which was this: to be the exemplar of a peaceable Return.

The next station after Pylos in the telemachy is Lacedaemonian Sparta.

24

HELEN AT TROY
AND HELEN AT HOME

HELEN IS THE CAUSE AND THE PRIZE of the Trojan War; Clytemnestra is the scandal and the bane of the Return; Penelope is
the aim and the anchor of Odysseus' odyssey. Each of these terrific women is in some way responsible for the deaths of men.
It is one of those Homeric reticences that we are not explicitly made to realize that they are in fact closely related, though
the knowledge throws a strange light on the Returns. Helen
and Clytemnestra are indeed sisters, married to the brothers
Menelaus and Agamemnon. They are the daughters of Tyndareus, who is, in turn, brother to Icarius, Penelope's father.
This fraternal relationship is not mentioned in the *Odyssey*
(though it seems to have been common knowledge); you have
to scrape these family involvements together from all the ends
of the poem.

Penelope is therefore cousin to that baneful sororial pair,
the Tyndarides, which makes her nobility the more affecting.
It is so felt by Agamemnon, who, in Hades by his wife's hand,
compares her badness to Penelope's faithfulness. And the relationship explains why Helen is so much on Penelope's mind
at a crucial moment: She fears succumbing, like her cousin, to
temptation; she is afraid of being too easy and doing something shameful with huge consequences, though it is only too

easy a surrender to her husband that this proud wife is on guard against.

All women of high station weave. Homer shows both Helen and Penelope at work, and their weaving distinguishes their characters. Helen at Troy weaves to pass the time and, apparently, for exhibition: a great purple tapestry displaying the horse-taming Trojans and brazen-coated Greeks fighting for her sake, a work of artful vanity. Penelope weaves to make time stand still, in secret: a shroud for her father-in-law, Laertes, upon the completion of which she has promised to give herself away in marriage; it is a work forever in progress because she unravels by night what she has done by day, a work of self-forgetful faithfulness.

Helen, her cousin, is on Athena's mind too as she remonstrates with Odysseus, who, literally on the threshold of his house and the recovery of his marriage, seems to be hesitating: You fought nine years for white-armed, high-born Helen, and by your plan was Troy taken—and now you hold back!

Who is this Helen? A perpetrator or a victim? Are the Greeks rescuing or harassing her? Are the Trojans detaining or protecting her? Is she good for anything except to look at?

HELEN AT TROY

In the *Iliad* the Greek chieftains, especially the older ones together with their favorable gods, resolutely keep up the notion of her unwilling abduction and so of the righteousness of the expedition. For them Argive Helen is "the Trojan boast."

But the younger generation is apt to show contempt and even hatred for her, especially Achilles, who calls her sneeringly that "all-over-beautiful" maiden—an adjective usually reserved for tripods and tables here gracing a woman of forty! Mourning for Patroclus, he bewails his lot, to make war for "coldly creepy" Helen; the Greek word *rigdanes* betokens a cold that makes you shudder.

And of course, back in Ithaca they hate her, especially decent Eumaeus, who had himself been kidnapped as a little boy by his nurse, the all-too-willing woman partner in a pretended abduction. He knows how these things work and places the blame: "Would Helen's clan had utterly perished," he says.

The older Trojans keep up the contrary side in support of their own cause. Paris/Alexander (he goes by both names), the young Trojan prince who brought her to Ilium, claims repeatedly that he is fighting for her and her *possessions,* intimating that she came willingly bringing a dowry along. They all insist on calling Paris "the *husband* of fair-haired Helen." Priam, the royal father, emphasizes that she is not to be blamed for the siege, the gods are—with some justice, for a connected cause of the war was said to be an incident barely mentioned in the *Iliad,* the infamous "Judgment of Paris," the beauty contest among the three goddesses at which Paris insulted Hera and Athena by choosing Aphrodite, the one who "serviced his trouble-making lust." It is part of the background knowledge of the Trojan world; they fight within sight of "Beauty-Hill" where the contest took place, and there Ares, Aphrodite's lover, and the gods of the Trojan party sit and watch the battle.

The old men of Troy find Helen enchanting. She has heard of an impending duel between her two husbands. After much prodding, Paris has agreed to meet Menelaus in a decisive duel to end the war then and there. She comes to view it on the wall because she has a yen to see her Greek husband—a pretty cool piece of curiosity. There sit the old gentlemen, good at talk but no longer at fight, "chattering like cicadas." They all wish she were gone, danger that she is to Troy, but they also love to see her; she seems to go, contrary to decorum, unveiled. Hector's Andromache, a real wife and mother, comes properly attired to the wall to say good-bye before the battle; she runs back to the wall after hearing of Hector's death, and on seeing him dragged around before the city, she faints, losing her veil, in a decent woman a sign of being utterly undone.

Helen, who is the best judge, blames herself. Indeed, she shows her shame almost shamelessly. "Hateful me," she calls herself, and "me the evil-devising bitch." She tells Priam that she "followed" his son, leaving behind her beloved daughter and the "lovely women-friends of her peer group"—death would have been better. She contrives to be pitiable without ceasing to be hateful:

> All Greece reviles
> the wan face when she smiles,
> hating it deeper still
> when it grows wan and white,
> remembering past enchantments
> and past ills.

I think she is the prototype of the hypernaturally beautiful woman who, forever looked at by all men, really likes none of them. What she likes is to be in a throng of Trojan women, the scandalous center of chat; when Aphrodite comes to her, the goddess wisely takes the shape of an old loved woman attendant.

She is most uninhibited with Hector, who is always kind—though severe—with the troublesome pair; he has built Paris his apartment. But he is impervious to her—though she tries. She calls him the brother-in-law of a bitch, evil-designing:

"Would a bad windy squall had swept me away on the day my mother bore me." Would I had married a better man, she tells him. And it is plain whom she has in mind—the solid big brother.

This second husband of hers, a bowman who fights at a distance (5) and who goes unaccountably absent from battle, who has to be jollied by his big brother into returning to the fight, who lets himself be called "woman-crazy" by him and a "virgin-peeper (*parthenopippa*), vain of your hair-do" by Diomedes, seems to be a charming, feckless fellow, captivating as a lover but tiresome as a husband, good at declarations of love, but in the long run not much of a man or a warrior, to Helen's shame. Aphrodite has to threaten Helen to go to him, as he appears in their bedroom, dressed more as someone returning from a dance than as a warrior back from battle. The reason that Paris is at leisure for lovemaking this particular time is that the duel between Helen's two husbands that was to end the war is aborted just as Menelaus is dragging him by the helmet into the Greek lines. For Aphrodite wafts her darling to safety to put him to bed with Helen. In human terms: His helmet strap breaks and he makes off, in an excited state. She is talked into making love with him then and there, because she is afraid to lose him in the fighting—he is, truth to tell, all she has. Yet, she can't stand him: *You* take him, she says to Aphrodite, get him to make you his wife or slave, leave Olympus and sit with him and take care of him.

Helen has landed in a sad and sordid situation, having neither the gravity of tragedy nor the lightness of comedy, and it is hard to imagine that after a decade of this hollow misery in Troy her aspect could anymore amaze an admirer:

> Was this the face that launch'd a thousand ships.
> And burnt the topless towers of Ilium?

The viewing on the wall mentioned above, one of the subtlest moments of the *Iliad,* will resonate in the *Odyssey.* It takes place at the Scaean Gate, the Left (perhaps "Sinister") Gate, where not long after the closing of the *Iliad* her lightweight husband will kill the grandest of the Greeks with that despised weapon, the arrow; Hector foretells that death in dying. When the dim old men ask her to point out the Greek heroes in the field, she readily discerns Agamemnon, her brother-in-law, and huge Ajax, and Idomeneus of Crete, whom she has met in Menelaus' house. She looks for, but sadly fails to find, her twin brothers Castor and Polydeuces, long dead in Sparta —an added note in her desolation. Menelaus, whom she ostensibly came to look at, she simply overlooks. But she is acutely aware of Odysseus, who had come into Troy more than once for negotiations. Old Antenor, his host on one occasion, describes his looks in detail (2); we may imagine Helen listening with avid interest: She knows Odysseus well, perhaps too well.

HELEN AT HOME

Telemachus and Nestor's Peisistratus enter the palace at Sparta to the sound of wedding music, just when Odysseus, deep in Hades, is telling Achilles of the glory gained by his son Neoptolemus (41). This same son, now lord of the Myrmidons, is at that very moment spoken of in Menelaus' and Helen's palace as the bridegroom of the "beloved" baby daughter Hermione whom Helen had left behind when she absconded, a daughter who has inherited the beauty of Aphrodite. Neoptolemus and Hermione, unlike Telemachus, lucky for all his troubles, are not the best-loved pair of children; Achilles says outright that Patroclus matters more to him than does his son, as Paris obviously, though long ago, once mattered more to Helen.

They are not heard of again in this epic, but they have one's good wishes.

To hear the wedding music must make us—though surely not young Telemachus—think of Helen as a prospective grand-mother, almost a contradiction in terms! We know she had been away from Sparta for twenty-seven years—twenty of them in Troy, for the expedition evidently did not get organized to pursue her until the tenth year of her elopement. In the tenth year after that Troy falls; she and her Greek husband then travel for seven years, getting home just in time for her sister Clytemnestra's funeral.

They have been to Cyprus and Phoenicia where—and this will be a key to the *Odyssey* (39)—the Returners seem regularly to have gone as marauders and merchants, in search of some booty with which to come home; Troy had evidently been too impoverished during the siege to yield much by way of the spoils of war. Menelaus also stopped in Egypt, as was usual. There he entered the fantasy realm briefly and heard of Odysseus—and grew very rich, while Helen obtained a store of drugs which she will draw on this very night.

There is a bizarre but revealing story, long known to the Greeks through the poet Stesichorus. It is again related by He-rodotus in the fifth century B.C.: The Egyptian priests he vis-ited claimed with a lot of circumstantial detail that Paris had stopped in Egypt with abducted Helen, that the straitlaced pharaoh of the time took Helen, the innocent victim, under his protection and seized Paris' loot, but let him go. It is in fact reported of Alexander in the *Iliad* that he brought home treas-ure from Phoenician Sidon when he returned with Helen—clearly the spoils of a common piratical venture. At any rate, the Trojan War, the priests said, was over a phantom, and the reason the Trojans wouldn't return Helen is that they didn't have her. These priests are at once giving the Greeks the moral right to invade Asia Minor (since Helen *appears* to be in Troy), and also intimating the childish futility of the exercise. Recall that Herodotus thinks that if you look far enough behind any great war you will find a woman who is its cause or instigator.

Now it is the tenth year after Troy, and Telemachus arrives. Helen is a woman of fifty or so, and surely the wedding festivities are a somewhat strained merriment for her, as the palace is generally a joyless place. There is the aging, burnt-out couple; Menelaus is unhappy amidst his wealth and often weeping for his murdered brother and all the men who died at Troy. His marriage with Helen is sonless, for Helen has no other children; he has only a slave-born son (who is also getting married).

If Menelaus, who was never very forceful, is now a reduced man, Helen of Sparta is certainly no longer Helen of Troy. She descends from her fragrant chamber like Artemis the golden-arrowed, the chaste goddess—she who used to be Aphrodite's girl! A later poet asks if this aged Helen has found love and repose at home with her husband:

> No one has cared to say. The story clings
> To the tempestuous years, by passion bound,
> Like Helen. No one brings
> A tale of quiet love. The fading sound
> Is blent of falling embers, weeping kings.

Another poet, similarly preoccupied, envisions the atmosphere—mistaken as to fact, but not far off in feel—by imagining the romantic moment when Menelaus first sees her again at Troy. This comes next:

> So far the poet. How should he behold
> That journey home, the long connubial years?
> He does not tell you how white Helen bears

Child on legitimate child, becomes a scold
Haggard with virtue. Menelaus bold
    Waxed garrulous, and sacked a hundred Troys
    'Twixt noon and supper. And her golden voice
Got shrill as he grew deafer. And both were old.

The incomparable glory of Homer is that he *does* care to say
and *does* behold, with subtlety and verisimilitude: Menelaus
remains a kindly, recessive man. Helen has no more children;
though nearly old (or worse, thoroughly middle-aged), she is
still capable, given the incentive, of working enchantments as
she presides in her palace stuffed with valuable souvenirs—
which Telemachus, tactfully eliciting their provenance, admires in a stage whisper to Peisistratus.

She does one great thing for her sad old husband. As Leda's
child by Zeus (Tyndareus is actually her human foster father,
since divine parents do no child raising) she gets Menelaus into
the Elysium of the immortals "where there is no snow nor
heavy storms nor ever rain," among the real heroes. But for
young Telemachus she does something truly wonderful, the
one thing most needful, not as a child of Zeus but as the
woman she is.

She *recognizes* him. Recall that when Athena tells him that
he has Odysseus' looks and beautiful eyes, he says uncertainly:
"My mother says that I am his." Menelaus half suspects who
the visitor is—it is discourteous to ask before a meal has been
served—because the son hides his face when Menelaus speaks
of him as a newborn and of Odysseus as missing. (Just so does
his father at this very time in Phaeacia while the song is of Troy
(41).) But Helen descends and recognizes him at the first
glance. She never saw anyone—awe seizes her as she looks—
so like another as he is like the son of great-hearted Odysseus,
this baby he left behind when he went to Troy, for the sake of

"dog-faced me." (She can't leave off revelling in her shame.) The lovely thing is this: She says she never saw any two, man or woman, look so alike as Telemachus and Odysseus' *son*. She doesn't say that he looks like *Odysseus* but that he looks like the *son* of Odysseus, like himself. Of course, she's never seen this son before, but she evidently has the intuition to recognize immediately what the son of Odysseus must look like, to recognize him instantaneously.

Moreover, she had taken one look and asked her husband, "Do we know who among men these claim to be who have come to our house?" And she points to him: "that *man*," he is the one who looks like Odysseus' young son. It may be the first time in his prolonged boyhood that he has been called a man, and by such a personage! I think that perhaps Helen is never more beautiful than when she gives this boy the recognition that makes him Telemachus, the son of Odysseus, a young *man*.

Here is the moment to think of Odysseus himself who is on this very day in Hades (41), where he has gone to discover the way home. He finds out nothing of consequence in that respect, but he learns, as we will see, something much more valuable (32). In a parallel fashion Telemachus, who has gone to discover his father's whereabouts, will get no useful information bearing on that question at either court, but he has just learned something that makes the trip worthwhile, even indispensable.

Helen is not working on mere intuition, because as it happens she knows Odysseus well, probably intimately, and her lovely gift to his son may be the fruit of an indiscretion with his father—that is Helen. She herself later tells of an odd episode, yet another Odyssean mission, a spying sortie we hadn't heard of, when he came into Troy in the very realistic guise of a beggar battered with self-inflicted blows. (So he has had practice in playing the role in which he will enter his own palace!) The Trojans were fooled, but not Helen. He tried to evade her, but it ended up—she does not say how—by her bathing and oiling him and his telling her all the Greek plans, a very old version of a situation spymasters dread. He escaped after killing some Trojans, and she ends the tale with a confession that Aphrodite blinded her when she left Sparta, coupled with some flattering comments on Menelaus' brains and looks, no doubt to keep him from wondering about that bathing session—such hospitable bathings are normally done by handmaids. Is this the first time she has confessed outright that she followed Paris from erotic passion? In any case, she is of all mortal women, besides his own mother, best qualified to recognize the son. I doubt he understands her story; he isn't meant to, she has seen to that. All in all, this is her finest moment, at Troy or at home, and a wonderful thought: that it is Helen, the cause of so much sorrow, who gives Odysseus the son he needs to accomplish his Return.

Menelaus now too receives Telemachus courteously and warmly, if ineptly. He tells of his plan to give Odysseus a city in Argos and to bring him and his household to live near Sparta. He clearly has no idea what rocky Ithaca means to the Laertidae (29). But his wish throws light on the politics of Ithaca (46).

Together they weep, each for his own lost or dead—in this world there is never any shame for men in such weeping. Peisistratus too weeps for Antilochus, the most lovable youngster at Troy, the brother he hardly knew. He turns out to be disarmingly like his father in sententiousness: "I take no pleasure in supper-time weeping . . ." Then he gets a little nervous and, I think, the youngster's diction slips a little just where ours would: "I do not blame who cries for the dead among mortals. . . . Indeed that is the only prize for woe-stricken mortals:

to cut our hair and let tears drop down our cheeks." These Nestoridae just have a touch of comedy about them in their ceremony.

Amidst all this sadness Helen goes to work, witch that she is, with her Egyptian drug, "pain-killing and wrath-reducing," that makes one forgetful of evils. It is only after having dropped this tranquilizer into their wine that she tells the young son and the old husband that risky story of Odysseus the beggar. Menelaus in turn gives a more detailed account of the Trojan Horse infiltration, Odysseus' great stratagem. Again Helen plays, by her husband's innocent telling, a very strange part, although she has claimed she is by now anxious to be a Greek again. This time, according to Menelaus, she mimics the voices of all the Greek wives, tempting the men inside the Horse to come out; it is self-restrained Odysseus who holds them back, even clamping his hand over one Greek's mouth.

The next day Telemachus tries to fulfill his mission of getting some news of his father. It is now Menelaus who tells stories, of his Egyptian adventures and of his brother's murder—like Nestor, leaving out Clytemnestra, perhaps because he thinks it is not the best thing for Penelope's son to hear. In Egypt, under magical circumstances—he too has been in fairyland—he had heard of Odysseus in Ogygia, but that is now several-years-old news.

Telemachus says gracefully that he could stay and listen for a year, but that he must urgently get home. He thanks Menelaus for his inept gift of horses—Ithaca has no flat pasture and is horseless—but he'll be glad to have portable treasure. Menelaus, smiling, gives him plate instead—he has plenty.

Here we leave Telemachus, Odysseus' grown-up son. It is really only for a very short night, but the interval takes up five thousand lines, that five-twelfths of the whole *Odyssey* which is devoted to the telling of the complete odyssey (27), until

Athena comes for the son in Sparta, in the middle of that same night, to fetch him for his convergence with his father and the denouement at the palace (41). She is full of instructions, about the ambush of the wooers in the straits of Ithaca and about the disposition of his treasure—by which means she comes to speak of the prospects of a bride for him. And she tells something new: The Tyndarid family, her father Icarius and her brothers, have been urging Penelope to take the richest of the wooers, Eurymachus—that Argive family has never liked her marriage into provincial Ithaca (46). Athena implies that Penelope is willing and may go off with some of the already diminished palace treasure. You know, she says to the son, how women are, they forget their former husbands and children and are eager to enrich the current man. All of which is pure inciting invention on her part: Odysseus isn't dead, and Penelope thinks only of him and her son. In human terms the young man can't sleep and is filled with hopes and anxieties.

In this state of mind he wants to get up and go, then and there. His friend knows you can't go driving in a chariot at night. In the morning he can hardly wait while the royal pair choose presents—Helen's own personal gift is the most apt one possible, to fit the night's thoughts: a bridal gown—what else? Just as they are at last leaving there is an omen that Helen anticipates ponderous Menelaus in interpreting: An eagle bears off a tame white goose from their barnyard. This eagle, "coming from the mountain," she says, means that Odysseus is even now at home to take vengeance on the wooers and rescue Penelope. She may be vaguely thinking of Orestes, whose name means "Mountain-man," and that Penelope's name, significantly deriving from the word for web (*pene*), is also, incidentally, the word for a kind of duck. However Helen comes by her insight, she is confident, and of course, she is right.

Telemachus' parting words to her are: "So may Zeus grant . . . and I will worship you at home as a divinity." He is full of her. She hasn't, for once, seduced him, but she has bewitched him, though benignly—the older woman helping a belatedly maturing boy. She has treated him as a man, the interesting son of an interesting father. When he gets home he tells his mother, in a comically by-the-way manner, about seeing her cousin. And, to her delighted amazement, he gives her self-assured orders: Mother, don't worry me now, "but take a bath and put some fresh clothes on yourself."

And finally he tells her about Calypso who is by force holding his unhappy father, since he is without ships or comrades.

So Penelope now learns first, that her husband is with a woman, and second, that he is alone—a personal and a political fact of momentous interest. But this conversation with his mother is subsequent to Telemachus' meeting with Odysseus, which, in turn, must wait till after the telling of Odysseus' own odyssey.

Telemachus' telemachy is now over, of all the *Odyssey* the part where stately diction and subtle wit are married to best effect.

25

THE STATIONS AND SIGHTINGS OF ODYSSEUS' ODYSSEY

THE ADVENTURES OF WHICH Odysseus is now to tell are so amply fleshed out with wonders that their elegantly articulated skeleton remains hidden from a first view. Here it is, an artful armature:

	Phaeacia	Sleep at arrival	
1	Ismarus		Ships lost
2	Lotus-land		
3	Cyclops		Men lost
4	Aeolia		
	Ithaca	Sleep	
	Aeolia		
5	Laestrygonians		Fleet lost
6	Circe		
7	Hades		
	Phaeacia		Phaeacian queen interrupts
	Hades		
	Circe		
8	Sirens		

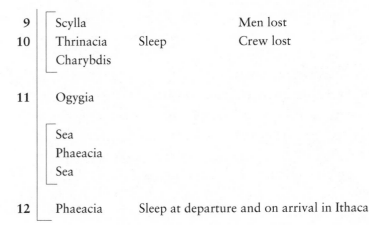

9	Scylla		Men lost
10	Thrinacia	Sleep	Crew lost
	Charybdis		
11	Ogygia		
	Sea		
	Phaeacia		
	Sea		
12	Phaeacia	Sleep at departure and on arrival in Ithaca

COMMENTS

■ Phaeacia is the magical land where the odyssey is told; it is Odysseus' *place of emergence,* forever inaccessible after him, from which he is returned, asleep, to Ithaca.

■ There are *twelve* distinct adventures, all but two of which take place in fantasy realms. Ismarus in Thrace is a real city, a convenient *point of departure.* Hades is *no fantasy place* either; its location is known to all Greeks, though only two mortals have returned from there alive, Heracles and now Odysseus.

■ Calypso's island, Ogygia, is the place where Odysseus passes *seven of the ten years* of his eclipse. Only two of the adventures ever appear in the *Odyssey* outside the odyssey: Thrinacia, where Odysseus loses the last of his men, is brought to our attention by Homer himself in the Prelude (14), but news of Ogygian Calypso has actually seeped into the human world of the epic: Menelaus, who has himself entered the fantasy realm, is there told of Calypso; he tells Telemachus, who tells Penelope: Menelaus' word is the only connection the two worlds have that is not through Odysseus; the odyssey is a nearly hermetic, that is, a sealed world.

■ The odyssey is a kind of *ring tale* that ends where it begins, with Odysseus leaving Ogygia. Odysseus breaks the cycle with the words: "Why should I tell you this tale? I am enemy to telling again a clear-told tale" (27).

■ There is an early *sighting* of Ithaca, a near landfall that is thwarted by Odysseus' sleep. There is later on a similar sighting of Phaeacia before Odysseus is swept out to sea. There are a number of other archings back, as shown in the chart.

■ Each such return represents two passages of *danger* separated by an interlude of longed for, sometimes treacherous, *rest*.

■ By the number of events, *Hades is the central adventure* of the *Odyssey,* especially if Ismarus the real is excluded or the magical arrival in Ithaca is included among the adventures.

■ By the measure of lines, *Thrinacia,* where Odysseus' own crew is doomed to the last man, *is central*. Their fatal deed is recorded in *the exact middle lines* (as best determinable) of Homer's *Odyssey*. Thrinacia, "Trident Island," is the crux of Homer's *Odyssey!* (33)

26

ASLEEP ON THE WATCH

A LOOK AT THE "STATIONS" OF THE ODYSSEY will show how often Homer reports Odysseus asleep at a crucial moment (25). "Sweet sleep" comes on him within sight of Ithaca after only a few adventures, and the chance of a landfall is lost; sweet sleep causes him to lose the last of his men in Thrinacia; it is while he lies in sweet sleep that he is wafted home to Ithaca.

Odysseus, so the poem's prelude says, strives to save his own *soul* and the *return* of his comrades. He succeeds in one and fails spectacularly in the other. The fact is first on his mind and increasingly colors his return. For the would-be usurpers in his palace are not only children of draft dodgers but also of men whom Odysseus led to Troy.

We might go so far as to say that his endeavor is just the opposite of that announced: to lose his comrades, to ruin their return. I would not wish to saddle Homer's people with an unconscious, a roiled reservoir of desires unknown even to themselves. But they *are* capable of a lot of psychic duplicity. As Odysseus sinks into the world of his imagination, he seems to require solitariness. Indeed, whatever we may think, this seems clear: The last adventures are not imaginable with companions, and *he* is not imaginable without these adventures.

Every skipper has a problem with sleep, but *his* sleeping is perfectly timed for disaster. Moreover this captain, who was so well trusted at Troy, has managed to lose his sailors' confidence—not in his competence but in his solid intention to bring them home. By the time they engage in the last, completely fatal act and broil the forbidden cattle of the sun from sheer starvation while their captain is asleep upland, they are in full mutiny, led by Eurylochus, the second officer. As any reader of sea tales has learned, whatever sea law says, sea sense knows that in a mutiny the captain is always culpable.

The crew's disaffection has been festering for quite a while, as early as his first sleep. It overcomes him because he held sheet and tiller for too long after they left Aeolia, "Squall Isle," with a bag given Odysseus by the king of winds; the men think it contains treasure he means to keep for himself. They open it within sight of home, and it is full of contrary winds. Eurylochus doesn't trust Odysseus' assignments; he refuses to go on reconnaissance into Circe's house, rightly scared of a snare. Later he cannot avoid seeing that on account of Odysseus' failure to stay alert himself, to alert his crew, and to obey Circe's instructions they lose six men to Scylla, the barking monster. Soon after this disaster they come to the island of Circe's father Helios Hyperion, "Sun On-high," which Circe has told him to avoid since the slaughter of the sun cattle on the island is taboo. But Eurylochus objects: You may be made of iron but we are tired and hungry. (Homeric folk say "iron" where we say "steel," as in "man of steel" or "steely-eyed"— it is how Odysseus looks when Penelope dissolves in tears.) They disembark and give oaths not to touch the cattle. They run out of ship's provisions and slaughter some of the animals from famine, while Odysseus sleeps inland (33). All but he drown.

Once more he sleeps when the Phaeacian ship bears him home; once more others pay, for Poseidon cuts the Phaeacians and their island off from the world for helping the man he hates (35).

Odysseus' sleep is dreamless, as far as we know. After all, he himself is in a sort of dream, and while people sometimes have so-called "lucid dreams," where they *know* they are dreaming, they don't seem to *dream* that they are dreaming—human consciousness rarely goes beyond the first levels of reflectiveness. Odysseus' sleep in the odyssey is indeed what Homer reports it is: "Sleep, the brother of Death." Odysseus' odyssean sleeps are such as might seize a man who is working at peak effort physically and imaginatively. They come suddenly, irresistibly, and inopportunely, like a brief restorative death.

Yet *are* they so inopportune? There is in Odysseus a strong streak of what one might call opportunistic passivity. There are these times when he lets go, somehow knowing that the thing that must needs happen will happen. Witness the loss of his comrades on his watch. So Athena greets him as he returns to his own, real island with the double-edged words: "I knew in my heart that you would return, having lost [*or:* destroyed] all your comrades." The odyssean Odysseus lives up to his name: hated, suffering, pain-bringing (21).

His wife at home is, wonderfully, an opportunistic sleeper as well (42).

27
THE POET OF THE ODYSSEY

HOMER COMPOSED THE ODYSSEY but Odysseus tells the odyssey. He tells it a first time to the Phaeacians on Scheria, the "Enclosed Coast," that art colony of the fantasy. He tells it a second time to Penelope in Ithaca, which is as real a place as ever was. No one else in this world ever hears of it, except that something has leaked out about Calypso the Concealer (24). To ask how Homer knows of the odyssey is to drive the question concerning the origins of poetry to dizzying extremes, though Homer's own answer is not obscure: Olympus takes a—distant—interest in Odysseus' sojourn in fantasyland, and so the Muses know, and they tell the poet of the *Odyssey*. The fact to be noted, a wonderful but perfectly reasonable fact, is that Odysseus himself, as he tells his tale, never calls on the Muses. This is *his* story, private, secret; *he* has lived it and *he* tells it. It exists, with small exceptions, only in *his* telling. It is a tale hermetically sealed yet also in close contact with the world (39). And since its telling is embedded in Homer's *Odyssey* as an interlude in what Aristotle regards as its basic plot, it is certainly poetry, sung as Homer sings, though Odysseus only *tells*—lyreless.

"Poet" is Greek and means "maker" (*poietes*). Odysseus is a poet in his own right insofar as he makes, shapes, his tale. He does it among the Phaeacians (*Phaiekes*), whose name carries in its sound (if not etymology) the word *phainein,* "to bring to light, to make appear." It is the word whence comes *phantasia,* "fantasy, imagination." Scheria is the place where things derealized shine out in their truth. Thus the odyssey is a voyage *of* the imagination though by no means merely *in* the imagination, a voyage which is first canonized in words, that is to say *told,* among the Phaeacians. Thereafter it is a work of epic art, *factually fantastic* and *actually true.* These oracular assertions will be given a sensible explanation below (39).

Singers call on the Muses to sing or tell them the fame of men, but the maker of the odyssey never, as I said, appeals to these goddesses, for he is telling a personal story, his own. That is the deep motive that drives Odysseus to "lose" his men; the deep recesses of the imagination from which this tale comes cannot imaginably be reached in the company of a fleet or even a flagship. These are—it is a cruel fact—sacrificed to the requirement of Odysseus' story. Such things happen. People sometimes sacrifice others, and do it moreover in no outrightly culpable way, that they may then do what they must and be what they are. I think Homer knows that about Odysseus and shows it in a light coruscating with some revulsion and much love.

In a camp without professional bards, Achilles sang to the lyre of the fame of warriors; he hoped the world would honor him too. Odysseus is an amateur as well, but he tells, lyreless, of the desires of women, dangerous, powerful, to be worshiped, dominated, and ultimately discarded for a true wife. And as I said, his tale is not for publication.

Those who hear him recognize him for a poet. King Alcinous and his Phaeacians, who are all artfulness, see in Odysseus "not a seducer or a thief" such as are the many men "who fashion falsehoods from places one cannot even see," a compliment to the poetic truth of his tale as well as to its brilliant

His Skills

visuality. Eumaeus, the well-born rustic, is so charmed by Odysseus' cunning concoctions—just those lies of which Alcinous holds him innocent—that he compares him to a singer "who has learned from the gods to sing to mortals songs of longing, and they are wildly eager to hear, whenever he sings."

This poetic gift is part of Odysseus' versatility: He is an athlete of power and finesse, a nimble boxer, a runner in his younger years, a discus- and spear-thrower, and, so disastrously for Ajax, a smart wrestler (6). But above all, he is an archer, not (as he claims) in battle where the bow is not the weapon of the great (5), but in the hunt where it belongs. His bowmanship is something out of the ordinary. With the deftness of a minstrel he strings his great ancestral bow, with the easy smooth motion of a skilled singer who inspects his lyre, trying the tuning of the instrument, and "it sang beautifully under his fingers, like a swallow in voice." Odysseus' archery is like that of the archer-musician Apollo, the teacher of singers, to whose altar in Delos he has made a pilgrimage and on whose feast day he will retake his palace by means of his lyrelike bow (43).

Like Homer, Odysseus loves and respects professional singers, especially the connoisseurs' own bard, Phaeacian Demodocus, the People-Enchanter, who sings a hilariously uncensored ballad of Hephaestus, how with his cunning net he—literally—caught Aphrodite and Ares in the act (8). But moved by the Muse, Demodocus sings also of the fame of men, of the quarrel between Achilles and Odysseus over the way to take Troy (7), and at Odysseus' own request, of Odysseus' greatest device, the Trojan Horse—Odysseus sends him a large gratuity, a slice of fat boar's back, and Homer too praises his sweet song. For all his admiration, however, Odysseus pulls an old café trick on Demodocus: The local musician finds that his fiddle has, so to speak, been borrowed by a guest virtuoso who eclipses him for that night.

Sometimes the singer conducts a circle dance from the center with the strokes of his lyre and the beat of his song, as Demodocus leads the well-trained Phaeacian boys. Sometimes a minstrel merely accompanies the freewheeling revels, as Phemius attends the antics of the Ithacan wooers. Him alone Odysseus pardons at his fatal reckoning with the wooers, and with him, at Telemachus' request, the herald who leads him.

So Odysseus is close to the singer's art, but he is no fame singer or people enchanter. "Seek the light as quickly as possible and learn these things so that you may later tell your wife," says his mother in Hades, and his wife alone will hear them, for the people of Scheria, the Enclosed Coast, hardly constitute the public.

For this personal, perhaps new, poetry, without Muse, accompaniment, or the intention of fame, Odysseus coins a new word, used in the *Odyssey* only by Odysseus for the telling of the odyssey: *mythologein,* "to-give-an-account-in-story-form." Odysseus, the poet of the odyssey, is the first original Mythologist, the teller of his soul's own tale, embedded in the Musical epic of the poet of the *Odyssey.*

28

THE FAME OF MEN AND WOMEN

MEN

ACHILLES, HAVING WITHDRAWN FROM THE FIGHTING, sits by his tent delighting his heart with his beautiful lyre and singing "the fame of men" (*klea andron*), while Patroclus sits silently facing him. There is a universe of concerns that goes with this fame: prize, honor, glory (*geras, time, kydos*). It is because his prize has been taken, his honor impugned, and his glory diminished that Achilles is at—self-imposed—leisure to sing of these things. The *Iliad* itself is a song of the fame of men; in it a myriad of names of men who perished is memorialized in the never-perishing song of the Muses, the daughters of Memory. Achilles, the chief object of this song of glory, is himself a glory singer, a singer of fame who has himself won fame.

Homer always furnishes events with more resonances than are immediately obvious, and so we can, if we pay attention, clue out the dark fact that the artfully made lyre on which swift-footed Achilles, the sitting singer, accompanies himself was taken when the girl Briseis, for whose sake he is at leisure, was captured, and that the city sacked for those two prizes was Eëtion's city. Eëtion, it turns out, is Andromache's father whom, along with seven brothers, Achilles has slain. It is why her husband is all in all to her—Hector, whom within just two days, Achilles will have killed as well. That is one aspect of the fame of men.

More modern authors will be proudly dismissive of the desire for glory—they and certain stoics of antiquity whom Montaigne cites in his essay "Of Glory." What they despise is the externality of it: Glory is a mere attachment to one's name, separable from deeds and virtues: "For my own part, I consider that I exist only in myself"; in life there is no enjoyment in glory that is not vanity, "and when I am dead I shall be still less sensible of it."

For the warriors at Troy these would be vain words. It is not that their self-esteem depends on others. A man like Achilles himself gives the estimate of his high worth, and he does not need the confirmation of the world: Patroclus silently looking at him is regard enough. It is more that enforcing the proper honor now and assuring fame beyond the pyre belongs to the competence of the hero; it is a part of the deeds that earn the fame, as, on a less magnificent scale, it belongs to being the author of a book to be concerned that people should want to read it.

Moreover, an antique hero cannot dismiss postmortem fame. Death is a sort of lesser life and fame its one enhancement, giving the shade its substance in Hades, the more so the briefer the life. Achilles is fully conscious of exchanging worldly time for underworldly fame. The irony is that a brief, glory-gaining life has an intensity that makes it, less than any other, death-congruent. It is irony upon irony that Achilles, to intensify what little terrestrial life he has, must sacrifice some of even that short span to self-neutralizing inactivity. So he sings of the fame of men.

All the heroes want fame; the honorific "hero" itself expresses that (4). If that is primitive, then we are primitive. Anyone who has read the *Iliad* with young students knows it is glory that grips and puzzles them. It puzzles them because their modernity requires them to think that only the deed and not its large shadow should matter, and it grips them because it is their suppressed longing. And that their glory should become visible in prizes—women (or *mutatis mutandis,* men), chariots, and golden cups—and audible in songs the world sings— would give them the deepest satisfaction. Don't we all carry in our imaginations a Hades from which to look on the afterlife of our names here?

Montaigne also says that the first charm with which the Sirens seduced Odysseus was an appeal to glory. It is true that they call him by a flattering appellation as he sails by: "Come hither, as you go, much-praised Odysseus, great glory of the Greeks." Glory, however, is not the Siren's lure, but it is something far more debilitating, as we will see (33). Indeed, Odysseus, who is in fact called "hero" only once in the *Odyssey* (29), is a remarkable exception to glory seeking, being for the ten-year duration of his odyssey quite purposefully out of sight and out of hearing—as Telemachus succinctly says: "unsightable, undiscoverable" (*aïstos, apustos*). I think he can be so unheroic because he is perfectly secure in the sufficiency of his hero's fame, as Achilles never seems to be. When he finally uncovers himself to the Phaeacians he announces himself grandly: "I am Odysseus, son of Laertes, who plies all manner of wiles among men, and my fame reaches heaven"— wiles among men, fame with the gods.

WOMEN

Now comes a gratifying complement to the "fame of men." There is a fame of women as well. Generally speaking, the *Iliad* is, after all, a memorial to the value an entire people has chosen to place on one of its women. The Achilleïs within it, whatever else it is, is the story of the value Achilles places on a woman he truly loves. The *Odyssey* is the story of a man's Return to his wife. The odyssey is the tale of that man's coping with female deities.

But it is not Helen, Briseis, Circe, Calypso, or even Nausicaa who are the bearers of the "fame of women." It is Penelope whose fame is particularly sung in the *Odyssey*. The report of her courage has reached Nestor's palace, and so it only makes us smile to notice that she is never mentioned in Helen's house. She is given her glory where it really matters, in Hades (32). The wooers whom Hermes has brought down tell of her deeds, and it is said that "the fame (*kleos*) of her prowess (*arete*) will never perish and immortals will fashion for terrestrials a graceful song for mindful Penelope."

She and Odysseus are thus full partners in their unsought fame. She says of herself: "If he would only come home and serve [!] this life of mine, my fame would be greater and so much more beautiful." And best of all, Odysseus says of her *exactly* what he has said of himself: No mortal could quarrel with you, he begins, "for your fame reaches broad heaven," and he goes on to give the fame its full force and dignity: "as does that of a noble king who, god-fearing, is lord over many and mighty men, and upholds fair judgments." This queen is kingly (42).

29
ODYSSEUS' ODYSSEY I: FIRST THROUGH SIXTH ADVENTURE

ODYSSEUS WILL TELL, THEN, not about the world in and for which the fame of men is sung, but about a realm, mostly of women, which is out of sight and beyond discovery, and to which he is, as he emerges from it, the only human witness.

His journey has twelve stations and events, or "adventures," some of which he revisits (25). It lasts ten years. Ten of these adventures—Odysseus would probably call them labors, likening them to Hercules' famous twelve, among which is a descent to Hades—take place in the first three years, three real years, of which the events take only days or hours. That is the truth of all adventure traveling, especially by ship: peaks of laborious eventfulness and long stretches of nothing much, intense happenings surrounded by months of unmemorable time.

What is Odysseus actually doing as he slowly loses his fleet? What could be more obvious? What they were all doing, these Returners meandering home after a profitless invasion of Asia —marauding, trading. All these merchant-pirates used the same route sketched out by Menelaus: Crete, Cyprus, Phoenicia, Egypt in the eastern Mediterranean. Perhaps some were driven far west, but always men were lost to rash incursions, shipwrecks, desertions. How many men did Odysseus lose? All but the largest ships may have had complements of fifty men, to judge by that great manifest of the expedition, the Catalogue of Ships in the *Iliad*. Odysseus came and left with twelve ships; replacements may have come when men fell at Troy, as Neoptolemus replaced Achilles. So perhaps about six hundred men left and never returned, a huge number from the small island kingdom of Ithaca, Same, Doulichium, and Zakynthos.

Someone might say that these lost men, including finally the crew of Odysseus' flagship itself, are only the mostly faceless and nameless extras of the voyage. Homer himself says in beginning the Catalogue that "the mass (*plethos*) I could not tell or name, not if I had ten tongues and ten mouths . . ." and unless the Olympian Muses remembered them for me. Yet it seems to me that these comrades' loss weighs on Homer's Odysseus. After all, ten years on land and three years at sea is a long time together. In any case, Odysseus does not cover up his casualties, and assigns blame for their loss, most often to the men themselves, sometimes to himself.

That Odysseus is really on a perfectly mundane cruise of wealth gathering is not a mere guess from generalities. He has actually been seen in geographically real places and he himself intimates it unmistakably (38).

What follows is an interpretive telling of the adventurous voyage as seen against the background of the real trip. Real-life travel supplies us with a myriad of sensations, for it consists of movements, each of which has its contingencies of safety, comfort, and expeditiousness, and of stations in between, each of which is, if nothing else, yet another place where things may happen: "There we met a man who . . ."; "there we arrived in time to . . ."; "there we bought some . . ."; "there we nearly. . . ." All this happens to Odysseus and we hear about it, but it is *not* the odyssey.

If the *Iliad* contains multitudes of similes (20), the odyssey might be thought of as comprising a dozen metaphors, in each of which a mundane fact is figured as a fantastic event. For Odysseus certain moments of his journey shine out, or better, he makes them appear—recall that the Greek word for the imagination, *phantasia,* is derived from *phainein,* "to make appear," "bring to light" (27). For him the mere fact shapes itself into a signifying fantasy, the mundane reality into meaningful truth. I want to say that the odyssey is *true,* and its underlying trip merely *real.* The adventures of the odyssey are so interpretable because they are already figures presenting extracted meaning:

> Like things produced by a climate, the world
> Goes round in the climates of the mind
> And bears its floraisons of imagery.

Odysseus begins his odyssey just as Homer began his *Odyssey,* with the question of the right beginning: "What shall I tell you first, what last?" He says to King Alcinous of the Phaeacians that first he will tell his name so that in the future he may be the king's host, though he lives far away. That, it will turn out, is never to be, for the land of the Phaeacians, Scheria, the Enclosed Coast, will be isolated from the world forever on Odysseus' account; Poseidon will enclose it with a mountain.

So he makes his famous, proud disclosure, his name, patronym, epithet, fame, provenance, and island realm. His Ithaca is rugged but "I for one cannot see anything sweeter than one's land." The beautiful nymphs Calypso and Circe have each tried to hold him, "longing for me to be their husband," but his heart remained unpersuaded, "for nothing is sweeter than the land of one's fathers and one's parents." Behind these asseverations is his tacit refusal, only the day before, of the hand of the princess of the realm, not an experienced witch or nymph but a girl and a noblewoman with a considerable dowry. This is his tactful, tacit apology.

Having begun for the Phaeacians as the Muse did for Homer, with Calypso, he now backtracks and begins the narrative of his Return in the order of time: "From Ilium a wind bore me. . . ."

FIRST ADVENTURE

The wind brings him to his first station, Ismarus of the Ciconians in Thrace, a real place, toward which set the prevailing winds from Troy. The Ciconians are listed as allies of the Trojans in the Catalogue; the Greeks at Troy raid there for horses and get daily deliveries of wine. Odysseus too raids, sacks, and takes away wine, which will soon serve for more than rations.

But "much wine is drunk" by his crews, and six out of each ship perish. The survivors sail off, having called thrice on each of the dead. It is their last landing in a real place—at least as far as their captain is concerned—and the beginning of their destruction.

They are driven south, make one unidentified landfall to sit out a storm, and there is one sighting of a real island, Cythera, at the south end of the Peloponnesus. There will be just one more such sighting, Ithaca itself, but though the crews may think they are in charted waters, their captain is now on the sea of adventure.

SECOND ADVENTURE

For nine days they are driven yet farther south, to Lotus-land, where live the Lotus-eaters. Odysseus sends out three men to find out who these people are "among grain-eaters." He is expecting them to be ordinary humans, since "grain-" or "bread-eaters" is what Greeks call mortal men. They aren't, however, bread-eaters but lotus-eaters, and far from killing the three, they persuade them to partake of their "honey-sweet fruit." They promptly forget their mission and their Return; they want to stay in Lotus-land and have to be dragged into the ships and bound down. The fleet gets off by rowing.

No one knows what plant this lotus is. They are way down south, perhaps in Egypt. In Egyptian wall paintings you may see large elegant lotus blossoms handed round at banquets for inhaling; perhaps the fragrance was mildly intoxicating. Half a dozen plants are later called lotus, but whatever they have ingested, they are clearly what we call "spaced out," their minds altered by a drug-induced, relaxed oblivion; they have thrown off the sailor's hard and incessantly death-facing lot:

> Hateful is the dark-blue sky,
> Vaulted o'er the dark-blue sea.
> Death is the end of life; ah, why
> Should life all labour be?
> Let us alone. Time driveth onward fast,
> And in a little while our lips are dumb.
> Let us alone. What is it that will last?

Here we see once more what will be a main theme of the odyssey and Odysseus' apology for its losses: the lack of restraint his men show as contrasted with his own much-enduring resistance. Lotus-land is always and everywhere the imaginative aspect of a place, be it African Egypt or American Atlantis beyond, where people succumb to drug-induced escapes from life and have to be forcibly rescued.

THIRD ADVENTURE

They immediately come to the land, probably an island, of the Cyclopes, the "Circle-eyes." Their habitation is fronted by a long, low island that to Odysseus' practiced eye looks eminently desirable; he lyrically describes its well-watered, fertile, arable land and its natural harbors, clearly mystified by its lack of habitation. It turns out that his misgivings are right. These Cyclopes, though the sons of Poseidon, have—ominously—no ships or shipwrights. The Greek fleet sails in under a moonless mist; they sleep, have an easy hunt, feast and sleep again.

Something in Odysseus drives him to cross the channel to explore. The fleet is to stay put while he goes with his own ship "that I may test these men" and find out who they might be. Here a second theme of the odyssey turns up: Odysseus' never-ceasing impulse to test, make trial—his huge, reckless curiosity.

They sail across and come on a dolmen-like structure where a giant, a "monstrous man," a shepherd, sometimes sleeps, one "who had no commerce with others but existed apart, knowing only lawlessness." He is put together like a monstrous marvel, unlike a grain-eating man—he will in fact be a cannibal —but like a wooded peak of a high mountain that stands all alone, away from others. He is also one-eyed. They have sailed out of the world coinhabited by ordinary men and Olympian gods into a strange demimonde of half-divine monsters.

He takes twelve of his comrades—they are always called comrades (*hetairoi*), though from now on mere adjuncts to his adventuring—and a skin of very concentrated Ismarian wine, which ought to be mixed twenty measures of water to one. He has precise forebodings of what they will meet: a being who knows neither judgments nor customs. They go on, climbing, I imagine, and come on an inhabited cave full of rustic supplies, cheeses, pails of milk, and pens of lambs, all lovingly and knowledgeably described. His comrades beg him to take some and go, but for all his forebodings he refuses—in retrospect he admits his error. He wants to *see* the man and *receive* his gifts, in that order. They make themselves at home until the Cyclops returns with his flocks, rolls an enormous stone in front of the cave's entrance, and sits down to his milking. Soon he sees them. Though terror stricken, Odysseus boldly introduces them as Greeks returning from Troy, Agamemnon's men (forsooth!), driven over the sea seeking home, but now on "another way, other paths"; they have been shipwrecked by Poseidon and seek the customary hospitality, suppliants in the name of Zeus. Zeus is nothing to this son of Poseidon. He seizes two sailors, dashes out their brains as if they were puppies, and prepares them for supper. They can't get out, but on the next day Odysseus forms a design and prepares a device. After the Cyclops leaves, having had two more sailors for his breakfast and blocking the cave, they sharpen a huge stake of the Cyclops' olive wood staff. That night after the monster eats two more of them for supper, Odysseus offers him bowl after bowl of unmixed Ismarian wine. The monster, who grows grapes but knows nothing of wine-making, can't get enough and promises gifts in return. Now Odysseus offers a name: "No-one, *Outis,* is my name"; the Cyclops announces his gift: No-one will be eaten last. While he lies in drunken sleep they drive the red-hot point of the stake into his one eye, twirling it as a shipwright does a drill in a ship's timber—technological know-how victorious over the brute primitive; it is a very gory business.

The blinded Cyclops calls to his neighbors in the surrounding hills. These troglodytes come to make a cursory inquiry. What is the matter, they want to know, calling him by his name, Polyphemus. This name is pure Homeric irony:

"Polyphemus" means "Wordy," the adjective used both of public assemblies and minstrels—this of an alinguistic semi-hermit!

When he is asked if anyone is harming him he cries out, "No-one is killing me by guile and not by force." So these fellow troglodytes tell him to pray to Poseidon since he must be sick if he is in trouble when no one is hurting him by guile or force. And they leave.

Meanwhile Odysseus is tying his comrades to the bellies of the sheep and himself under a great ram; thereby they escape the groping hands of the blinded monster when he lets his flocks out to graze. They make for their ship and shove off, with Cyclops heaving boulders after them. His comrades beg Odysseus to be silent, but he *will* shout his real name in triumph: If they ask who blinded you, say it was city-sacking Odysseus, son of Laertes whose home is in Ithaca. It is his last bid for fame in fairyland, and he will have a long time to be sorry for it, for he won't arrive home very soon.

From now on he is the identified target of Poseidon's hatred, which fact will combine with his own insatiable curiosity to drive him farther into this realm of monsters and witches, and to effect the loss of his comrades.

From the point of view of the fairy realm, the odyssey is a foregone conclusion. Polyphemus remembers an old Cyclopean seer's prophecy that Odysseus would come to blind him, only he didn't expect so puny a creature. Circe has been told of his coming by Hermes, and the Phaeacians have an old prophecy about him.

What is the inner meaning of this monster tale, the most notorious of all Odysseus' adventures? In general, it defines Odysseus' quest, this gratuitous labor that loses lives, attracts persecution, collects no profits but teaches him concerning the kinds of existences that are to be found in the world.

And more particularly, who might they be, these moon-eyed monsters whose land he approached in a moonless mist, who "do not know"—the verb equally means "have not seen"—customs and laws? What is this monocular half-blind seeing?

The Cyclopes are beings that lack the perspective of depth perception, for that requires binocular vision. They are enclosed in the near isolation of a narrow, asocial, uncommunicative primitiveness. They don't distinguish between human and animal flesh, being themselves neither one nor the other. However, their shared brutishness and rusticity do not bring them closer to one another but rather to their beasts. They have no unifying customs, no objective judgments of right. They don't sail—sons of Poseidon unable to enter his enlarging element—and they are vulnerable to the guile, versatility, and technical craft of a civilized man.

Their lack of linguistic aptitude and perspective is shown in their inability to interpret Odysseus' name ruse: They cannot differentiate pronouns from proper names, much like children who take general nouns for proper names, as when they call their kitten "Kitty." And they are far from decoding the truth in Odysseus' trick name, that *outis,* "No-one," hints at *metis,* "craft," the mark of Odysseus (18). For they can't hear in depth any more than they can see.

His comrades have been brought by Odysseus to a dangerous, unprofitable, wild place, good for nothing to the sailor, certainly not for the gratification of their reasonable desire for goods, but only for Odysseus' greed for new experience—the Germans call curiosity *Neugier,* "news-greed"—inquisitiveness as a form of acquisitiveness. It has gained for him knowledge of the nature of the primitive—not of some one distant tribe dubbed "primitive" by anthropological misunderstanding, but the Primitive wherever it turns up—here right in Poseidon's Greek sea. It shows itself to Odysseus, and to us, as idyllic in its way, close to nature, far from exploiting natural resources, innocently rustic when left alone, revoltingly savage when invaded, and pitifully vulnerable before human craft: Odysseus has loaded himself with a crime against elemental nature.

FOURTH ADVENTURE

Odysseus divides the flocks stolen from Polyphemus equally; they eat, sleep, and sail on to Aeolia, "Squall Isle," a floating island fiercely fortified by a sheer bronze wall. There lives the large, quick-moving family of Aeolus, the "Blower." They enjoy a month of hospitality. Odysseus is given the parting gift of a sack containing all the contrary winds. On the tenth day of sailing he falls asleep, having been on watch too long. The crew undoes the silver string, suspecting their captain of having sequestered treasure. Out rush the winds, and within sight of Ithaca they are driven back to Aeolia. On this leg of the trip Odysseus is in despair and ponders whether to throw himself overboard—the sight of home has been too much—but decides to endure in silence and stay among the living: "I endured and stayed, and covering myself lay in the ship." Here are his most marked traits of character and his odyssean *modus vivendi* in capsule form: endurance and hiding.

Aeolus angrily refuses help; he cannot aid a man who has come, as you have, "hated by the gods." In this adventure Odysseus has his first experience of three cooperating evils: his own finite energy, his crew's distrust, and the directed hatred of Poseidon. He learns a strange fact about the world: When authority and trust fail, the elements are freed to become rambunctious. He sees, moreover, that the bag that tempts his men to insubordination—he has not explained its contents to them—serves to project him into isolation.

FIFTH ADVENTURE

They sail on, and as, perversely, the wind now dies, row on. On the seventh day they come to Telepylus of the Laestry-gonians, the "Roughpelts," another giant folk, way up north where the nights are short and the herding is good. Odysseus lets the fleet run into the harbor enclosed by sheer cliffs. (Such sheer inaccessibility plays a large role on these hermetic island stops—Aeolia, Telepylos, and finally even Phaeacia.) He himself wisely stays outside the cul-de-sac. He again sends three men. They find a monstrous girl drawing water and her mountainous mother who calls home her husband King Antiphatis ("Against-speaker") from the assembly; these are sociable giants —among themselves. The whole city of man-eaters comes and spears up sailors from the harbor basin like fish from the sea. The whole squadron, except for his own ship, is lost, and eight of his own crew as well. He cuts cable and they row for their lives. This adventure takes care of his fleet; to an admiral losing control this event looks like the aggression of xenophobic northern roughnecks and a corroboration of his own, by now solitary, prudence.

SIXTH ADVENTURE

They sail on, grieving, and come to Circe's Aiaia, the "Isle of Wails" (as in "aiaiai!"). The nymph, the "Circling Hawk" or "Encircler," whom they will shortly meet, a "dread goddess giving voice [to human sound]," is a witch, a literal-minded enchantress.

Who are these nymphs of Odysseus' odyssey? They are minor deities that people the elements, here the sea and its islands. Nymph means "bride"; these intensely female beings are in fact unattached, powerfully single, but they are also eminently unvirginal. They are in the fairy realm what a sailor in real life would look for—to his grief—in a harbor brothel but his captain would find in a high-class house. Later such courtesans, free, experienced, knowledgeable, and powerful, were called *hetairai,* "she-comrades."

For the first day the crew rests by the shore, overcome with weariness and sorrow. Odysseus goes exploring for human habitation and sees smoke. He takes down a stag and carries it to the ship "to give his comrades their dinner," a phrase showing their dependency. Then he tells them something prophetically false: "Friends, not yet shall we descend to the House of Hades, though we are sorrowful." He admits that he is well and truly disoriented; they are out of charted waters, in regions that old maps used to mark "Here Be Dragons." He tells them of the smoke, and they, thinking of his past exploits, weep; "but no effective action came of their lamenting," he observes coolly. He divides them into two squads. The lot for reconnaissance falls to Eurylochus. As he takes his people to Circe's house they find themselves surrounded by wolves and lions that fawn on them. They see Circe inside weaving, and Eurylochus alone, suspecting a snare, refuses her invitation. She serves them a sort of barley mush with cheese—and wine with a "miserable" drug mixed in. Once again they forget the land of their fathers. She strikes them with her wand and, as their heads now have the bristles and snouts of pigs, she puts them in pens. Now they get cooked acorn mush, for they are not even wild swine, just domestic pigs. Eurylochus reports back: He could not tell whether he saw a goddess or a woman, only that the men vanished. Odysseus takes his sword and sets out to help. Eurylochus begs not to come, and his irritated chief tells him to wait by the ship, eating and drinking.

Hermes Argeïphontes, the thieves' helper, appears to him in the guise of a charming young man. He is, *nota bene,* the only Olympian to appear in this demimonde of semidivine magicians; he is the liaison with Olympus, the not-very-willing bringer of orders and news from the real world.

He now tells Odysseus how to ward off Circe's magic. He gives him an antidote to Circe's animal-making drug, a milky looking flower that he pulls out of the ground; it has black roots and is called *moly*. He tells Odysseus to jump the witch with his sword when she attempts to strike him with her wand. She will ask him to go to bed with her, but he must hold off until she swears there will be no more mischief when she has got him "completely naked and unmanned," spent, that is.

He does as told and jumps on her as if to kill her, but she gets out from under, amazed at his powers of resistance. No one before him has ever failed to succumb to her drug "once it has passed the barrier of his teeth"—a phrase usually applied to speech that should not come out, but here to a drug that should not go in.

So by his hardness she recognizes him, for like others in this realm she had known from Hermes that he was coming. They go to bed, and then she wants to have a meal prepared for him; her servants are nature spirits. Unlike Calypso, who is solitary, this nymph is surrounded by creatures half-animal, half-human.

He refuses until she has de-magicked his men. By now they have turned into nine-year-old, butcher-ready hogs, but at a touch their bristles fall away, and his new and improved men cling to him sobbing. He goes to get the other squad and nearly decapitates Eurylochus when he refuses to come and wants to hold the others back, recalling just in time that his second officer is a relative by marriage. They stay for a whole year, the crew feasting and he enjoying Circe's attentions.

At last they remonstrate; now *he* seems to have forgotten his Return. They are right. He is a man of intense vitality and of long periods of lassitude. And though steadfast in the face of seduction, he is always ready for an experience on his own terms. What is the significance of this adventure with the she-raptor, the Circle-hawk?

As ever, his own restraint and resistance contrast with his men's dependence and susceptibility. They, given the chance, make pigs of themselves.

This almost laughably literal, proverbial understanding of the episode is not only obvious, it is also ancient. Xenophon, the Athenian general who wrote anecdotal reminiscences of Socrates, has him say jokingly of Odysseus: "I think that Circe made pigs [of men] by serving dinner with many kinds of savories, and that it was partly by Hermes' alert and partly because he restrained himself and refrained from excessive indulgence in such things that he did not become a pig."

In fact, the men succumb to some sort of womb food, and he resists temptation of a different sort, not only the drug, but her sexual aggression; sword drawn, he shows who is the man. No one knows what *moly* is or does; some say it is a type of garlic, and that makes good sense to anyone who has been a girl in certain ethnic neighborhoods in bygone times, when mothers would serve up garlicky meals to daughters about to be picked up for a date.

Now Circe fulfills her promise to speed them on their way, but there is a shock in store for them. They will have to do just what Odysseus said they would not do yet: sail to Hades. He must go there to consult the blind seer Teiresias, and "he will tell you the way and the measures of your paths and your Return." The inhabitants of this half-world seem to carry their human visitors' itineraries in their heads, for it won't be the seer Teiresias who has this information but the witch Circe herself.

Odysseus is devastated. No one, he says, has ever arrived in the House of Hades and Persephone on "a black ship," a man-made ship, before. She tells him just how it will go. The ship will run before a north wind all by itself and cross River Ocean to a grove of poplars and willows. There he will disembark and enter the House of Hades just where Acheron receives the other rivers of the netherworld. He must dig a pit, sacrifice a ram and a ewe, and collect their blood in the pit. Those whom he allows to drink will be able to talk to him; he will also have to hold off hordes of unwanted ghosts, so as "to keep off the impetuous impotent dead." This is when Circe, speaking to him with awe and respect, calls him "Hero," the only time he is so called. This is a voyage like no other, not even the circuit through magic-land; the man who makes it is marked.

The geography, disorienting before, is now truly upside down: The Cimmerans who live near Hades in perpetual murk seem to be northerners, but Odysseus' ship is to sail south. Yet Hades is not in fairyland. It is a real place with a location known to all Greeks, at the margins of the world beyond the encircling River Ocean. It is not accessible—or rarely—to living mortals, but their souls will inevitably go there: It is as real a place as ever was, the common destination.

After Hades, Odysseus circles back to the Encircler, who is the point of departure for and of return from Hades, not the least reason for this return being that one Elpenor, not the brightest or the bravest of the crew, has killed himself by failing, when he hears the bustle of departure, to take the ladder as the way down from the roof where he is sleeping off a drunk. Odysseus owes him a sailor's funeral, for Elpenor, who as a shade has preceded the ship to Hades, meets Odysseus before any other shade and extracts a promise that his captain will perform the proper funeral rites, raise a mound for him, and plant on it his rower's oar. In the characteristic Homeric way, this poor stupid kid's burial will gain an unexpected importance much later (48).

30

ODYSSEUS IN HADES: SEVENTH ADVENTURE

THE HOUSE OF HADES ENCOMPASSES BOTH of Homer's poems. It is there in the third line of the *Iliad* as the place Achilles' anger sends so many heroes; it is there at the end of the *Odyssey* as the place Odysseus has sent so many nonheroes (31). It is again there figuratively at the end of the *Iliad,* when Achilles, as Lord of the Dead, receives Priam (13).

It is also the central adventure of the odyssey, the more exactly so if we discount the first adventure, the departure from Ismarus, which is still in the real world, or balance it with the magical arrival in ever-real Ithaca as a thirteenth adventure. Hades is thus the event of events of the odyssey. And here really "labor" in the sense of Herculean Labor is the better word, especially since Odysseus is vying with the half-god Heracles who came back out and who has even now, after his second, real death, a strange double existence—a double death, a double life: Heracles' phantom has gone down to Hades forever, but "he himself is with the immortal gods." It was the half-god's task to bring the infernal watchdog Cerberus out of Hades. (Later a third descent will be made by Orpheus, a singer, to retrieve his dead wife Eurydice by his singing; Homer does not mention him.)

What does Odysseus bring up? Certainly his own soul—we learn what those lines in the prelude of the poem meant by his "striving for his own soul." But what besides his sheer escape, having been in death's house and come back to life, does he bring back?

His ostensible business is quickly done: to get an itinerary home and advice on the aftermath of his Return. For Teiresias, the second soul he speaks to, has nothing practical to tell—except about a strange and mystifying ritual Odysseus is to perform on his Return, a ritual which will take him on yet another voyage. He is to march inland, carrying a sailor's oar on his shoulder, until some local mistakes the oar for a winnowing shovel. There, making a sacrifice to Poseidon, he is to plant his oar in the earth and go home to live in peace (48).

So he begins to have colloquies with the shades, first with poor young Elpenor, who makes Odysseus promise to bury him with sailor's honors, planting his oar in the earth that covers his ashes. We might stop to imagine the murky weirdness of the place—the gibbering, incommunicative souls drinking blood, perhaps going slightly ruddy, and gaining speech, yet remaining intangible, the sorrow of seeing but not touching, of trying to embrace a corporeal nothing which is yet the being you long for. We learn later that the Land of Dreams lies on the way to Hades, and we may imagine Odysseus as being in a dream mode, though not dreaming. The house of the dead contains the human residue when the body is separated out: the soul; and the dead have the gauzy properties of dream figures, except that they are not private; there is no more public domain than Hades.

The third soul to come forth for Odysseus is his mother, Anticleia—as if to display to us the poignancy of the souls' inability to exchange endearments, she cannot clasp him. She had tried to approach him before, but he, with iron-hearted self-control, has held her off until he has completed his business with the seer. She died some years before of sorrow for him—yet another soul he has sped to Hades. She has old but comforting news of Penelope's faithfulness; perhaps even happier is the fact of his wife's absence here.

Eventually Agamemnon comes. Odysseus learns, for the first time—and at about the same time as does his son in Sparta (41)—of the terrible Return of Agamemnon—from the shade himself. In the *Iliad* the great overlord is awkwardly pompous, ill-judging and in constant need of propping up by Odysseus (5). Here in Hades he has the pathos of a victim, since the crime imputed to him by his wife as told by Aeschylus is not part of Homer's story (23). What Odysseus learns from Agamemnon is partly useful: to approach his palace alert for treason; and partly not: to suspect his wife.

From the Elysian Fields the other heroes come over. The memorable encounter with Achilles has been told above (13): how in comforting Achilles with news of his son's bravery Odysseus both establishes himself in Hades as the sacker of Troy and tells there as news the wonderful tale of his greatest device, the one that fits his epithet *polymechanos*—the Trojan Horse. The sadly sullen appearance of Ajax has also been told (6). Then appear to him the grand shades of the mythmakers of the older generation, the superheroes: Minos, Orion, Tantalus, Sisyphus, and Heracles.

I have omitted the first and largest crowd of shades that come for Odysseus' viewing, right after his mother. Persephone, Hades' queen, sends them up for him, the tribe of famous "female women," "very womanlike women"—in his mother's honor, I imagine. Here Odysseus sees Oedipus' mother, who was also his wife; Phaedra and Ariadne; Alcmene, the mother of Heracles; Leda, the mother of Helen; and six more. We now learn some facts necessary for reading the *Odyssey;* for example, the seer Theoclymenus, who turns up out of the blue but so opportunely on Telemachus' return from Argos, is there given his bona fides by Homer in a long story involving a daughter of Neleus; in Hades we find out who she is. But the main effect is that these women are seen and remembered. Three centuries later Pericles will end his famous funeral oration by speaking to the widows of the fallen: She will be best thought of "whose fame (*kleos*) among the males, for virtue or for blame, is least." How much closer Homer is to us!

Here, between the appearance of the women and the men, Queen Arete interrupts as all sit silent, spellbound. Suddenly we are back at the Phaeacian court, which here interjects itself right into the underworld adventure, the last fairy state into the ultimately real realm. She is very pleased with Odysseus, praises his looks, and promises gifts, and Alcinous too chooses this moment to express his appreciation of Odysseus' poetic gifts (27). Phaeacia is listening avidly.

So what Odysseus brings back *up* is the fame of women and the myths of men—and he also brings *down* some of the latest additions to the stock of stories. About his Return he learns almost nothing; it is clearly only the pretended aim of whatever divinity decreed his descent—a matter left obscure. What he brings up is not the watchdog of the House of Hades, Cerberus, but its very treasure: the myths of Greece, the matter of poetry (32).

And his crew? To them it is just another wild goose chase into dim and frightening parts as they sit waiting by the black ship.

31

THE WOOERS IN HADES

TO SEE HADES' FULL SIGNIFICANCE in the *Odyssey* it is necessary to fast-forward to the end of the poem when a second descent to Hades is told. In the ancient division of the *Odyssey* this episode was called the "Descent of the Dead" (*Nekyia*). Just before Laertes' reunion with his son, Odysseus, and the final battle against the fathers of the slain (14, 46), we see Hermes conducting the souls of all the dead wooers into Hades. This descent of the horde of dead complements the descent of the one living man, because we see what remains the same.

While dead Achilles and living Odysseus dominate the Hades scene of the odyssey, this last scene is very much Homer's, who makes it one of the several climaxes the *Odyssey* develops before it fades away.

The scene opens thus: "Cyllenian Hermes called out the souls of the wooer-men," men no more. He wields the same golden wand which he used when bringing Priam to Achilles (13). With it he rouses the souls and "as in the recess of a marvelous cave bats flit about gibbering, when one has fallen off the rock from the cluster by which they hold on to each other," so, gibbering, they followed Hermes the Conductor and Deliverer.

Hermes is the inventor of the lyre, the swiftest of travelers and their guardian, a messenger and go-between amongst the

Olympians and other realms, the god of heralds (such as on earth lead about blind poets), the only Olympian who enters fantasyland. As son of Maia the Midwife, he is the guardian of generative production; he is the protector of thieves and liars, and had taught Odysseus' grandfather Autolycus these skills; he is the god "who lends grace and glory to the work of humans"; he is the only Olympian god who enters Hades, and it is he who will in later times be the god of the art of interpretation, known to the ancients and to us as the Hermes-art ("hermeneutics"), and of literature in general.

Above all Hermes is the conductor of souls from the place of the living to the realm of the dead—one might say that is his signature capacity, which sums up all the others. Following him they go past the streams of Ocean, past the demesne of dreams, to the meadows of asphodel where dwell the phantoms of the great heroes, who toiled once but are now at leisure—*beyond* the land of dreams: the House of Hades, the last destination of all souls, is deeper and more remote but also more public than dreamland; death is the deeper brother of sleep.

Here they find first the greatest ghost, Achilles, reunited with Patroclus, in company with young Antilochus, and Ajax, next greatest to Achilles in physique, and a whole throng of souls. Agamemnon too comes up, and Achilles addresses him in a more sympathetic spirit than he had on earth because of his terrible, tombless fate. In death these antagonists are comrades.

Agamemnon responds, here at the end of the *Odyssey,* with an account of Achilles' funeral, for his death had fallen between the two epics. His mother Thetis came out of the sea with all her fifty sisters, Achilles' aunts—this swarm nearly frightened the grieving Greeks out of their wits; for Patroclus' funeral they had mourned discreetly underwater. The body was burned by Hephaestus' flame, with fat sacrifices. It was wrapped in garments from the gods, drenched in oil and honey, while the Greeks in armor dragged themselves around the pyre. The funeral lasted for twice nine days and the bones were laid in a golden urn together with those of Patroclus, as Patroclus had begged and Achilles planned in the *Iliad*. My Return was doomed, says forever-grieving Agamemnon, while "you in your death did not lose your name, but your good fame will be forever among all men."

For there were nine other guests: The Muses themselves came down from Olympus to lead the dirge. A heroic death draws the Muses, and *Achilles dead* is their dearest subject, it seems; all the Greeks are in tears.

At this point in the rousing of memories and telling of stories the souls of the wooers arrive, their bodies still unburied in the Ithacan courtyard. As the dwellers in the House of Hades had just heard the climax and completion of the war at Ilium, they now hear the consummation of the last Return in Ithaca, Odysseus' killing of the wooers and retaking of the palace—the public aspect of the story, as it is seen very vividly from the wooers' point of view, who were totally taken by surprise. We learn some new facts: how reluctantly Odysseus had gone to war, that to the wooers the chief wooer was already "King Antinous." It is a nice touch that they think Odysseus ordered his wife to bring out the bow and don't realize that the stratagem issued from the mind of the woman for possession of whom they died (42).

Agamemnon, ever mindful of his miserable end and faithless wife, who will have a "hateful song" among men, responds with a praise of Penelope "the fame of whose prowess shall never perish and the immortals shall make a graceful song for men on earth about mindful Penelope."

Why does Homer give us a vision of the newly dead wooers arriving in Hades, there to tell the story of "Odysseus' Return"? Why is Hades the place to tell "Achilles' Funeral"? Because Hades is the safe-depository of tales, the treasure house of myth.

32

THE TREASURE HOUSE
OF THE GREEKS

LIVING PRIAM RETRIEVES HECTOR from Achilles' terrestrial Hades (13), but no dead Trojan ever appears in the real House of Hades—not Hector or Priam or Paris, though Trojans too go to the "murky darkness" of death. Greek Homer is generous and sympathetic to the Trojans, establishing a noble tradition. Perhaps three hundred years later, the Athenian Aeschylus, who had himself fought the Asian invader at the first great victory over the Persians, the battle of Marathon, would write a play, *The Persians,* which would see the great war and its losses from the Persian perspective, an amazing deed of fellow feeling, surely not unmindful of Homer's poem.

Nor does Homer think of the Trojans as barbarians. We do not know what language he thought they spoke among themselves, but for him they speak Greek. In fact, the overtone of something not quite human that the word "barbarian" bore later (the *barbaroi* were the people who said "bar-bar-bar," and uttered unintelligible noises instead of human speech) is quite absent in the epics; indeed the word itself occurs only once, when the Carians are said to speak in a barbarian, that is, an uncouth voice. So the Trojans are fully civilized for Homer even though they are not Greeks, not Achaeans. Why then is Hades reserved for Greeks?

I think that the House of Hades is the treasury of *Greek* myth. As it is not the demesne of private dreams such as are occasional manifestations of the personal soul but of durable, coherent public stories, the ones we think of as "the Greek myths," so it is not of the stories of the Trojans or, for that matter, of the Phoenicians or Egyptians. They may figure in the myths, but it is the Greeks who tell them as *their* stories.

Thus not for its subterranean veins of gold alone was Pluto (meaning "Wealth") an ancient name of Hades—more valuable and more communal treasures than gold are laid up there. To Hades are consigned the stories that will become the common property of the Greeks. And from its depths they can be mined as is precious metal; they can be retrieved as from a place on the far side of mortal habitation; they can be brought back to life by a singer, a poet. The raw material of Musically crafted song comes to a poet by conversation with the souls of the dead, achieved by a sailing to the realm beyond and below.

These stories, the fame of Greek men and women, are what Odysseus comes to hear, or at least gets to hear. He accomplishes his other business in a very small part of the time of his descent, or more accurately, of his excursion to the extremities of the world (30). He takes his departure for this excursion not directly from the real world, but gains access to it from within the marine fairyland of his odyssey. For Odysseus is no professional minstrel or teller of public tales, and what he has learned in Hades will not be the matter of the odyssey. This trip to the treasure house of the Greeks is granted him as an acknowledgment that, though not of the craft, he is in his soul a poet and merits a look into their sanctum.

One last observation: Hades, the Unseen, is the place of the shades, those mortal "bread-eaters" who are now blood drinkers. To bring these gibbering phantasms to living communicative speech, the odyssean poet has to infuse them with blood;

unincarnadined shadows ordinarily have no common world with each other or the living. The greatest, most extraordinary souls, however, who dwell laborless in the Elysian Fields, seem to be so indefeasibly alive that they retain the power of passionate speech; they come companionably, striding vigorously forward over the meadows of asphodel, the lily fields of inner Hades, to speak to Odysseus or to receive the newly dead. These figures live in death even without their poetry, for the world remembers them apart from the artfully composed songs in which they figure. Think of the people who have heard of Achilles and Odysseus and the Greek gods but who have never read the Homeric epics: They have heard tell of the matter without the form, the plots without the poetry.

Hence none of these beings, whether they live through a poet or their fame reaches the world as common knowledge, is a fiction, in the sense of being poetic creations. They preexist poetry as its matter; they are the subject of poetry—I mean Homer's poetry.

In the *Odyssey*, the treasure house that contains the matter of poetry, Hades, is stocked by the deaths both of lesser men and of heroes. The very young, the wooers, remember recent events vividly and intensely; those who died old will remember mutedly but extensively—just imagine Nestor in Hades telling stories by the aeon. And the heroes of Troy who died in the prime of life have all the leisure to tell and retell the great canonical stories of that glorious and terrible time. When Hermes, the conductor of souls, the inventor of the lyre, and the god (one might well say) of the arts of the word, conveys new souls to Hades he is, so to speak, bringing new accessions to libraries-to-be.

What I mean, soberly speaking, is that the two times the invisible Hades appears to us in the *Odyssey*, it is the place where the great dead are to be encountered and where stories are avidly received and amply retold.

I do not think Odysseus' odyssey will be told in Hades, the depository of public myth. He will find a place suitable for shaping his adventure into a told tale, a place devoted to shapely appearance, well-wrought artifacts and artful song (35), but it is a private sort of tale not meant to be broadcast, as is the fame of men and women (27, 28). Yet, though an amateur and a personal poet, he is, as I said, given a chance to go to the source of Greek common memory.

The Muses on Olympus are the teachers of the singers, teachers of the story as well as of its mode and order of telling. On earth singers teach singers the craft of song. In the netherworld the dead keep alive the canonical matter of poetry. Seen mundanely, the terms are reversed: It is not the dead who remember but who are remembered, and that is how our myths survive. But a poet might say—Homer seems to say: If there is no place we can speak and listen to *them,* how will *we* remember? Poets require access to the dead. Yet another way to put it: The Muses are the daughters of divine Memory who lives on Olympus (as Homer must have known, though he does not mention it). Human memory, however, lives in Hades, and to its House the singer must sail over the formless elemental sea.

33
ODYSSEUS' ODYSSEY II: EIGHTH THROUGH TENTH ADVENTURE

THEY SAIL BACK TO AIAIA. Circe addresses them:

> Bold men who have gone living down into the House of
>   Hades—
> Twice-dead, when other men die but once!

Odysseus will be marked as twice-dead—and so once reborn —for the rest of the odyssey, but his comrades will be returning to Hades, dying their real second deaths, in little more than a month. Circe leads Odysseus apart by the hand, where they sit together very decorously while he reports. (Penelope will hear the same story lying in bed.) Then she gives him the route home in much more detail than could Teiresias, and she adds sober cautions and warnings.

They embark, and on board Odysseus tells his crew of Circe's decrees, since, he says, it isn't right that one or two alone should know of them. But it will appear that he, ever guileful, doesn't tell all.

EIGHTH ADVENTURE

The ship speedily approaches the island of the Sirens, who beguile men; now the wind fails and they must row. Odysseus has omitted to tell them how deadly these creatures are—whoever succumbs to them will nevermore return to his wife and little children. And he pretends that Circe actually ordered him to listen, when she only said he might—curiosity overtakes caution again. He packs his crew's ears with wax and orders that he himself be bound to the mast and, should he ask to be let loose, should only be bound tighter.

The Sirens, sitting in a meadow heaped with the moldering remains of men, call to *him:* "Come hither, much-praised Odysseus, great glory of the Greeks." They know and will sing to him a seductive song of the toils of Troy and of everything else. He does try to get loose but Eurylochus follows orders and tightens his bonds till they row out of hearing.

It was a conundrum for ancient Sophists "what song the sirens sang?" And much beyond antiquity the question is still alive: "What Song the *Sirens* sang, . . . though puzzling Questions, are not beyond all conjecture," says Sir Thomas Browne. The imaginative retrieval of things left to us to clue out is thus ever inviting to readers who read realistically; I mean readers who think that epic is about a world that is nearly completely realizable.

This, then, is what I conjecture the Sirens' deadly song is: The Sirens offer to ensnare Odysseus by a flattering and seductive song of *nostalgia,* "return-ache" (15). They claim that men who hear it sail away the wiser, but in fact no one gets away. He too will forget the Return that leads homeward to wife and child by changing the direction of his longing to the past. He will molder in pity for his lost comrades-in-arms and in self-pity for the glory gone, wallowing in veteran's reminiscences, aching to turn back to Troy. Those who have lived through terrible though stirring times sometimes do conceive this debilitating nostalgia for the bad old times, for the intensity and comradeship of living close to death and horror. In the spirit of this conjecture a poet-translator renders the Siren Song in hurdy-gurdy waltz time, a parody of the stately heroic dactyls:

> Argos' old soldiery
>> On Troy beach teaming,
> Charmed out of time we see.
> No life on earth can be
>> Hid from our dreaming.

But Odysseus sees himself in this adventure as quite literally self-restrained by the precaution of his physical bonds. This is how he shapes his experience of an attack of nostalgia and his resistance to it. The crew does not hear the Sirens' Song, and to them the wax in their ears is just another captain's crotchet.

NINTH ADVENTURE

Next, and on the same day, there is booming and bellowing, and the crew is too frightened to row. In this situation Odysseus makes, in quick succession, four false or at least doubtful moves. First, he has again omitted to tell them of a choice. Circe had given this choice, lengthily described: *either* Scylla-and-Charybdis *or* the Planctae, the Wandering Clashing Rocks. He silently decides against the latter. That means he decides to avoid the famous route taken by the Argonauts, who manned the only ship, the Argo, the "Swift," ever known to make it through. They had gone, led by Jason, in search of the legendary Golden Fleece; it was an enormous operation with all the superheroes of an earlier age, including Heracles, on board. Without asking his people, Odysseus decides not to follow in the wake of the Argo; he will be no Argonaut, no second Jason, who went for golden pelts and brought back Medea, the madwoman who killed their children. This is the only hint at the Argosy, the great predecessor voyage, in the *Odyssey*. Odysseus has implicitly rejected it in favor of his own odyssey with its finer prize and sounder end: an imagination freighted with adventures and a Return to a faithful wife.

Second, he ineptly tries to encourage the crew by reminding them that he had, by his ingenuity, saved them from the Cyclops, when they must remember that his rashness lost them six comrades to the monster's cannibalism—which is indeed the number they are about to lose to Scylla's maw. Third, he deliberately withholds from them the knowledge of the Scyllan cliff while warning them only of the Charybdean whirlpool. And last, forgetting Circe's explicit orders not to do so, he arms and stations himself on the foredeck to look out for yelping Scylla, the "Mangler." She lives in a cave in the cliff, a six-headed, twelve-footed monster; Circe has told him that the greater danger is on her side. As they are shooting through the narrows guarded by this duo of monsters, he loses concentration and looks out for Charybdis who is sucking down the waters from a lower opposite cave; meanwhile Scylla reaches down, and he turns to see her draw up out of his ship six sailors, writhing like fish on hooks. As they call on him one last time and stretch out their hands to him she devours the shrieking men. This event is Odysseus' imaginative rendering of a human situation for which Scylla and Charybdis have become proverbial: a choice of dangers, being "between the devil and the deep blue sea"—a captain's version of a confoundingly tough spot in which all choices are wrong and all decisions fatal.

TENTH ADVENTURE

They come to Thrinacia, "Trident Isle," where they hear the lowing of the beautiful herd belonging to Circe's father, Helios

Hyperion, "Sun On-high." She has been emphatic: Leave those 350 head each of cattle and sheep alone. They are untouchable: "They neither have a birth nor do they perish." Else the crew will lose its Return, and you will return late and after many hardships. Odysseus intends to obey, but now Eurylochus is in full mutiny: *You* are cruelly hard, made of iron; *your* limbs never grow tired, he says—a fatal overestimation, as it turns out. You want to sail through the dangerous black night, but we need rest and food. Odysseus, who at Troy was the commander most mindful that the troops be fed, knows he is alone in his urgency to sail on. He makes them swear not to touch the cattle if they land.

But a contrary wind keeps them on Thrinacia for a month, and ship's provisions run out; they can't find game; they even take to fishing—a very last resort for these meat eaters—but without luck. Famine has set in. Eurylochus persuades the men that it is better to take a chance at placating the sun god later by building him a temple in Ithaca than miserably to waste away. They kill some cattle and roast the meat.

Where is their captain? He has gone upland to a sheltered place to pray to the Olympians, and "they shed sweet sleep on my eyelids"—one of his fateful sleeps (26). "You lulled me into a pitiless sleep to my ruinous blindness," he complains, inconsistently, to Zeus, exactly as early on the god had said men always will.

As he comes back he smells the savor. One of the shepherdesses, Circe's half-sister, complains to the Sun, who appeals to Olympus and threatens to go and shine in Hades if there is no redress. Zeus dooms Odysseus' last vessel. "This I heard from Calypso of the beautiful locks, and she said that she herself heard it from Hermes the messenger," Odysseus interrupts himself to tell the listening Phaeacians, for how else would he know what the Sun said or Zeus commanded? He is not making this up, after all. (Since we actually have Hermes' report, we know that the god got it wrong in part, perhaps on purpose. For he tells Calypso that Odysseus had offended Athena on his Return, when he had in fact offended Poseidon; it was indeed a matter of well-known song that Athena had made some of the Greeks' Returns difficult because they had sacked her temple at Ilium, but Odysseus seems to have been exempt from her anger. Perhaps this island nymph is not to know about Poseidon's hatred of her human companion.)

On Thrinacia the hides of the cattle crawl, the meat "rare and roast" bellows on the spits, but they feast for six days and sail on the seventh. A shrieking west wind blows up, Zeus throws a thunderbolt, the pilot's skull is crushed by the mast, the crew goes overboard, and Odysseus, straddling the keel and mast lashed together by the backstay, is alone on the seas, shipwrecked little more than a month after leaving Circe.

The wind changes, he is driven back to the Charybdean side of the narrows. He saves himself by clinging like a bat to a fig tree in the cliff, from morning until the time "when a man gets up from the assembly to his supper" and Charybdis vomits up the water. He floats for nine days rowing with his hands and on the tenth fetches up on Ogygia.

Here is something worth remarking a second time (25, 26): This tenth and last self-told adventure is in the numerical middle (by lines) of the whole poem. The *Odyssey* has 12,109 lines; at 6,055 Odysseus returns from his sleep when the meat bellows "roast and raw, and there was a voice as of cattle," as creepy a line as there is in the poem. I have to say again that since, because of disputed lines, this count in uncertain, the *exact* middle might fall somewhere nearby. But by any count, Thrinacia is central. That explains why the event there and no other from the odyssey is mentioned by Homer himself at the very beginning, in the prelude of the *Odyssey* (14).

Why is Thrinacia central? It is the place where Odysseus finally achieves the certainty of solitude, where Circe's prophecy will begin to come true: "And if you yourself will escape, late you will return and in a bad way, having lost [or: destroyed] all your comrades." On Thrinacia Odysseus shows together the two features of his leadership: a self-control incommensurable with his men's simple creatureliness, and a recklessness that expresses itself sometimes in provocative curiosity and sometimes in dangerous lassitude. He is disciplined, hardy, and mystifying to his men in his hidden purpose to see, hear, experience, know, and apprehend the world imaginatively. To them his leadership must look like aimless drifting into continual hazards. They have been falling away from him for quite a while now: They are urgent where he is dilatory, they are slack where he is impulsive. They depend on him but distrust him; he cares *for* them occasionally but not *about* them steadily.

Whatever Thrinacia is in real life (the ancients thought it was Sicily), it is for him the place where his comrades finally do themselves in by a fatal mutiny in behalf of their natural needs—here, as on Aiaia, overcome by the desire for food.

He is relieved of their company and floats off on his upside-down ship into the concealed recesses of the world his imagination is construing.

HERE HE COMES UP FOR AIR in his story. It is with Calypso that he began, and his tale has now returned to her. But we will pick up now the adventure that is reported much earlier in the poem, because the Calypso episode had been told by Homer on his own, outside of and before Odysseus' odyssey—as the Phaeacian adventure will be told by Homer himself, for it includes within it the telling of the odyssey.

34

CALYPSO WHO CONCEALS:
ELEVENTH ADVENTURE

FOR SEVEN EMPTY YEARS ODYSSEUS LIES "unseeable, undiscoverable" in Ogygia, the navel of the sea, with the nymph Calypso, who dwells in a hollow cave in claustrophobic luxury (18). She is a solitary minor deity, though, like Circe, a "dread goddess of [human] voice"—which may mean either that these deities do not use the divine vocabulary of which the *Iliad* gives intimations, or that they don't make weird, inhuman sounds but speak as women do.

Calypso's name means "I will conceal," or "cover" or "hide." We may imagine that Ogygia is the first place where Odysseus gives way utterly to that withering away, the spiritlessness Circe had noticed in the crew, to sink into passive luxury after the strains of piracy, trading, mutiny, and loss, and the intensities of imaginative experiencing.

Things become critical toward the end of this dead stretch in this luxurious limbo. He seems to be in a deep depression, weeping every day on the rocks by the sea. His endurance undermined by inaction, he doesn't know how to extract himself; Odysseus of many devices has no designs or devices left, and energy and ingenuity fail together, as will happen to people intensely active in the inner and outer realm at once.

Every night he goes to bed, "he unwilling, she willing"— that most skewed of human situations—and he longs ever more urgently for his wife. Calypso in her solitude is so anxious to hold him that she offers him immortality and agelessness. Later it will be a source of pride, especially as he tells Penelope of this affair, that he rejects both her and it:

> You give the choice
> To hold forever what forever passes,
> To hide from what will pass, forever. Moist
>
> Moist are your well-stones, goddess, cool your grasses!
> And she—she is a woman with that fault
> Of change that will be death in her at last!

She is luring him from the mortal moving world in a place of unvaryingly sensuous beauty, the kind of beauty that turns as painfully insipid under restraint as lovemaking does under routine.

He needs help, and for the first time in a decade Athena looks after him. She doesn't yet come to him, because no god but Hermes, the bearer of decrees and tales, goes into this island realm of half-and-half beings. But she sees to it that his umbilical cord to the navel of the sea is cut. So Hermes, none too pleased to have to go to so uncosmopolitan a sea-waste with no cities to offer savory smoke sacrifices, comes to Ogygia, is served nectar and ambrosia, gossips some, tells some falsehoods (33), and delivers the Olympian order to a nymph very resentful at not being allowed to keep her human companion.

She goes to get him, and he can hardly believe that she isn't plotting more mischief. She swears a very powerful oath by earth, heaven, and Styx below to be generous, "I don't have an iron spirit in my breast, but I am merciful." Together they go to the hollow cave, "the god and the man." Homer suddenly gives her masculine gender as if to signal the end of the affair. They sit down for a meal, he in Hermes' chair—a happier tête-à-tête than any recently. She makes a last attempt to hold him, and only now Penelope is mentioned; he admits readily that she is less beautiful than Calypso and only mortal, but he longs every day "to see his Return-day"—not, as the modern poet thinks, because she is mortal but because she is Penelope. And he will willingly endure all the dangers the nymph prophesies.

This versatile man, once back in action, turns out to be quite a shipwright, and the raft he builds!—Well, one could almost build a replica to Homer's specifications; he loves this sort of description. She provisions it, tells him to sail by the left of the North Star (which I figure to be due east), bathes and dresses him luxuriously, and provides a favorable wind. As happens so often, at the moment of leaving all the original sweetness returns.

This is Odysseus' experience of exhausted holing up, of intentional obscurity. Ogygia, of primeval sound, is the navel of the sea, Calypso's cavern is smooth and womblike; it is beyond my power not to put two and two together: Ogygia is a place of gestation, and when Odysseus casts loose he, who is to be twice-dead, has now been twice-born.

Calypso's name is all over the *Odyssey:* The Muse begins with her; on Olympus Athena complains about her; Menelaus tells Telemachus, who tells Penelope of her; Homer describes her island to us; Odysseus tells the Phaeacians and Penelope about his time with her. His stay on Ogygia signifies "addressee unknown" to the real world and arouses the suspicion that world entertains of anyone lost to sight: that he must be illegitimately luxuriating somewhere.

Now Homer takes back and embeds the odyssey into the *Odyssey*. This, the eleventh, and the last, twelfth, adventure, are told to us by him.

ODYSSEUS HAS SEVENTEEN DAYS of smooth sailing, and sights the Scherian coast on the eighteenth. Then all hell breaks loose. For Poseidon, who has been away visiting the Ethiopians who live at the edge of the world, has come back and espies the object of his hatred on the raft sailing over his own element: "For I know," says Odysseus, "that the glorious earthshaker hates me" (*ododystai moi*), fulfilling the omen of his name (21). But he is about to see the last of Poseidon's uncultivatable and chaotically formless element; he will fetch up in a land of high culture.

35

PHAEACIA THE ARTISTS' COLONY: TWELFTH ADVENTURE

THE ISLAND OF THE PHAEACIANS is the last station of the odyssey, the place where it is composed into a tale and the place whence Odysseus emerges, as he had taken his departure from Thracian Ismarus a decade ago. It is altogether different from the monster-and-witch islands, be they beautiful or baleful, that he has visited. It is light, bright, highly polished, with girl-princesses instead of ageless vamps, a kindly sessile king rather than man-eating aggressive monster chieftains, a civilized public life rather than xenophobic or solitary existences. And yet Odysseus brings tragedy to Scheria. For these fast-traveling, communicative sailors, "whose ships are as swift as a wing or a thought," having delivered him home, are punished by Poseidon, their own god, by being themselves cut off by an upheaval, closed off by a mountain. Their island is now truly Scheria, the "Enclosed Coast." Poseidon, recall, is the "Earthshaker," the god of earthquakes as well as the god of the sea. Cultivation and its propagation are at his mercy.

A previous king had resettled these Phaeacians, away from their plundering neighbors, some Cyclopes of Hyperia, the "Beyond-land," so that they might live "far from wage-earning men." They are the aborigines of leisureland, though we can only hope that their *dolce far niente* will retain its relish when enforced by isolation.

This is the most telling mark of their difference from the other islands—the Olympians do willingly come among them: "The gods . . . ever appear clearly to us, . . . and they dine with us, sitting where we sit." When the gods meet one of them alone on the road, they don't conceal themselves, for the Phaeacians are close to them—as are the Cyclopes and the wild tribe of giants, among whom, however, we might add, the gods don't appear. So in Phaeacia (Homer never uses this place name, but it's convenient) Odysseus will meet his goddess again after a long decade of occultation.

His arrival itself is wonderful. Through Poseidon's hatred, Odysseus is thrown from his raft in a tumult of seas but hangs on—*nota bene,* the craft he built does not break up. He strips off his fine robes and slings on a saving veil given him by a sea goddess—*toujours la femme.* Poseidon sends a huge wave, and he lets go, reciting to himself a version of the beginning of his poem: "So now, having suffered many evils, go I wandering over the sea." And now Athena intervenes, though not yet manifest to him. She reconfigures the winds and gives him the sense to cling to the rocks of the Phaeacian shore like a cuttlefish, much as he had made himself a bat at the Charybdean cliff. He gets through the surge and swims into a calm river. He is in terrible shape, waterlogged, with swollen flesh, but remembers to return the magical veil to the sea before going to earth under two bushes in a pile of leaves, like a brand, a seed of fire that a farmer hides under the embers because he lacks neighbors to rekindle his hearth. He is near death, but Athena gives him a dreamless restorative sleep.

Meanwhile the young princess of the land, Nausicaa, beautiful as the Graces, also sleeps, but she dreams: Athena comes to her like a breath of air in the form of her best friend and chides her carelessness. Her marriage is near (in a general way) and her wardrobe lies unwashed. Taking care of this kind of thing is what brings good reputation! She is to pack her things and ask her father, the king, to let her have a wagon so she can go to the seashore to do her laundry. Athena flies off to her limpid Olympus.

Nausicaa awakes and goes down to see her parents who are already up and about. "Papa" (the same word in Greek), she says, "Papa dear," can't I have the wagon, because you and my three bachelor brothers will want clean clothes when you are in council with the first of the land and they at the dance. Alcinous understands perfectly, and they prepare for a wash-and-picnic party. She takes the reins and with her handmaidens comes to Odysseus' river where the washbasins are. They launder, bathe, and picnic. Then they throw off their veils and have a romp, playing ball and singing. It is a characteristic Homeric moment; one might call it idyllic realism: Every detail is familiar and homely and the whole is a vision of beauty.

They are ready to go home, and Athena wants Odysseus to wake up. Nausicaa tosses the ball to another girl but misses her—*she* misses; she is the agent here—and the ball rolls into an eddy. They shout; he awakens. Again it is a characteristic Homeric event: Nothing happens that does not happen to us all; balls get tossed wide and land in the drink; people are woken up by shouts. Yet nothing happens that is not under Athena's aegis—*both* at once. In effect human life is imbued with divine attention, and whether that is piety, poetry, or prosaic fact is what we are left to think out. They may all three come to the same thing.

Odysseus wonders, is he among savages or god-fearing people? Is he hearing "the female cry of girls or nymphs" or of "human-speaking people"? He has presumably had enough of these nymphs. He covers his nakedness with a leafy branch and issues forth, like a briny, weather-beaten lion, who, eyes ablaze, raids the sheep, drawn by hunger. All the other girls run from the sight—not Nausicaa. Odysseus has the sense not to try to touch her, even in supplication, and he makes a wonderfully tactful speech. He addresses the girl as "Milady." If she is a goddess, she must be Artemis (the virgin huntress), if mortal, her father and Madam-mother and brothers are thrice blest, but most blessed is he who will lead her to his house. Never has he seen such a mortal, man or woman, though once on Delos he saw such a palm shoot coming up by Apollo's altar. And he tells her of his shipwreck while wishing her all she desires, husband, home and in it "like-mindedness" (*homophrosyne*). For nothing, he thinks to say, is better than this, that a man and a woman should keep a household being of like mind in their thoughts. He is speaking through the preoccupations of his Return to her young dreams. And he has said the right thing.

There follows a scene full of charmingly delicate comedy. She is a little sententious with the rugged apparition: Zeus has given you your lot, you have to *endure* it—she has found the adjective of his character as a man. She introduces herself: Nausicaa, daughter of Alcinous who is in authority here. She calls her maids, reassures them, and orders them to feed and bathe him. He modestly declines and washes himself. As the brine and scurf come off and he is oiled in the customary way, Athena works the first of those transformations to which he is prone and she is party (2), overlaying his silver hair with its old gold and making his body more erect, glistening with grace and beauty.

Nausicaa is clearly struck with love. She marvels: "If only a man like him would be called my husband," she says unashamedly to her girlfriends, "settling in this place, and it might please him to stay right here." She slips smoothly from "like him" to plain "him." She offers food and drink. The

Greek words for "drink" and "husband" happen to be homonyms; they sound the same (*posis*), and her talk—it makes
one smile—rings with this sound. Odysseus is ravenous,
though, we may imagine, mannerly. Then she offers to lead
him, "and when we are about to come to the city around
which runs a high wall"—she loses her thread; it's the only incomplete sentence in heroic hexameter that I've noticed. But
she gets it out: She doesn't want the whole harbor and assembly, all the low lifes of the town, saying "Who is that handsome and tall stranger Nausicaa has in tow? Where did she
find him? Now this one will be a husband for her." And they'll
be offended because she is scorning her many noble Phaeacian wooers for a stranger. So he is to sit awhile by a spring in
this particular grove of Athena until she is back in the palace.
Then he is to follow, and when he enters it, he is to pass right
by her father and to go straight to kneel at her mother's feet.
We learn who counts at this court.

Odysseus does as told and prays to Athena, who, though
busy in his behalf, has not yet appeared to him, from fear of
Poseidon and his realm. Now finally in her grove she comes
to the spring as a young noblewoman with a pitcher, as girls
and goddesses do over and over in an old, old scene: Rebecca
at the well. Odysseus addresses her avuncularly as "Child."
She is with him, but he is not with her, yet. She confirms to
him, as she shows him the way, that he is among a sea people,
Poseidon's people, whose young nobles sail and have sea-and-
ship-derived names—*naus*, as in Nausicaa, means "ship." The
royal house is directly descended from the enemy god. Queen
Arete, "She-Who-Is-Prayed-To" (or "Prayed-For") is his progeny by a giantess; she is King Alcinous' niece. All that said,
Athena is off to Marathon and her temple in her own city, here
called not in the plural, Athens (*Athenai*), but just "Athena."

It must have given an Athenian a thrill to hear his city so named in the work that united Hellas and of which his city had assumed the stewardship.

As they are going, wrapped in mist, Odysseus marvels at the cityscape: the harbor with its stately ships, the great walls fitted with palisades idly defending a city not interested in bow and quiver but in shapely ships to cross the sea, a city without enemies. The landscape too is marvelous: orchards of trees bearing all year, cultivated vines, and irrigated garden beds. At the palace he stands still, struck at how everything flashes with bronze, silver, gold, and blue glass: the gold and silver dogs made by Hephaestus guarding the door, the golden youths bearing torches, the rich robes and throw rugs. It is the highly crafted counterpart of Ogygia's luxuriating nature.

This is a land of sophisticated superfluities, of expressive art, of advanced technique—a land of leisure and of connoisseurship. It is an artists' colony; here Odysseus will get the chance to produce his kind of poetry.

No sooner has he reached Arete than the mist about him evaporates. He is well received; they wonder if he might be a god; he had looked like one to Nausicaa. As he will later in Ithaca, so here he makes a forceful disclaimer; yet there is some look of a god about him when the occasion is right.

Once Arete has recognized his tunic and coat—they belong to Nausicaa's brothers—he tells her how he came to be on the shore and of Ogygia and his departure thence. He praises Nausicaa's courteous and correct conduct, and when her father chides her for not bringing the stranger directly home, he claims her precaution as his idea. We can imagine how Nausicaa feels about him now, and how her heart beats as she hears her father, to whom her wishes must be clear, offer him marriage with her. But Alcinous too is tactful; he does it so lightly and tentatively that Odysseus can evade a direct reply to an offer a thousand times harder to refuse than ever was Calypso's. Alcinous generously promises Odysseus protection and Return on the next morning; the wanderer will be asleep as they sail without labor and in no time.

He has not yet had to utter his name, such is their politesse, that ancient hospitality with its unquestioning tendance of strangers for their mere common humanity before the curiosity of the hosts is satisfied. Games and contests are put on; there is a delightful contretemps with an impertinent young sailor-prince (2). Demodocus sings a hilariously uncensored story of a divine affair (8). There is solo dancing and leaping with a purple ball; treasure is collected for Odysseus, packed and made secure by him with a magical knot Circe taught him.

Nausicaa stands at the doorpost looking at him and asks to be remembered as a reward for being the first of those to whom he owes his life. May Zeus grant me my Return-day and homecoming, and "there will I pray to you all my days as to a deity, for you, maiden, have given me life." He will *never* mention her name again, not even, or especially not, to his wife when he relates his adventures to her in bed (48). The girl is not an anecdote or even an adventure to him, and his silence is the token of a promise kept: He will never speak of her and always worship her. The adoring love of a young princess might well give an aging man life. She is the quintessence of girlhood, and there is, I think, none like her until Natasha Rostov of *War and Peace*.

Demodocus sings again, by Odysseus' request of the Trojan War. Odysseus moans under his cloak. He had deafened himself to the Sirens' seductively sentimental call to nostalgia, but he surrenders to sorrow—this man of feeling—when he hears a true poet sing of Troy. And now Alcinous forthrightly calls for his name. Odysseus reveals himself: "I am Odysseus, son of Laertes who plies all his *wiles* among *human beings,* but my *fame* reaches to *heaven.*"

And then he tells the odyssey, for the first time.

Who are these water-borne artificers, the Phaeacians? The name has no certain meaning, but meanings ring in it: "shining out" and "making appear" (*phainein*), "speaking" and "saying" (*phanai*). Phaeacia is the place for plying the wiles of the imagination, for making appear the visions of the mind and for telling artfully the meanings of events. It is a perfect place for productive composition. Here then Cyclops the Circle-Eye, Circe the Encircler, Calypso the Concealer, and a band of other beings who are neither Olympian gods nor mortal women are bodied forth and given a local habitation and a name. The figures belong to fairyland but the odyssey is not a fairy tale. King Alcinous has said of Odysseus that he does not fashion lies from what no one can see. He is right in a somewhat intricate way (39). These Phaeacians are discerning listeners, and they are at once his *first and last public.*

THE MAGICAL PHAEACIAN SHIP with its material and human freight shoots over the formless element of the resentful god and deposits Odysseus at home. On the way back the ship is turned into stone outside the Scherian harbor by a stroke from Poseidon, on Zeus' advice and in accordance with an ancient prophecy. The Phaeacians, at least, won't soon be broadcasting Odysseus' odyssey. At the very moment, however, when he has a sort of resurrection in Ithaca, awakening from "a sleep much like death," the Phaeacians are offering bull sacrifices to propitiate Poseidon. Some day Scheria may again be open.

36
THE LOCALES AND SETTINGS OF HOMER'S ODYSSEY

AS EVERYTHING HOMER COMPOSES, the locales of action have their own symmetry. I am thinking here not of the places we hear of *from Odysseus,* but of the settings about which we hear *from Homer himself:* the geography of the *Odyssey,* in its narrative and therefore not always in its temporal order of occurrence:

PRELUDE
Ogygia
Olympus

TELEMACHUS
Ithaca
Peloponnesus
Ithaca

ODYSSEUS
Olympus
Ogygia
Phaeacia

RETURNS
Ithaca
Peloponnesus
Ithaca

EPILOGUE
Hades
Ithaca

COMMENTS

■ The sea is the all-surrounding element of the *Odyssey*. All places but Olympus are reached by ship. Olympus and Hades, albeit the one is reached by no mortal while the other, though the destination of every mortal, is reached by few before death, are real places in the Greek geography: Olympus is a snow-capped mountain, over nine thousand feet high, in what is later known as Thessaly (the region of Achilles' Phthia); Hades is beyond River Ocean at the—probably northern— margins of earth.

■ Homer himself speaks of two places in Odysseus' magical island world: Ogygia, which is the navel of the sea, is inhabited by the solitary nymph who "conceals," Calypso, the daughter of Atlas who bears the pillar that separates the sea and the sky. Scheria, the Enclosed Coast, the island of the Phaeacians, will be "concealed all around," cut off, and prevented from commerce with the real world by Poseidon after Odysseus' departure.

■ These are the events that take place in these locales:

BOOK

i	In Ogygia Odysseus is detained for seven years. On Olympus there is a plan to release him.
	In Ithaca Athena activates Telemachus as Penelope's wooers infest the palace.
ii–iv	In the Peloponnesus Telemachus establishes himself as Odysseus' son.
	In Ithaca the wooers plot and Penelope worries.
v	On Olympus the plan for Odysseus' release is set in motion.
	In Ogygia Calypso helps Odysseus to sail off.
vi–xii	In Phaeacia Odysseus relates his ten years' odyssey.

xiii–xiv In Ithaca the wooers plot and Penelope copes.
xv In the Peloponnesus Telemachus is fetched home by
 Athena.
xvi–xxiii In Ithaca Odysseus, with his son's and wife's help, carries
 out the plot to repossess the palace.
xxiv In Hades the slain wooers tell of the Return.
 In Ithaca the Laertidae make peace with the nobles of
 Ithaca.

37

THE LIAR'S GODDESS

ATHENA HAS NOT BEEN MANIFEST to her own favorite for ten years, from fear of Poseidon and because Olympians don't go in person to the fairy realm. But now that he has returned to Ithaca she is there to welcome him. Here, on his home soil, she speaks to him as no god has ever spoken to mortal man, not as a propitious deity but as a soul mate.

She has always been more intimate with him than with her other protégés. In the *Iliad,* when Diomedes prayed to her before that dreadful night patrol (5), he asked her formally to help him on that exploit as earlier she had helped his father. Here, in contrast, is part of Odysseus' trustful prayer: "I am never out of your sight as I move about. Be my friend again, now especially!" Even in these ten occulted years she has kept a watch on him and has got him free when the time was ripe. Nestor tells Telemachus: "I have never yet seen the gods love so openly as Pallas Athena stood by *him* openly."

The Phaeacian ship slices through the sea and bucks the night billows like a team of four stallions on the plain rearing under the whip; it is "carrying a man like to the gods in plans," a man sleeping sweetly now but "who before suffered very many pains in his heart." It is the plosive fourth line of the poem again (18), but now the sea is relegated to a later line and the new word "before" is heard: He has come within a few days of the end of all his griefs, and the end of his sea wandering is right now.

The swift craft runs into the harbor with a speed that drives her halfway up the beach. The crew is familiar with this place, called the Harbor of Phorkys. They have clearly chosen it because it is not the island's working harbor and because at its head there is a cave, the Cave of the Naiads, who are water nymphs. But there is also irony in the choice. Phorkys is the grandfather of Polyphemus, the Cyclops whom Odysseus blinded and for whose sake Poseidon hates him. Polyphemus is the son of Phorkys' daughter, the nymph Thoosa, by Poseidon, and, for all I know, she is herself a Naiad. In any case, one late ancient writer thought that Homer wanted there to be some reminder of Odysseus' offense reaching even to his homeland. And this is neat, because in truth his peace with Poseidon is yet to be made, so a reminder is indeed in order (48).

Homer takes time out to describe the harbor so that we may see right away what Odysseus won't see at first, because Athena will have enveloped him in a mist. It is a place of Greek beauty: There is a long-leaved olive tree and behind it the lovely, shady cave with mixing bowls and jars. And here the bees lay up honey, and there are stone looms on which the nymphs weave purple webs, "a wonder to behold," and there are ever-flowing springs. One door toward the north wind is for humans and the opposite one is for the gods.

The Phaeacians leave Odysseus on the shore still asleep in a rug, unload the gifts, stow them out of the way so they won't be stolen, and depart.

Odysseus awakes in "the land of his fathers," but all is strange: "Oh to the land of what mortals have I come now again?" Athena has shed that mist about him to make him in-

visible to all, wife, townspeople, friends, but by the same device his own homeland seems strange to him, "its lord," as he
jumps up and looks on it.

It is the alienation of twenty years' absence, hanging like a
mist between him and his home. How many of the Returners
must have felt just that dimness of the finally real, the distance
of the utterly familiar:

> But everything trite and strange,
> The peace, the parceled ground,
> The vinerows—never a change!
> The past and the present bound
> In one oblivious round
> Past thinking trite and strange.

Odysseus does the characteristic thing: Talking to himself,
he sets about counting his tripods, cauldrons, and woven
goods. To acquire these, he had told Alcinous, he would have,
for all his impatience to get home, stayed there yet another
year, so that he might return as a more respectable and well-
loved man. He is devoted to the material realities with un-
ashamed candor.

But then he walks, lost and moaning, on the shore, and now
his goddess meets him, in the guise of a nobly dressed, refined
young shepherd. Odysseus appeals to the first being he has met
in this strange, mist-hidden land: Save this treasure; save me!
Tell me this, am I on an island or on the mainland?—in that
order. She tells him: "You are a fool or from very far" to ask.
She describes Ithaca: a rugged island, not good for horses—
recall how young Telemachus got Menelaus to give him plate
rather than equine treasure (24)—but with grain, grapes,
goats, cattle, and rain aplenty. And finally she gives its name:
Ithaca—a name that has reached even Troy "which, they say,

is far from the land of the Greeks,"—a neat bit of playing the untraveled young local.

Now "much-enduring, divine Odysseus" is glad and rejoices in his land, the "land of his fathers." It is a brief, dry statement for so great an occasion, the end of Odysseus' seafaring, the hour of his Return. But the word for "land of his fathers," native land, fatherland (*patris*), has been in the poet's mouth repeatedly to lead up to this brief moment when Odysseus *knows* that this is not yet another fairy island nor an alien mainland but *his* island home.

He is about to reveal himself to the shepherd/goddess when he holds back his words and instead tells a lie. It is the first of that series of ingenious lying tales he will now produce, with variations for every occasion (38). This first time he is already a Cretan—Cretan he will remain—in flight for manslaughter.

Now Athena—a major moment—smiles and caresses him with her hand—this is going pretty far for the virgin goddess who goes about in armor—and changes into a stately woman. For all we know she looks like the goddess herself. She speaks to him winged, loving words such as surely no deity has ever said to a man: "Cunning must he be and thievish who would outdo you in all wiles, even if a god confronted you." That is just how he had announced himself to the Phaeacians, as one who plies wiles among men while his fame goes to heaven.

> Dangerous man, dapple-devising [*poikilometis*: diverse-planning], ever-avid for wiles! You are not about to stop—even though you are on your own soil—your deceitful and thievish tale-telling that is dear to you from the ground up.

But come, she goes on, let's not talk of that, since we both know how to be crafty, for you are among all mortals the best in counsel and tales as I am famous among all the gods for design—she borrows *metis*, Odysseus' own word—and craftiness.

She trumps him at their game: "Yet you didn't know Pallas Athena, Zeus' girl, who has always stood by you in all your toils and guarded you; it was I who established you as friend with all the Phaeacians." She says it with a little note of triumph.

She has come, she says, to "weave a device" with him—echoes of Penelope—and to help hide his treasure. And she repeats his signature words: You must endure and tell no man or woman that your have come back from your wandering, and in utter silence you must suffer many pains—the beginning lines of the poem once more, but now with the end in sight.

Odysseus of Many Designs answers, but by no means submissively: It is hard for a mortal to know you when he meets you, especially for this one, since you used to be kind to me, but I haven't seen you since we left Troy. In retrospect he recognizes her in the Phaeacian girl at the spring. But, he says, I have a sense that this is not *clear-seen* Ithaca at all and you are making these announcements to cajole me. "Tell me if I have in truth come to the dear land of my fathers." "Clear-seen" (*eudeielos*) is Ithaca's chief epithet, but of course she has at the moment obscured it in mist—a most ironic Return.

She answers with another paean to the features of his character that appeal to her: That's how you are, and that is "why I cannot leave you in your unhappiness—because you are soft-spoken [he wasn't to her] and keen-witted and mindful." Anyone else returned from wandering would have rushed to see his children and wife, "but you don't care to know or find out anything before you have tested your wife"—who is, she hastens to say, still in the palace, weeping. Thus she announces

the theme of the second part of his Return and his poem: Testing. And we will see who in fact tests whom (46).

For herself, she has never doubted that he would return,
having lost [or: destroyed] all his comrades. She apologizes: I
couldn't oppose Poseidon whose son you blinded. "But come
now, I will show you the site of Ithaca." She draws aside the
veil of mist, and the site described before appears to his view,
clearly seen. Odysseus kisses the grain-giving earth; he is in his
mortal home, clear-seen Ithaca. He prays to the Naiad-nymphs
and to Athena whom he calls for this purpose the "Booty-
Bringer." She helps him bring his treasure into the cave and
stow it; the cave has, after all, a special door for her. He prays
that he may live and his son grow up. That growing up has
just taken place (22), and his son and he are converging.

She tells him that the wooers have for three years besieged
Penelope with gifts and that she is encouraging each man with
messages while her mind is set on his Return. This is, of course,
the moment for him to think of Agamemnon's catastrophic
homecoming. If you had not warned me, I would have met the
same fate! He is thinking of Aegisthus, Clytemnestra's lover
and Agamemnon's murderer, but perhaps a doubt about Penelope herself, first planted by Agamemnon in Hades, remains.
He begs Athena to "weave a plan" and to give him the courage
that he had when "they loosened the bright veil of Troy." This
warrior's figure for sack and ravage has sexual overtones; there
is a woman to be repossessed in the palace of Ithaca as there
was in the citadel of Troy. With the goddess at his side he could
fight even three hundred men, "if you would stand with me as
eager as you were then, Gleaming-eyes!"

She promises help and a bloody end to the wooers. For se-
crecy she now hides him again in a novel way: She reduces him
to a beggarly shape, shrinks his limbs, thins his hair, gives him

rags to wear. She tells him where to find the faithful swineherd while she goes to Sparta to fetch Telemachus who—this is the first he hears of his son's journey—is there to hear news of him. This is when keen-witted Odysseus asks her acerbically why *she*, who knows everything, didn't give his son this news herself. Athena tells him a part, but only a part, of the true purpose of the telemachy: "I sent him to win good fame."

She touches him with her wand and, shriveled, he begins his real Return, encouraged by his goddess to lie for his life. Gods seduce mortal women and goddesses take mortal husbands all the time; it is always amorous love. But that man and goddess should be one in soul, with the same gifts and practices—and such unconforming ones, too—that is a new thing, a bond only Odysseus has with a deity.

Later on, in the tragedies and comedies of Athens, Odysseus was to be in bad repute for his low cunning (3). But low is what Homer's Odysseus is not. Keen intelligence, versatility, competence, and endurance are what Homer and Athena admire: Who is there that has managed a lot of life sagaciously and has not told controlled lies? But Odysseus does not lie *to* himself, as does noble Achilles, nor does he lie *for* himself in a mean and narrow sense. He lies royally, as a king sometimes must who is returning a people in part run wild to its old and just constitution. But there is no denying that he also lies exuberantly, like a natural of the imagination.

38

THE CRETAN LIAR

EPIMENIDES WAS A LEGENDARY CRETAN wonderworker of uncertain but early date, who said: "The Cretans are ever liars, bad beasts, lazy bellies." Hence arose a paradox still infamous among logicians: Suppose the Cretan says, "All Cretans are ever liars." Then, if this Cretan speaks the truth, it is not true that all Cretans always lie, and so he is lying. But if he is lying, then all Cretans—for he is included—might indeed always be lying, so he may be telling the truth. But if he is telling the truth . . . etc., etc.

I do not know whether the Cretans already had a reputation for lying and verbal trickery in the Homeric world, but I would bet that something of that sort was said about them and that Odysseus was assuming the right provenance when he set himself to lying his way into Ithaca. Moreover, Odysseus' kind of lying has something of the Cretan Liar's logical merry-go-round, which comes from his reflexiveness: He includes himself in his claim. Insofar as Odysseus includes himself among the Cretans, all these stories are lies because he is from Ithaca, but insofar as he (and no doubt many Cretans) did these things, the tales are true. They are facts really lived become lies in the telling—real facts falsely related.

Our hero is, as we have seen, an Olympic-class liar, and as a liar, then, he thinks it plausible to present himself as a Cretan in almost all of the elaborately concocted stories he will tell about himself.

This lying self-presentation, all of which takes place after his arrival in Ithaca, is not only condoned by his goddess; she in fact started it long before when she presented herself to Telemachus as one Mentes, a Taphian, who claimed to have seen Odysseus when the latter came to get some poison for his arrows. She was even then foreshadowing Odysseus as the deadly bowman, though of course he will use no poison on the wooers.

Odysseus, however, begins lying quite fluently on his own the moment he awakes in Ithaca, and he goes on to tell six more such tales. In all but one he is a Cretan: outlaw, fugitive, exile, kidnapped victim, but above all, merchant—as that impertinent young Phaeacian observed, he can look the part (35). The tales will be cunning fabrications tailored to suit the addressee, but they will also display sheer exuberant mendaciousness; here is one realization of Odysseus' epithet, "much-designing."

FIRST TALE Odysseus, as we have seen, checks his first impulse to candor and opts to be crafty with the shepherd/goddess: He is a rich Cretan who has secretly killed a son of Idomeneus, the king of Crete (and one of Odysseus' comrades who is, like himself, of the older generation at Troy). This son was going to rob him of his Trojan loot. He takes passage on a Phoenician ship for the Peloponnesus; they are blown off course and land; he falls asleep (an Odyssean propensity) and the Phoenicians sail off, having honestly unloaded all his treasure. The point here is that he has to account to this ostensible Ithacan for the heap of booty lying under the olive tree. Then Athena reveals herself.

SECOND TALE   Odysseus is now incognito, holed up with his faithful swineherd at his outlying farm with its pigsties. Here he has been received with generous, simple hospitality and feasted with roast piglet and rustic cups of wine while Eumaeus tells him of much that he needs to know: of the wooers' depredations, of Penelope's sadness, of Telemachus' newfound independence and his risky trip to the Peloponnesus, and above all, of Eumaeus' own mourning for a kindly master who has died for Agamemnon and for Helen—would she "and her clan had utterly perished." Odysseus intimates he might have interesting news—he's been around—and asks the master's name. Eumaeus is politely skeptical because he and Penelope have too often been deceived by vagabonds lying for their supper and announcing Odysseus' survival or arrival. "And quickly you too, old man, would fabricate a narrative (*epos*)" for a cloak and a tunic, says Eumaeus in a kindly way.

Odysseus swears that he, for one, will tell the truth and asks for this reward of a cloak and tunic for his "good news" (*euangelion*) as soon as Odysseus has in fact come back. He echoes Achilles' famous words in the *Iliad*: "Hateful to me as the gates of Hades is that man who, yielding to poverty, tells a deceitful tale" (10). What he now says is both fact and deceit, factual deceit: Odysseus will return this very day! To which Eumaeus makes the first of those double-edged replies that will now keep coming, a skeptic uttering unwitting truth: "Old man," he says, I will not pay you a reward for your good news, "nor *shall* Odysseus come home anymore." Of course he won't, he is already there, and what's more, he will in fact get that reward from the generous swineherd.

Only then does Eumaeus ask the customary questions that have to wait until hospitality has been offered: Who are you, and whence? How did you get here, and who are your parents? Odysseus' answer is leisurely; he could talk a whole year of his woes of spirit and his toils. I will retell his story in summary, interjecting the veiled truths in the plausible details.

He is, again, the son of a rich Cretan, the son of Castor, son of Hylax, "Beaver, son of Bark"—not so farfetched a pseudonym for the scion of "Wolf-Himself" (Autolycus) and "Bear-Man" (Arceisius), his maternal and paternal grandfathers. He himself got only a small inheritance, but he gained a wife from a great family because of his own excellence—exactly Odysseus' case with Penelope (46). I wasn't, he says, so decrepit then, when I went on many campaigns even before going to Troy. He had returned from Troy for only a month when he left again. Odysseus, as we know, will also soon leave again (48). He takes a fleet to Egypt, where he orders his crew to stay quietly by the ship. But they ravage the land and carry off women and children, until the local army comes out and kills all the crew except himself who sues for protection from the king—this seems to be a mundane version of the Ciconian and Laestrygonian adventures combined. He stays seven years with this king—his time with Calypso—and is persuaded by a cunning, evil Phoenician to go home with him to Phoenicia where he stays for a year—his time with Circe. He is deceived into sailing for Libya, ostensibly in charge of a cargo but really to be sold into slavery. They come within sight of Crete—as they once sighted Ithaca after leaving Squall Island in the odyssey—but are driven off and shipwrecked by a black thunderstorm, the survivors lashed to the mast— the description is taken directly from the shipwreck after Thrinacia. On the tenth day, he arrives in Thesprotia—a real land way up north near an oracle of the dead and near Acheron, the great river that flows into Hades; this is the commonly accepted geographic location of the underworld, opposite to that given in the odyssey, which appears to be south. There rules King Pheidon, "Stingy," and the tale-teller is received and given hospitality by his young son as he washes ashore, cold and weary—Nausicaa in male form, with her generous father turned into his opposite, at least in name. There he hears of Odysseus—it belongs to the Cretan ingenuity of these stories that Odysseus keeps running into Odysseus. This Odysseus had accumulated enough treasure to feed his children to the tenth generation—this very treasure is right now lying below in the Cave of Nymphs (37). He had gone to Dodona, Greece's oldest and most remote oracle, to learn how to manage his Return to Ithaca, whether to arrive in open or in secret—this is the descent to Hades; the oracle Odysseus consulted in real fact, which worked with the rustlings of a local oak, was probably about as helpful as was Teiresias in Hades—not very. Pheidon swears that he has a ship ready to return the teller to his native land—the promise of Alcinous. But he is sent instead in a boat being launched for Dulichium, a part of Odysseus' island realm. The crew tries to enslave him, but when they put into Ithaca for the night he gets loose from his bonds, slides down the side of the ship and hides in a thicket, as he had on the Scherian shore. After searching for him in vain the evil crew leaves.

It is comical that in this melange of local allusions, gender transpositions, temporal scramblings, and plain fact, Eumaeus fails to believe the one thing which *is* the case, that Odysseus has returned, and he takes as true that which is a tissue of half-lies.

But he has been beguiled too often by stories like that of a visiting Aetolian who claimed to have seen Odysseus in Crete at Idomeneus' palace mending his ships and saying he would soon be home with his comrades. The report, we may speculate, was perfectly true, albeit nearly a decade old.

Eumaeus, though not convinced enough to give then and there the reward of the cloak, is moved by the stranger's hardships to serve a second, even better supper of roast boar. His guest chooses this moment to tell the trickster tale of how Odysseus got the teller a warm cloak on a cold night (3). Eumaeus finds this anecdote flawlessly told and not implausible, and in fact Odysseus has now got, by his pleasing tale of Odysseus getting the teller a coat, a warm covering of coats for himself, which Eumaeus smilingly provides on this cold night. One wonderfully "Cretan Liar" aspect of Odysseus' Cretan lying tales is just this involved reflexiveness. The teller keeps running into Odysseus and even having exploits with him.

The long, leisurely lying tale to Eumaeus is the most closely keyed to the adventures. In it everything from the odyssey turns into its associated opposite: deities into mortals, women into men, kindness into danger, generosity into stinginess, north into south, first into last. So for all the major odyssean adventures there is a this-worldly incident as underpinning, taken from the inventory of reports likely to be given by ordinary, unimaginative merchant-pirates of the Mediterranean sea.

This second story Eumaeus repeats in summary to Telemachus, who has arrived and has asked the swineherd, calling him "Dad," about the stranger: How did *he* get here? Later on Odysseus will tell him how: The Phaeacians brought him. It is the only time *he* mentions the people of the odyssey to anyone but his wife.

THIRD TALE This one is told to the wooers in the palace where Telemachus has introduced his father as a beggar. Odysseus knows who is who right away. He begins by begging from Antinous; "for you are like a king," he says, combining observant realism and silent sarcasm. Again he is a rich man who sails to Egypt, again his comrades, "yielding to wantonness (*hybris*)," maraud and are killed. But this time, just for variety, he ends up in Cyprus, another port of call for traders. Antinous, the vulgar wit, tells him, in plain Greek, to scram, or he'll come to a "bitter Egypt and Cyprus," and shies a footstool at him.

FOURTH TALE   Before the next Cretan tale, there is a short warning tale to Amphinomus, apparently the oldest and certainly the most decent wooer. But Odysseus goes about it sententiously:

> Nothing feebler does the earth nurture than man
> Of all things that breathe and walk upon earth.

These two lines ring like the epic antithesis of the most famous lines in Greek tragedy:

> Many things are awesome, but nothing more awesome than
> man walks [on earth].

Odysseus means to convey a message to the good man, although as both probably realize, escape is no longer possible: You are in a situation beyond your power; leave now; Odysseus is near, and there will be bloodshed. He tells how he himself was once a prosperous man but did deeds of violence and came to grief. He seems to be surreptitiously apologizing, certainly not for the killings at Troy, but for the destruction of his Ithacan comrades, among whom may well have been some relative of Amphinomus.

FIFTH TALE   A similar warning story is later told to the most insolent of the maid-servants, Melantho. It is an angry recital of the beggar's former possessions, including slaves, and how he lost everything. Odysseus means to scare her with the thought of Odysseus' Return and the possibility that she, who lords it over him now, may find herself losing her position in the house. In fact, she will lose her life.

SIXTH TALE   The next Cretan tale is told to Penelope, at her urging: "Respected wife of Odysseus, son of Laertes, won't

you stop quizzing me about my parentage?" Since I imagine
that she penetrated the beggar's incognito long ago (45), this
telling has the special object of conveying truth to her covertly.

Odysseus begins by namelessly introducing himself, that is,
with an allusion to the well-known meaning of his name, "man
of woes" (21): "I am indeed a man of many groans," he says,
and she can hardly fail to catch on. She responds with her own
sorrows, beset as she is with wooers, and she tells him of her
"wiles," the weaving that is unraveled every night. "Wiles" and
"weaving designs" is what Odysseus does, so he can see that
they are in accord; they have the marital like-mindedness he
had prognosticated for Nausicaa. We also learn what we had
already imagined, that the wooers are young. For Penelope reports herself as addressing them, in her account to Odysseus
of the device of the shroud, as "youths (*kouroi*), my wooers,"
perhaps here causing him a little—unnecessary—anxiety.

His tale begins with yet another version of the beginning of
the poem. It is with me, he says, as with anyone absent for so
much time as I have now been, "wandering through the cities
of many mortals, suffering pains. You will give me over to yet
more pain by making me tell of my lineage: There is a certain
Cretan land. . . ." And he gives her a Cretan geography and
genealogy lesson; she cannot help inferring that he has in fact
been there.

This time he presents himself as actually a brother of the
Cretan king, Idomeneus, a more plausible relation invented for
bright Penelope. He now gives himself a name, a "glorious
name"—no one has ever heard of it except as a horse's name
in the *Iliad*. It is Aethon, "Ruddy-Blaze." He is being funny
about his incipient baldness; his hair, which was once reddish
gold, is now silver and sparse, and that wit Antinous had
joked that there was not a hair left on his head, not one, and
that a glare as of torches seemed to emanate from it.

As Idomeneus' younger brother, Aethon was charged with putting up Odysseus, who had been driven out of his way to Troy—twenty years ago. Aethon/Odysseus now sets himself up for the Test of the Brooch (46), which interrupts the tale. Then Aethon goes on. He has lately heard that Odysseus is quite near, in Thesprotia, alive and bringing great wealth gotten, of all things, by begging. Here both of them surely suppress a smile at his present getup. Now he introduces certain elements of the odyssey that he claims to have heard: the loss of all the crew after Thrinacia and its cause, and Odysseus fetching up on Phaeacia where he gets more gifts. Calypso is, for present purposes, suppressed. King Pheidon of the Thesprotians told Aethon that Odysseus would have been home long ago, for the Phaeacians were ready to convey him, if he hadn't thought it most profitable to gather wealth all over the earth. So much beyond all men whom death carries off does Odysseus know how to turn a lot of profit; no other mortal could compete.

So he is covertly conveying to her the two thoughts very much on his mind besides regaining the palace: the fact that he has lost his contingent, which spells trouble with the town, and the fact that he's come back rich, which is comfort for the future to prudent Penelope.

The rest of the tale is the same as that which he told Eumaeus. But most of Penelope's lying tale, oriented to the issues of his Return, is much more practical than are the sailor's adventures Eumaeus gets to hear. Unlike his swineherd, however, his queen is vouchsafed hints of the parallel voyage, the odyssey.

SEVENTH TALE   His last lying tale is told to his old father Laertes from murky motives (46). It is mostly pure invention, with made-up names. He claims to have entertained Odysseus and describes in detail the presents he gave him. Laertes weeps and wants to hear more from the stranger: How many years was it since you gave hospitality to that unfortunate guest of yours, "my child, if ever there was," and who are you? It was, says Odysseus, five years ago—when the liar was with Calypso! He himself comes from Alybas, "Roverland," and is the son of Apheidas, "Unstingy" (a twist on Pheidon of the Eumaeus tale), the son of Polypemon, "Much-Possessing." His own name is Eperitus, "Strife-Ridden," an allusion to his real name, the "Hated" (21). Alybas is supposed to be in Sicily, and that is the one touch of grace this story has, for the decrepit widower is tended by an old Sicilian woman. Lying tales seem to be a habit with Laertes' son by now, and he is beginning to strain for usable elements.

I have no doubt that Odysseus was in fact in all these places, except perhaps in Sicily, about which he seems to be improvising. That Aetolian who had long ago visited Eumaeus and Penelope did evidently see Odysseus in Crete at Idomeneus' court, a likely destination for a veteran of an unprofitable war. Athena has placed him at Ephyra, later called Corinth, a trading city. The Phoenicians that figure so much in these stories are the acknowledged sea traders, slavers, and pirates of that time; Eumaeus, born the son of the palace, was himself kidnapped by Phoenician pirates who seduced his Phoenician nurse who had herself been kidnapped. So the swineherd knows this sea world of trade routes and pirate incursions from personal experience, and he finds Odysseus' elaborate tale movingly plausible—except for the sightings of Odysseus. But above all, the tale-teller, Odysseus himself, had seen, or better had *been*, Odysseus in these places.

The Cretan tales are therefore very plausible variations on the routes of the Returns. One might say these lies are a tissue of fact.

39

LYING TALES VERSUS FAIRY TALES

ODYSSEUS IS A VERSATILE AND CONTROLLED LIAR. His lying tales are collages of fact; they have verisimilitude because they are a neat mosaic of probabilities, facts that surely happened to someone, some time, probably to him. What Odysseus was in fact, in *mere* fact, doing all this decade belongs to the realm from which these tales are told, the world of generally known sea routes with their piracy, marauding, trading, guest friends. Some such things he was in fact engaged in, and if he wasn't in Crete, he was in Cyprus, and if not in Egypt, surely in Libya. No doubt he was subject to storms and shipwrecks at sea, kidnapping and capture on land. These lying tales are built on the commonplace factual ventures of the Returners who were in ships and avid for loot to bring home.

But the adventures are truths told in figures devised by that one latest Returner. We may speak of "mere fact," but never of "mere truth." For truth always has the gravity of *meaning*, of which facts may be devoid. At certain stations of his utilitarian wanderings the truths revealed in the mere facts of his profit-seeking ventures shape themselves into fairy form. There are the curiosity-driven adventures, in which the sailor's world of harborfronts, helter-skelter raids, of plundering men and depredatory women, turns into a sea realm of magical islands. This realm is the submythical demimonde of half-deities, those beautiful and terrifying monsters that are the imaginative expression of the human condition and of human nature. This imaginative realm is both: hermetically sealed from public view because intimately private *and* in the closest contact with the real world to which it is *in fact* identical.

The *Odyssey* is the story of a man in his world; the odyssey is the tale of his soul in *its* realm. In sum, the lying tales relate the—cleverly scrambled—facts of his reasonably expeditious Return in their brute reality; the fairy tales tell the circumstances of his delayed homecoming in their psychic actuality.

Many valiant efforts have been made to give a place and a name to the stations of the odyssey, beginning with Libya for the Lotus-eaters and ending with Corfu for the Phaeacians. It is love's labor lost, since Homer is willfully indifferent to real geography in this voyage of the soul. For

> as imagination bodies forth
> The forms of things unknown, the poet's pen
> Turns them to shapes, and gives to airy nothing
> A local habitation and a name.
> Such tricks hath strong imagination,
> That, if it would but apprehend a joy,
> It comprehends some bringer of that joy;

and except that this poet probably had no pen, the comprehension of an apprehension seems to me to describe the odyssey accurately.

Homer says in the third line of the *Odyssey* that (translating precisely) Odysseus "knew the towns (*astea*) and the mind (*noos*) of human beings (*anthropoi*)." In the odyssey proper there are only three towns (those of the Ciconians, the Laestrygonians, the Phaeacians) and the beings are, except for the Cicones, not human and mostly not men. So if we wish to look for the rule of transformation by which mere incidents become experienced events, here it is: What he learns to know rather than the *mundane cities of mortal man* are the *magical islands of half-divine women.* That is the world as reflected through his imaginative soul, and that is the realm in which his man's mettle is tested and his poet's imagination is realized. [P.S.: Should readers doubt that our earliest poet—though what has time got to do with it?—and an epic poet to boot is capable of being so "psychological," let them recall that the even earlier epic of Gilgamesh similarly combines the fact of a plundering venture, the cutting of cedars for Gilgamesh's building program at Uruk, with the truth of a soul's voyage, the incurring of guilt in the battle with badness.]

40

TELEMACHUS RETURNS

WHEN YOU'RE YOUNG even an overnighter can bring you back transformed. The telemachy lasts just a week, but when Telemachus returns he has changed from an uncertain boy to a self-assured young man. On a smaller scale, he now has something to match the veteran's Return (15). He has had a very abbreviated but intense "year abroad." Greece's most beautiful woman has recognized him and seen in him a man deserving her attention (24); he has been received with respect in the courts of Argos, especially by the family that has the overlordship of the Greeks. To the strange seer who turns up to accompany him home (30) he, before so unsure of his parentage, says in a new voice: "I am of Ithaca by birth and my father is Odysseus, as sure as ever there was such a one." To his father, before he reveals himself, he says "Odysseus begot me as his only son in his halls," in a line of only sons. So once he knows who the beggar is, he is sure enough of his parentage to meet his father with self-possessed deference. He is ready to become his father's co-conspirator in repossessing the palace and modest enough to know that he could not do it by himself, especially in view of what he regards as his mother's wavering and the wooers' aggression, displayed when he called the first assembly since Odysseus' departure—the right move in conception though one beyond his youthful powers (43).

The young man does not only look like his father, but he *is* like him, though in toned-down form. He has his father's courtesy, his restraint and his feeling, his ability to practice deceit, to be slyly tactful, to keep a secret, to be hardily firm and cleverly kind, to be circumspect—as when he wisely consigns his newly gathered treasures to a friend's house rather than taking them up to the unsettled palace. Like his father he has a talent for mimicry—one can fairly hear him mimic old Menelaus' voice as he recites his tale to his mother; he is physically deft—as shown in his expeditious setting out of the axe heads needed for the Contest of the Bow; he is powerful—his father thinks him capable of stringing this great bow (though he is still too young to desist from making the tactical error of an attempt); and in his first battle he shows himself to be a valiant fighter.

He himself feels changed. He boldly tells the wooers to behave: "This is no public house but the home of Odysseus, and he gained it for me." We can imagine the shamefully promiscuous openness of the palace that excites this outburst:

The door flapped open in Odysseus' house,
The lolling latches gave to every hand,
Let traitor, babbler, tout and bargainer in.
The rooms and passages resounded
With ease and chaos of a public market . . .

"I observe and know what is going on now, the good and the bad," he now says, "though before I was still an infant." Consequently, his relations to the wooers are newly exacerbated, particularly with Antinous, the most intimidating of the lot, who is only a little older than Telemachus but just old enough actually to remember Odysseus from his own childhood. Telemachus now tells him shortly to keep quiet and adds with heavy sarcasm and hidden meaning that "you care for me as a father for his son," since you order me to drive the stranger —his father in disguise—from the hall.

Everyone else senses the change too: The housekeeper sees that he is growing a beard. Penelope sees his new maturity and expects more of him. It is a wonderful moment to imagine: the relieved and proud mother appears, as always, modestly and royally flanked by two handmaids, and faces her handsome, confident prince who appears similarly flanked by his swift dogs. She is even genuinely happy when Eurycleia tells her later that Telemachus has known all along of Odysseus' arrival and kept the secret—not only happy for the Return but for her son's prudence, his "soundmindedness" (*sophrosyne*). Of course he knows nothing she doesn't also know, but he doesn't know *that*.

The relations of this newly assertive son of the house to his mother naturally are quite changed, more masterful, if still boyish. When she greets his return—she has been very anxious —with feeling, he sends her upstairs to bathe while he marches off to regulate things. She goes without argument: "Her word remained unwinged"—a pleased silence, I think. He had been a little rebellious before he left, but now his independence is more adult. Later he assumes public responsibility for her marriage plans. With Odysseus home there is no actual question of her leaving the palace, but he asserts his authority convincingly. The wooers want to think of this new tone as funny, but they are made very uneasy by it.

It is clear that the older generation dotes on him. "Mother" sits with him spinning while he eats; Eurycleia, "who of all the women servants loved him most," can't do enough for him; his grandfather has been fasting and groaning (*odyromenos*) since he heard of Telemachus' trip. Those who observe him closely see the change.

He is, as I said, still very young in some respects, especially in not sensing the subtle understanding between his parents and the covert drama that is playing out. Twice he interjects himself between them into arrangements he doesn't divine: He is critical of his mother for having had a bed made up for the stranger on the porch rather than in the house; he has no clue to the complexities of that night, Odysseus' first in the palace (45). And after the killing of the suitors he tries to speed up his parents' mutual acknowledgment (46), nescient of the restraint needful between these two in their marriage of equals. "Mother, Bad-mother," he says to her, why do you keep your distance from Father, why don't you talk to him? "No other woman would stand aloof in so enduring a spirit." He uses for her Odysseus' own epithet "enduring" (*tlemon*), though without quite seeing the point: His two parents are locked in a well-matched holdout.

His father diverts him by turning his mind to their common danger: Exile is the punishment for killing even one man, he says, and they've just decimated the city's younger generation. So, very aptly, Odysseus gives his son the commission to mount a mock wedding as a ruse for the neighborhood. The city, hearing wedding music, will think Penelope has accepted one of the wooers. It will, as it happens, also be the night on which Odysseus and Penelope are first together after twenty years—something like a silver wedding anniversary. This is a triply Odyssean device: The son is diverted, the town fooled, and as they prepare to go upstairs the house sounds with marital music.

Nonetheless, this son is also a true partner, and early on he saves his father from a strategic mistake. When Odysseus wants to canvass the island to find out who is of his party, Telemachus, here more sagacious than his father, points out to him the dangerous impracticality of the move. The father follows the son's advice.

I have left to last what really comes first, the actual convergence of father and son and their mutual Recognition. Telemachus has escaped the wooers' ambush by taking, as had the Phaeacians, a back route and avoiding the city harbor. He lands near Eumaeus' cottage and comes up. The dogs, which had gone fiercely after Odysseus the stranger, fawn about the familiar son, and that is how the father is alerted to his son's first appearance: It is a case of the dogs that didn't bark. Suddenly the prince stands in the doorway; the beggar rises for the young master. Telemachus treats him with noble courtesy. After some exchange about the current Ithacan situation, Odysseus, made to look older than his generation by Athena, says: If only I were as young as Odysseus' son or Odysseus himself, with the spirit I have now, I would wreak havoc in Odysseus' hall, or anyone may cut my head off. Before long Athena appears, visible to the father only. She signals him to go outside. His time has come, and she rejuvenates him (2).

As so often, Homer leaves this great moment largely to our imagination. Telemachus, at first a little standoffish, is quickly convinced that this glorious stranger is his father. They weep, as Homeric men freely do, and start planning for the recovery of the palace. The father gives the son detailed instructions. And he finds, like Helen, the perfect thing to say, almost as a throwaway: "When I nod my head, you take note of all the weapons of war that lie in your halls" and hide them. Odysseus has said "*your* halls." Telemachus is now the acknowledged crown prince.

41

ODYSSEUS AND TELEMACHUS: CONVERGENCE

AS SO MUCH IN THE ODYSSEY, the way father and son are brought home from their parallel journeys and finally converge is both artful and natural:

Day	Odysseus' odyssey (end)	Telemachus' telemachy
1	Shipwrecked in sight of Scheria.	Sails clandestinely.
2	On the seas.	Pylos; wooers plan ambush.
3	Beached in Phaeacia, sleeps out.	Night at Pherae.
4	Meets Nausicaa, goes to palace, mentions Calypso.	Meets Helen in Sparta, identified by her; ongoing marriage festivities for Neoptolemus and Helen's daughter.
5	Gifts; identifies himself, tells odyssey: meets Agamemnon in Hades and there tells Achilles of Neoptolemus; finally stays with Calypso.	Menelaus tells Return tale, with odyssean elements: murder of Agamemnon, Odysseus with Calypso; gifts.
6	Returns to Ithaca asleep; meets Athena; hides out with Eumaeus.	Awoken by Athena; returns to Ithaca; evades wooers.

7	Reveals himself to son; sleeps in his palace.	Meets father at Eumaeus'; sleeps in palace.
8	Strings bow, kills wooers; to bed with Penelope; retells odyssey.	Sets out axe heads; arranges mock wedding.

COMMENTS

In the three or four days before father and son's convergence and cooperation on Ithaca, the odyssey and the telemachy run parallel—one might say, in sync. When Odysseus meets Princess Nausicaa, Telemachus meets Queen Helen, each of whom gives the traveler something of great value: one the gift of life and the other the gift of recognition. Both men reveal themselves to their hosts and receive material gifts. Odysseus tells the odyssey of his Return at about the time that Menelaus tells the tale of his Return; in both stories appear helping and hindering nymphs of the magical sea world. Just about when Odysseus in Hades relates his account of Neoptolemus' bravery to Achilles, the music for this young warrior's coming wedding is sounding in Sparta; the stories of Odysseus' survival in Ogygia and of Agamemnon's murder in Mycene are told on the same day. Just when a middle-aged Odysseus tells a young princess that he will pray to her as a deity all his life, a youthful Telemachus tells an elderly queen that he will worship her as a divinity when he gets home. Father and son arrive on Ithaca on the same day clandestinely, both shepherded by Athena, and so, on the eighth day after Telemachus sets out on his journey, he is by Odysseus' side as together they recover the palace.

42

PENELOPE THE KINGLY QUEE

THE AIM, THE PURPOSE, THE END OF the *Odyssey* and the odyssey within it is Penelope. What is she like, the woman who sits quite literally at the focus—the hearth—and at the heart of the poem? Here she is, seen in one mirror:

> Sole at the house's heart Penelope
> Sat at her chosen task, endless undoing
> Of endless doing, endless weaving, unweaving,
> In the clean chamber. Still her loom ran empty
> Day after day. She thought: "Here I do nothing
> Or less than nothing, making an emptiness
> Amid disorder, weaving, unweaving the lie
> The day demands. . . ."

There is no penelopeia to match the odyssey and the telemachy. She is not a Returner but a Resister. She sits and spins and unravels, manipulates and manages, watches and weighs, balances hopes and chances. The mistress of a palace and a large demesne, with unruly servants to be supervised, aging parents-in-law to care for, and a son to raise, will have her hands full, doing, in mundane fact, a great deal. It is no quiet or retiring life that she leads.

Her chief troubles, however, come not from her household but from the kingless gentry, the ambitious, neglected, and spoiled progeny of the Trojan generation—she addresses them as "youngsters" (*kouroi*). An unlikely number of them—108—pretend to be serious pretenders to the throne of Ithaca. We know that she is in touch with Eumaeus who takes care of her outlying possessions and comes when called, and that she is mindful of Laertes who, alone since Anticleia's death, has isolated himself on a remote farmstead at the other end of the island. We may imagine that she has daily disciplinary run-ins with some of the insubordinate young women servants. We know that she tries to keep close watch over her fatherless adolescent son with the help of the older house servants who hear things before she does. But her most difficult—though also exciting—moments must be her descents, when she comes down into her hall to deal with the infestation of young wooers feasting there. She is keeping things stable by balancing promises and procrastination.

So "sitting" and "doing nothing" are hardly the words for her busy, difficult life, though "doing less than nothing" does catch the canny evasiveness by which she keeps her beleaguered house open for its master's Return. Penelope has pathos about her, but she is in no way pathetic. And now she undertakes something that gives new meaning to the old saying that "a woman's work is never done."

She has devised a grand multipurpose stratagem, much sung in later poetry, the worthy counterpart to her husband's Trojan Horse. During the day she weaves a tapestry that is to be Laertes' shroud. She has promised that upon its completion she will choose one of the wooers as a husband. But each night she unravels the day's labor. This apparent futility is really a powerful action:

Taking apart the cover of darkness fabricates
Light, and Time itself goes forward by unravelling:

So the queen's dismembering hand weaves the images
Of faith and remembrance on the bared warp of her lo[
Arachne ignores the lessons of nay-saying that
Lurk in what she sees there in the midnight's unworking.
Her eyes are only for the energies of resolve,
Of what is spun out of oneself in devout silence.

Arachne, the observant spider (though for my part I doubt that spiders' webs were tolerated in her chamber), sees what is first to be seen about Penelope, the sheer force of marking time, of undoing for the sake of safekeeping, of holding out, enduring, to secure her husband's kingship and her son's patrimony. She is the exemplar of covert resistance and of purposeful procrastination.

This web she weaves—a work resonant with the Greek locution, dear to Odysseus and Athena, of "weaving a design [or plan]"—serves several ends. By its sympathetic magic, it is staving off the death of the old king who, though ineffectual, is still the progenitor of the house, of the Laertidae. It is also her secret solace, by which she maintains herself and passes her nights as she longs for her husband to come and "be in service to her life." But above all it is her way of keeping time from running out, of keeping the wooers under her control while holding them at bay. She has told them to be patient; the women of Greece would be angry with her if—this queen thinks of her fame—Laertes "who had won so many possessions" (the first we hear of his accomplishments) "were to die without a shroud." And, *very* disingenuously: "I would not wish my spinning to be in vain."

Whom will Odysseus see—we are not told but may imagine —when she unveils herself to him on the great night of the Foot Washing (45)? She is a woman in her early forties, not bewitchingly beautiful like her cousin, Aphrodite's Helen, probably more severe-featured, like Artemis, and in her middle age handsome in a way that is more splendid than beauty—his match and counterpart in this too (2). She is somewhat careworn; both son and servants tell her on important occasions to make herself up. And as women will, who know why they look as they do, she resists: Don't beguile me to wash and oil myself; all my beauty is gone "since *he* went away in the hollow ships."

She is, in that remarkable epic locution, a "very female woman." It means women who are women according to their kind—essential women. It is said of the great women in Hades and otherwise (with one derogatory exception) only of Penelope—by Odysseus when she won't easily yield to him. We might say she is a real woman.

Which means she is both Odysseus' complement and his counterpart, his silent confederate and his active co-conspirator. She has aspects of manhood just as he has aspects of womanhood: He is the one wooed and the one who resists, by Circe, Calypso, and even by modest Nausicaa; he knows about lonely crying and in public too he weeps, in Homer's simile, like a woman who is beaten about her shoulders as the enemy drag her off her husband who is giving his life to ward off her captivity. And he has on occasion that delicate sensibility often attributed to women.

She on the other hand has, like any real woman, a man in her, of which Odysseus is proud. He attributes to her that fame he claims for himself, and in a remarkable simile he compares her to a noble *king* who is lord over mighty men, and all the earth is fruitful for him, and even "the sea supplies fish because of his fine leadership."

In her anxiety to guard her son, servants, possessions, her
\d's bed, and "the voice of the people"—she evidently
ʔar to the ground, beyond the gentry—she dreams one

night of twenty white geese who warm her heart; a great
gle comes forth from the mountains to kill them, and they lie
in heaps about the hall. It is a dream version of the portent Helen had interpreted for Telemachus (24), as Odysseus now
does for Penelope, nearly twenty-five hundred lines later: The
single goose seized in Sparta by the mountain eagle is also
white, and this adjective reveals its gender; it is female, and so
will the dream geese be. Yet they are her suitors, of whom she
dreams as female and as a joy to own and a sorrow to see die—
as if she were the wooer.

But the most remarkable indication of her manliness is the
simile for the seafaring Odysseus' Return to her, which, it
turns out after all, is as much her Return to him:

As welcome as appears the earth to swimmers
Whose well-built ship Poseidon has broken up
On the sea, driven by the wind and the robust wave,
And a few escape from the grey sea to the dry land,
By swimming, and a lot of brine encrusts their skin,
And with a sense of welcome they step on the earth, escaped
    from something bad—
So welcome was her husband to her as she gazed at him,
And for a long time she did not let go her white arms from
    around his neck.

She too is a briny sailor, seeking home—though a white-armed
one.

They are alike in so many more ways, superficial as well as
deep. He tells stories; she dreams (as we have just seen). He is
hated and hating by his very name (21); she can hate as well—
to her, Ilium is always "Ill-ium (Kakoïlion), not to be named,"
and she (united in this with Eumaeus) feels aversion to her
cousin Helen, whom she mentions but once, with perfunctory
charity and subdued hatred: "Prompted by some god, she did

a shameless deed, a foolish deed which was the origin of sorrow for us"—though neither her husband nor her son would concur in these objects of her hatred (24).

Both know that sweet deep sleep which overcomes them just when most of us would be sleeplessly anxious and watchful. Both undergo physical transformations for great moments. Both are masterful procrastinators. They are, moreover, alike and equal in that intensification of feeling by restraint that makes them co-players in the memorable event they make of their mutual Return (46). But above all they are alike in this: They are both beings of many motives, beings whose natures have not only highways but also byways. The husband's essential faithfulness does not preclude his being with other women. Reciprocally, her utter devotion to him does not prevent her from regarding these tempestuous youths of hers as pleasures as well as pests: She descends to show herself in the hall not only to protect her son, but at least once she appears almost provocatively before them, though denying such an intention. Practical motives—gaining time, eliciting and receiving gifts (a practice approved by her husband because it replenishes the coffers)—dictate the double game of neither refusing nor choosing, which she evidently does not *altogether* hate. Here her motives are as divided as her son's who, filial love apart, does not wish to see her dowry leave the house, yet boyishly, though reasonably, also worries about the depletion of his inheritance by this protracted wooing as well as about his own accession to the throne. He must be confused at getting advice to the same effect from the most opposite quarters, for both Athena and the most lavish wooer, Eurymachus, tell him he should assert himself to get his mother to choose a husband. She, on her part, is alone, aging, with a moody, frustrated boy to manage and protect, and there may well have been moments when, in the midst of domestic and political embroilments, she thought the unthinkable. But not seriou and not now. Things are suddenly moving and there is a crisis brewing (44).

Let me end the topic of the kingly queen with Homer's most subtle and most definitive tribute to the oneness of this pair. When Athena sings her paean to Odysseus' wiliness she uses three words to describe his nature, two of which are never used of anyone else: "urbane" (*epetes*) and "mentally present" (*anchiphron*). But the third word *is* used of one and *only* one other person. It is Penelope's very own epithet, said of her by others often and by herself once: "thoughtful" (*echephron*), "mindful" with the fullest force, which signifies being in complete possession and control of one's mental powers. I think the word has a kind of sober glory about it for Homer.

So they are equals and partners. But, at the end, this matchless woman conceives two devices even his cleverness cannot match: the Test of the Bow and the Test of the Bed (46).

43

SUITORS AND SERVANTS

SUITORS

WOOER OR SUITOR, THE GREEK WORD for this character is *mnester*, meaning "one who has something in mind, who has intentions"; we used to speak of the betrothed as "the intended." There are, as I said, 108 of these—Telemachus counts them for his father, together with their islands, all Ithacan dependencies—infesting Penelope's palace. What do they *really* have in mind? They cannot all truly expect to marry her.

They are the sons of the Ithacan gentry, run wild in the absence on the Trojan expedition of the king and their own fathers and older brothers. Eurymachus, Aegyptius' son, is one such; because of his ability to give large presents, he is favored by Penelope's family—her father, Icarius, and her brothers (except for their crass misjudgment in this matter, reported by Athena, we don't hear much of them). In the *Iliad* are mentioned evaders of Agamemnon's call, men who buy themselves off, and there are obviously some of these older stay-at-homes on Ithaca. But most of the youngsters at the palace, many not much older than Telemachus himself, are, we may imagine, under no adult control, since their fathers are missing. What is more, the city's political life is suspended in Odysseus' absence, since there have been no public assemblies for twenty years until Telemachus calls one: a move wise in conception (it is in fact Athena's idea) but chaotic in outcome. The mischief done by this cessation of public meetings can be gauged from the simile Homer uses to describe the wait Odysseus endures, clinging to a fig tree, suspended over Charybdis' vortex until she vomits up the waters to float him off; he waits until that hour "when a man rises from the assembly to go to his dinner." The assembly, the *agora,* the simile shows, is the daily occupation particularly of the male aristocracy, by which it measures its laborless day. There, issues are debated, quarrels are settled, and control is exercised, and above all, leisure is absorbed. These youngsters have no occupation, nothing to do with their time.

Out of this large crowd only a few are serious suitors for the queen's hand and possible candidates for the kingship, the main prize. There are in fact two principal contenders. One is the aforesaid Eurymachus, who, though involved in the plot to kill him, seems not to intend to seize the kingship from the crown prince but just to have his mother. In his evidently wealthy family one son is off to the war and has indeed, as we alone know, long since been devoured by the Cyclops. The other two quietly manage their father's farm. The four sons mirror the Ithacan divisions: the absent at war, the quietly neutral, the rambunctiously demanding.

The other wooer-in-chief is Antinous, whose very name says "Opposition-Minded." He does have kingship in mind. He is violent, sarcastic to and about Telemachus, inhospitable to strangers even in another's house, and rude to servants. He is the initiator of the plot to assassinate Telemachus. (This is serious business, but since it miscarries, Homer allows himself to wax witty: The opportunity for the ambush is suggested when a clueless citizen called Noemon, "Mindful," son of Phronios, "Thinker," gives Telemachus' departure away by coming to inquire of Antinous when he might get back the ship the prince has borrowed from him.) Antinous' plot, which the palace and certainly Penelope soon know about, is not abandoned till the end, and it clearly exacerbates Odysseus' avenging fury. There is also a decent but weak-willed wooer, Amphinomus, whom Odysseus tries to warn to get out, but who just can't pick himself up to go. So the nameworthy wooers are finely differentiated.

The wooing crowd goes home to sleep, but spends its days hanging around the palace, feasting daily at the palace's expense (such war exploitation was probably rife at the Greek courts; witness Agamemnon's Mycene), drinking far too much, playing sports, and dancing to constant loud music for which purpose they have impressed the palace minstrel.

To be sure, they are kept unbalanced by Penelope's promises and Telemachus' young impotence as well as their very real conviction that Odysseus is lost, as are some older brothers and fathers. This beleaguering the palace did not, after all, begin until seven years after the end of the war, three years ago, when it had begun to seem that nobody was returning. Anticleia, Odysseus' mother, reported in Hades from earlier in the decade that Telemachus' inheritance was safe and that he was well treated by the town. By the time father and son converge on the palace things are getting seriously out of hand. Besides the criminal attempt on the prince's life, there is drunkenness, throwing things about, hysterical laughing. Antinous arranges a mean punching contest between the itinerant beggar—Odysseus—and the palace beggar and instigates other indecorums that shock even his fellow wooers. Near the end his wit becomes ominous. Himself half drunk, he compares ragged Odysseus to a drunk centaur, a beast half-horse, half-man, one of those who, in a famous myth, got drunk and started a fatal brawl with the human Lapiths and their king

Peirithous. In making this upside-down comparison, in which he figures himself as the king of the palace, Antinous forgets that Peirithous went to Hades alive but did not return. He himself is about to make that one-way descent. And of course, he does not know that he is dealing with a real king who in fact descended to Hades alive and returned. Antinous is not even very brave; when the Test of the Bow is upon them he wants to hold off and weasel out.

In the great killing that follows, Antinous takes an arrow through the throat while lifting a wine cup. Eurymachus tries to blame all their misdeeds on Antinous, admitting that the real issue was the kingship after all. He acknowledges Odysseus in his last moments by according him overtly the appellation which must have been in the wooers' ears in his absence; it must be sweet to *his* ears now: *Odysseus Ithacesius:* Odysseus of Ithaca. Nonetheless, he gets an arrow through his nipple. The rest is mass slaughter; no wooer survives. As so often, Homer puts a consecrating background behind the event, here a bloody consummation: It is the feast day of Apollo "of the Glorious Bow," the archer god.

SERVANTS

The most palpably evil ripple effect of the wooers' degeneration is the corruption of the servants. The queen's household is divided into the same factions as the town: the faithful, the treacherous, and the uncommitted. The more than loyal, the loving swineherd Eumaeus, though his serf name betokens his skill as breeder—"Good-at-midwifery"—is of noble birth, abducted as a child and practically a son of the house; he was a favorite of Anticleia, Odysseus' mother, and was brought up by her together with her daughter Ktimene, therefore as Odys-

seus' brother. The reason Odysseus does not reveal himself to
Eumaeus until the day of the final battle is clearly that the
swineherd is emotional about his fraternal master and might
not be able to maintain the charade in the face of the insults
Odysseus suffers at the wooers' hands. As it is, he angers Antinous with his weeping. His evil counterpart is the brutally
vulgar and loudly lewd servant girl Melantho, the "Black" (as
in "black fate") who has lascivious Eurymachus as a lover. She
was similarly brought up by Penelope, and surely that accounts for some of Telemachus' savage treatment of her and
her lot (22). Each of these two, good and bad, is part of a pair.
Eumaeus' counterpart is Philoetius, the loyal cowherd. These
two are all the army the royal father-and-son team has—but
then, as Odysseus has said, with Athena at his side he could
face three hundred; he is in fact facing less than half that
many, serving men included—still, terrific human odds. When
he recruits these two for his battle, he promises them not only
wives and establishments but fraternal standing with Telemachus. Eumaeus is, of course, already as an uncle to him, and
the young prince calls him "Dad" (*atta*). Melantho, on the
other hand, has a brother, also gone bad, a goatherd named
like herself, Melanthius, "Black." I am sure there is some reason known to a farmer why swineherds and cowherds should
be more given to loyalty than goatherds.

There are also two loyal old house servants. There is Eurynome, the sensible housekeeper, and there is Eurycleia, the
honored old nurse, well born like Eumaeus—her lineage is
known, and when Laertes bought her he did not use her as a
concubine, respecting her and avoiding his wife's anger. She
notices everything, is utterly discreet—"as close as hard stone
and iron"—and can be depended on to carry out orders without any back talk: "Her word went unwinged."

Eurycleia keeps a mental list of the transgressors in the servants' hall, as Telemachus does of the wooers. She offers to name them to Odysseus, who doesn't really want to hear about them before the young nobles are dispatched. But immediately after, he does get her to talk, and from her we get a look behind the scenes. Twelve of the fifty household servants have gone bad, one reason being that his mother would not let Telemachus, too recently come to manhood, take charge of them.

There is also a pair of fellow travelers: the court minstrel Phemius, the Voice, who is impressed into singing for the wooers' parties and whose pleas the father will hear on that day of terrible retribution, and his guide, the herald Medon, for whom the son will speak.

That is the palace as things ripen to their bloody fruition, and this domestic situation and that of the whole island realm mirror each other. Thus when the small Odyssean party has finished inside they still have to face the outside (46).

Meanwhile, with the execution of the wooers, their own servants, and their hangers-on within, the palace is purged of its infestation—for that is how the killing seems to the four victors—and sulfur smoke purifies the hall of pollution by their corpses. Odysseus of Ithaca has Returned.

44
CRISIS

LIKE A POINTILLISTIC PAINTER building up the picture, point by tiny, hardly noticeable point, Homer lays on the crisis that is brewing in Ithaca. After years of increasingly uneasy quiescence, all hell is about to break loose, and in the last days there are signs and portents, arrivals and rumors, coming thick and fast. We may be sure that anything we notice the palace takes note of too.

Penelope's stratagem for making time stand still for three years, her daily weaving and unraveling of Laertes' shroud, has been discovered, and the wooers have forced its completion and a decision. At that chaotic and yet catalytic first assembly called by Telemachus he has found himself saying that he is angry with the wooers—whose parents are also present and presumably somewhat sympathetic to this complaint—because they won't apply properly to his grandfather Icarius with bridal gifts. The wooers think they too have a genuine grievance in Penelope's trickery and her wavering. Antinous, as their spokesman, points out to the son that his mother's dithering is costing him. Telemachus feels stymied all round, unready to make her go, unable to make them leave, unwilling to be the loser. It is hard to think that he hadn't seen something of his mother's secret activity, but easy to imagine that he hadn't till recently known what he was seeing. Before, in his late boyhood, it may have seemed to him that she was just dawdling destructively:

> Slowly, slowly did they come,
> With horse and chariot, spear and bow,
> Half-finished heroes sad and mum,
> Came slowly to the shuttle's hum.
> Time itself was not so slow.
>
> . . . .
>
> Instead, that jumble of heads and spears,
> Forlorn scraps of her treasure trove.
> I wet them with my childish tears
> Not knowing she wove into her fears
> Pride and fidelity and love.

Now the end of Telemachus' boyhood is confirmed through Helen's clairvoyance. She also told him with certainty that Odysseus was back, and her prophecy is now confirmed. It is *the* fact of facts that he keeps from his mother when he reports to her about his trip. She tries repeatedly to get more from him about Odysseus' Return. He says he'll tell her all the truth, but he doesn't, and what mother wouldn't divine that! Indeed in the Homeric poems, as in the world, the announcement "I'll be honest with you" is always cause for suspicion. Halithersis, the local seer, prophesied to Odysseus when he left, and now tells this assembly with assurance, that Odysseus was to return in his twentieth year, "having lost [or: destroyed] all his comrades." No doubt every public word gets reported to Penelope who has her ear to the ground. But now a new seer comes on the scene, Theoclymenos, opportunely picked up by Telemachus on his return trip, and he tells Penelope directly what her son had suppressed: Odysseus is home to kill the wooers and even now is "creeping about." The palace singer Phemius suddenly has a new and therefore more exciting song in his

repertoire, a song of the Returns from Troy. And assorted va-
grants have been about telling of Odysseus' imminent return.

The wooers are yet more urgent with Telemachus to influ-
ence his mother for his own good—and very jittery. There is
a lot of misplaced hysterical laughter—at Theoclymenos'
spine-chilling prophecies, at Telemachus' self-assertion—and
uproarious behavior such as footstool flinging.

Penelope who, according to Telemachus, had descended
only rarely to appear before the wooers, has begun to come
down more often and to speak out. She comes when she hears
of the attempt on Telemachus' life—Eurymachus vainly tries
to lie to her—and speaks furiously to Antinous for his arro-
gant violence (*hybris*). She seems to be close by when she hears
about the footstool flinging and the abuse of a stranger in her
house, and she denounces Antinous to Eurynome as a "black
fate." And in an aside: "So may Apollo of the Glorious Bow
smite you yourself."

Right after, when Eumaeus, who is rarely in town but is
now installed in the hall, tells her that he wishes they would
all keep quiet because this stranger can "tell tales that would
charm your very heart," she becomes *very* interested. She talks
more optimistically of the event of Odysseus' Return, while
now there is no man like him to keep the ruin out. She doesn't
yet have much faith in Telemachus' maturity. Telemachus is listening, and, knowing better on all counts, sneezes loudly. He's
tickled, but for his mother it's an omen; she laughs, reassured.
She sends Eumaeus to fetch the stranger and promises a coat
for a true report, for he has claimed to know Odysseus well
(and that, for once, is no lie). But Eumaeus returns without
him. What does this wanderer—she calls him "wanderer," not
"stranger"—mean by it? Queen, says Eumaeus, he wants to
see you alone. She consents to this bold request. It has begun
between wife and husband—the drama of mutual Return.

Once more she comes down to appear to the wooers, now to set *their* hearts beating, as Athena has put it into her heart. But first she falls into a transforming beauty sleep sent by Athena, who seems to be for this couple the goddess of personal beautification. Like her husband she sleeps at crucial moments, and like him she goes all beautiful at important times. Athena anoints her with an Aphrodisian balm, makes her taller and statelier, with skin whiter than new-sawn ivory. As she descends, modestly veiled and flanked by handmaids, the wooers' knees go loose with love, their hearts are enchanted, and they all want to take her to bed. It is probably their finest moment. Odysseus looks on gladly, because *he* sees it all as a ruse for gathering in presents. What a couple!

In this atmosphere she reveals a crucial fact to the wooers, especially to the most prodigal one, Eurymachus. When he went off to war Odysseus left Penelope instructions for the care of her parents and his son in case of his non-return: When my son is bearded, marry whom you will and leave the house. It is just the sensible provision for Telemachus' own establishment and succession that the son himself has, somewhat hesitatingly, in mind. Well, as everybody can see, Telemachus is now bearded, and the critical moment has come.

She will descend one last time to sit off on the side, watching the graceless last supper the wooers will eat in the palace. Then she goes off to get Odysseus' bow. We may pinpoint the moment that the thought of the Test of the Bow first comes to her: when amidst her handmaids she finds herself uttering that wish for Antinous, "So may Apollo of the Glorious *Bow* smite you yourself."

45

FIRST SIGHT

WHEN DOES PENELOPE RECOGNIZE ODYSSEUS? At first sight, of course. Is it likely that a woman who for a score of years has thought of nothing but her husband and his Return, who has in her house a son the spitting image of a very distinctive-looking man (24), would not know him on sight? Even though he has aged? It is not only unlikely, it is beyond belief. But to recognize and to acknowledge are very different matters.

The full, overt mutual recognition—recognition here in the sense in which one sovereign recognizes another—does not take place until the end, when the slaughter of the suitors and servants is done, and then only after she administers that test of tests: the Test of the Bed (46). Going by human likelihood alone, I would guess that she knows who the beggar in her halls is even *before* she sees him, for she must have heard his voice before ever she looks on him in the flesh: She has heard him being abused as he roams the hall begging, and so she has heard *his* voice too, probably from her upstairs apartment. Later she descends in the beauty given her by sleep and Athena; the motive of this visit she is not willing to state very clearly. She says that she has come down because her heart longs for her to show herself to the wooers to "flutter their spirits," and she also says that she wants to warn Telemachus about them, and she laughs a "pointless laugh." The palace has been ringing with such laughter these last days. Of course she wants to see *him*. He could not quite see *her* face, as she leans, decorously veiled, against the doorpost, even if he committed the indiscretion of looking, but nothing prevents her from seeing *his* face.

The real reason she has to come down, I imagine, is that she had taken the bold step of inviting him to come to her, and he has done the unheard-of by refusing—and won her approval for it as well as that of Eumaeus, the go-between who fears a scene from the suitors. She says of him, "Not without thought —that stranger"; "thoughtful," recall, is their common and exclusive epithet (42). She certainly has at the very least an inkling of the stranger's identity.

Why does she nonetheless deny herself to him over two days and a night? The chief reason is that they are co-conspirators in a plan requiring the utmost security and that the intimacy following mutual recognition would be hard to hide; in addition, once embarked on roles requiring mutual reserve it is not so easy to find the transition, especially since restraint is deep in both their natures:

> Is it Ulysses that approaches from the east,
> The interminable adventurer? . . .
>
> . . . .
>
> She has composed, so long, a self with which to welcome him,
> Companion to his self for her, which she imagined,
> Two in a deep-founded sheltering, friend and dear friend.

Just so, but not so fast. That is how they will finally find each other, but the decades of "composing a self" have surely something to do with the two days' delay. There is probably also something at work of the withholding effect seen most nakedly in dogs and children: If they await you, having missed you too intensely, then, when you do appear they won't even look at you, blocked by their very emotions. The dogs at Eumaeus' farm nearly killed strange Odysseus, but fawned quietly on familiar Telemachus. Odysseus' old hunting dog Argos ("Speedy"), however, lying neglected, decrepit, and dim-eyed in the dung, drops his ears as if going off duty, wags his tail, and dies when he senses his master near—the ultimate in being stopped dead by feeling, and the only *spontaneous* acknowledgment the returned master will get.

But the most inward cause of Penelope's wariness is simply this: Odysseus' looks are in fact unchanged "in stature, voice and feet," as observed by Eurycleia, who has, as we shall soon see, a reason for being fixed on Odysseus' feet. But that cannot tell Penelope whether his heart is unchanged.

General surmises are not, however, all we have to go by. There are dozens of clear, if subtle, indications that she knows; Homer is at least as fond of indirection as is his couple. First there is the wonderful double-talk they all engage in once he is on Ithaca—some doing it unwittingly, she wittingly and, one might say, wittily.

It begins with Eumaeus' insistence, in Odysseus' presence: "nor shall Odysseus *anymore* come home" (38). It is interpretatively echoed by Odysseus himself when he reveals himself to his son: "nor shall *yet another* Odysseus ever come here." Then Penelope says, knowing full well, I think, the meaning of her words: ". . . but him I shall never *again* welcome as one returned home," and later once more: "nor will Odysseus *anymore* come here." Of course not; he's right there. Best of all, she tells Antinous by way of getting him to agree to the Test of the Bow: "Do you expect that if that stranger strings Odysseus' great bow . . . he will lead me home and establish me as his wife?" And again, of course not; they've been married these twenty years. Her double tongue is anybody's match.

When she descends to show herself, she clearly speaks for her husband's ears: When Telemachus grows a beard, she announces, she is to marry and leave the house. Now he knows that she has been mindful of his instructions and that he has arrived just in time. She rebukes the wooers for eating her out of house and home and solicits the gifts proper to the wooing of a "good woman"; they promptly send for robes and brooches and other jewelry. Odysseus is impressed (42); she is his match too in acquisitiveness. To persuade ourselves that such solid good sense was then and ever after not only compatible with, but a condition for, lovableness, we may leap two and a half millennia forward to Jane Austen's women.

The wooers go home to sleep—most of them—and Telemachus, not without a certain pleasure, I imagine, employs his royal father as torchbearer while they stow away the weapons. Now comes the moment: Odysseus sends Telemachus to bed so he can talk privately, "and she, *grieving,* shall tell me about everything in turn"; he attributes to her his own telltale word, *odyromene* (21).

Penelope, chaste as Artemis *and* lovely as Aphrodite, comes down and sits on her throne. That shameless hussy Melantho is again being offensive to Odysseus; he threatens her with action by Odysseus' son Telemachus who is now, "by favor of Apollo, such as he himself once was." In response to Penelope's announcement he covertly acknowledges to her that the time is ripe, that Telemachus is now indeed a fully grown man. We may even surmise that the Feast of Apollo is something like Telemachus' birthday or name day: His name, "Far-from-Battle," might also be construed as "Fighting-from-Afar," as bowmen do; Odysseus thinks him capable of handling the Great Bow. All in all, Apollo may well be the adoptive ancestral god of the house, as Athena is Odysseus' personal goddess. Recall that Telemachus' maternal great-grandfather is Autolycus,

Wolf-Himself, and Apollo is called *Lyceios,* the "Wolf-God" (though, to be sure, not by Homer). At any rate, Apollo appears in this event as the scene-setter.

For the first time Penelope hears her husband up close. I imagine his voice as having an unmistakable timbre and range: ringing in command, dulcet in love, a clear tenor with moments of baritone when he is moved. The beginning of their first colloquy is—a wonderful touch—through this persistent wench Melantho, the vilest medium. Penelope tells Melantho to leave them alone: You've heard me say that "I am about to question the stranger in my own hall about *the* husband," not "my" husband—a curiously demonstrative locution. Chairs are set, and they sit face-to-face. Neither the son whom he left as a baby nor the swineherd who was then a young man recognized him spontaneously. He is still in beggar's rags, still aged and shriveled. Does she recognize him on sight? Of course.

She begins formally with the customary interrogation— Who are you, whence, of what parentage? He likens her to a king (42), but asks not to be questioned lest she fill his heart with grief; he again uses his name-word: *odynaon.* So she is, after all, told who he is. She expresses her need for him, and tells him—the first he's heard—of the stratagem of the daily weaving and nightly unraveling of Laertes' shroud and its discovery: "But now I cannot find another design." She too uses *his* word, *metis,* "plan, design." She insists on being told who he is, "for you aren't sprung from an oak or a rock"—fairy-tale language. He responds not with a fairy tale but a lying tale, the long one in which he is called Aethon and which sets up the Test of the Brooch (38, 46). He prophesies that Odysseus will be here before the month is out; she promises gifts (and we know from Eumaeus' offer that cloaks and tunics are first

among such presents to beggars) *if* what he says comes
and yet she promptly provides cloaks for his bed that night and
intimates that there will be tunics for the morning. Contrary
to all custom, his camp bed is to be made up "inside the
house," in the fore-hall of the palace. Even Telemachus had
to sleep on the outer porch in Argos; strangers always do.

Now he is to have his feet bathed. Things here are all out
of the customary order, which is: first bath, then questions. But
since he has denied himself, Penelope is going to show him that
she is a device ahead of him. This device is the Foot Washing,
though *he* gets to specify who is to wash his feet: his old nurse,
Eurycleia. And now Penelope intimates to him by a half-slip
what she knows. She gives the order to the nurse:

> But come, get up now, circumspect Eurycleia
> And wash your lord's—age-mate; and perhaps Odysseus
> By now has such feet—and such hands.

She reveals that she knows him

She catches herself and says not "feet," but "age-mate," that
is, peer. Then she oddly says that his feet must be such as are
Odysseus' because of their shared old age, but quickly adds
"and hands," thereby at once revealing and covering her insight.

The catch in the line is made audible by Homer's use of a
common hexametric verse scheme. Every epic line has a caesura, a clearly heard cut in certain standard places of the dactylic foot (18); sometimes there is a subsidiary division between feet called a diaeresis. In Penelope's line there is both a
caesura, the kind called trochaic because it comes after a
trochee, the long-short part of the foot (¯ ˘), and a diaeresis,
the kind called bucolic because it turns up later in pastoral poetry. The two can be combined, as they are here:

nī- psŏn | sŏi- ŏ ă- | nā- ktŏs ‖ hŏ- | mē- lĭ- kă; ‖ kāi pŏu
Ŏ- | dȳs- sēus

Here *anaktos* is "lord's," *homelika* is "age-mate," and you can hear at the double strokes where she stops, catches herself, substitutes, and then names her husband as if he were an afterthought and his feet as if her interest needed masking.

Why *is* she intent on Odysseus' feet? That quickly becomes clear. Eurycleia, the one who can usually hold her tongue, chatters excitedly as she makes her preparations. That's when she exclaims that she has never seen anyone so like Odysseus in stature, voice, and feet. He is laconic, deprecating: That's what everyone says.

She mixes cold and warm water, and he draws away from the hearth into the shadows. She begins the washing and sees the mark, the mark of his suffering, prevailing, and healing. Then, a second later in real time, his foot has clattered back into the basin. She has barely a moment to cry out: "Yes, you are Odysseus, my dear baby, and I didn't know you before I had felt my lord in the flesh," and he has her by the throat. An indiscretion now can cost them their lives, especially if that slut Melantho is still hanging around.

In the second between her feeling the scar and the foot crashing into the basin and turning it over, a long story has been told, the story of the scar that marks him (47).

Where is Penelope? Eurycleia seeks out her eyes as she speaks to Odysseus, trying to signify "that the dear husband is within." But his wife "is unable to meet her glance or to pay it any mind, for Athena had turned her mind away." Humanly speaking, she is exercising tight self-control; she won't even glance in their direction. She is his wife in this.

Odysseus, washed and oiled, draws up his chair, and she
er dream of the twenty geese (42), in which the eagle

self controlled like odysseus

comforts her in a human voice: "I who was before an eagle have now come back as your husband and will let loose destruction on the wooers." We know that the voice which now confirms the eagle's message is the same as the voice in the dream, and it says: "Odysseus himself has shown you how he will accomplish it." She plays the skeptic while at the same time confirming him in turn; she *says* that tomorrow will be the day of evil name which will cut her off from the house of Odysseus, but she prepares for the opposite to happen: She plans to set up the Test-and-Contest of the Bow, an exercise of tricky indoor archery that Odysseus used to practice. She wishes the stranger could stay forever to talk but on this night of all nights they must sleep, she upstairs, he in the hall.

She sleeps, but he can't. He tosses about, kept awake partly by the laughter of the women servants making love with those wooers who have not gone home, partly by the fatty sausage Antinous had given him (20), but most of all because he is planning tomorrow's battle; Homer can't even let Odysseus have insomnia without a multiple motive. Athena comes to calm him, and he finally sleeps. Now it is Penelope's turn to awaken from a dream in which he finally lies beside her. It is just before dawn, and Odysseus too is awakened by a most poignant disturbance—her weeping. It is for him a night spent between sounds of loud laughter and heartbreaking crying. It seems to him that she had known him and come to stand by his head. He packs up his bedding and moves outside to sleep on an oxhide. Has Penelope in fact been down to look at him? —a dangerous move if both should lose control, but I think she was there. Yet they escape this premature rendezvous.

Now comes a second touching Homeric moment: The weakest of the women servants hasn't got to bed at all because she is still grinding her assignment of barley meal. She prays in Odysseus' hearing that this may be the last day for the wooers, who have loosened her knees with heart-aching toil. The servants always know what's in the offing. Her prayer is answered by a thunderclap, and he is glad. Homer, ever mindful of everyone, shows in this brief vignette what the absence of a good master means to the weak.

In the morning, all arise and Telemachus asks the nurse why the stranger isn't better accommodated. She invents a plausible excuse for a situation she understands well: He isn't used to a nice bed. This is a real household, one where people are always telling each other little lies because for all their love, they don't trust each other's temper. With Telemachus, Eurycleia is probably wise. He doesn't quite get the point of his parents' reserve (40).

The wooers convene, and Penelope goes to the strongroom to get the bow, a voyage through the palace into the past, lovingly described. She offers herself as the prize for the contest or "labor" (*aethlon*), the word used in the premier Greek story, the Heracles myth. Antinous, who is old enough to have as a child known Odysseus, says that no one there is up to him, and no one will string the bow. Everyone, including Telemachus, is overexcited; he catches himself laughing witlessly and has a little public contretemps with his mother: She wants to make sure that Odysseus gets his chance at the bow, and Telemachus sharply tells her he'll manage that: "My mother," he says stiffly—it used to be "Mother"—"no Greek is more empowered than I to give it to, or withhold it from, whomsoever I will." He tells her, as is now his way, to go upstairs. She obeys, and like her husband, who can let go in moments of decision, she sleeps through the great slaughter.

When it is all over the loyal servants are brought in to kiss their master. Eurycleia goes to awaken Penelope and tells her that the palace is retaken by Odysseus. Penelope, aroused from the sweetest sleep ever, pretends that the old woman has lost her wits and is doing some "out-of-bounds talking." Eurycleia stops her by telling her what is surely no real though it nonetheless makes her glad: Telemachus knew all along who the stranger was. Assured that the time has come to admit facts, she happily leaps out of bed. Yet she keeps up a pretense that the nurse is not telling the truth and that not Odysseus, who has lost his Return far away, but the gods have wrought the wooers' destruction: "You know how welcome he would be to all were he to appear in these halls, and especially to me and my son, whom *we* love." She says out loud what Telemachus went to Sparta to learn (22) and what we never doubted: He is *their* son. And even when the nurse tells her of the sign of the scar as proof of Odysseus' presence, she says evasively: "Nurse dear, clever though you are, it is hard for you to clue out the arts of the gods that are forever." Not a word about her husband's part in the restoration!

She goes down and now for the first time looks him—perhaps not yet quite—full in the face. Familiarity comes and goes as it will with even the closest friend dressed out of character, for Odysseus, stripped of his armor, is still in rags. This is when Telemachus gets impatient with her, wanting her to stop being aloof (40). We shall soon know truly, she says, if this *is* Odysseus. She and his father have "signs which we alone know, hidden from others." Odysseus smiles and tells him to let his mother do her testing. Meanwhile he is to mount the mock wedding. And so begins the Test of the Bed (46). But it has nothing much to do with his mere identity.

These two, so perfectly alike and so perfectly complementary, play out a denouement that has its own tempo, which Telemachus is just too young to grasp. Odysseus prolonged his Return for ten years; now Penelope postpones his Homecoming for ten minutes.

Before they had refrained from embracing, being co-conspirators. Now as they sit face-to-face he is in mere *fact,* unquestionably, the master of the house, but is he in *truth* her

Tests his loyalty + memory

husband still? That is the *private* question yet to be answered. The *public* question will then be whether he is still king of Ithaca and the other islands, and when it has been answered the poem can end.

In tragedy the pivotal moment is the Recognition, the revelation of identity; that seems to be true of folktales as well. But in this epic poem, so full of marked moments, there is no one Moment of Recognition. Penelope has known at first sight that this beggar is Odysseus. What she needs to learn is something far beyond that mere fact.

46

TESTING

PENELOPE AND ODYSSEUS BOTH RAISE TESTING, trying out, putting to proof, to a heroic virtue. Odysseus, with a natural bent that way, is, on Ithaca, advised to do it by his wily goddess; but Penelope does it on her own, and does it better. Tests of identity are the staples of folktales and a standard part of tragic plots, but this pair takes the device to new heights of subtlety. So the question is continually: Who is being put to the proof by whom and for what reason? It is not even clearly the case that this testing is a matter of caution, of prudence; for Odysseus on his odyssey, it is often a reckless trying out (29), as it is for Penelope at home a risky holding out.

One might indeed say that Odysseus' whole odyssey is driven by the urge to try things out, to put situations to the test. But once he returns under cover, warned by Agamemnon in Hades and seconded by Athena on Ithaca, the testing acquires a practical purpose, though he carries it out with such flair as to drive it way beyond the needful.

It starts on a dark and stormy night, his first on Ithaca, when he tests the swineherd's generosity with that comical tale in which, acting a little drunk, he, the beggarly stranger, claims to have been saved from freezing on a snowy night out by Odysseus. They are on patrol, and he has left his cloak behind; Odysseus tricks the eager young Thoas, "Fast," into running

Penelope tests Odysseus

ne lines for reinforcements, leaving his cloak behind,
sto!—the stranger sleeps warm. For Odysseus' clever
su... of Odysseus' cleverness, he is rewarded with one of Eumaeus' thick extra cloaks. The generous man would have given
it anyhow, but Odysseus had to try him out. This is in good
fun, but thereafter all his moves are to test the loyalties of his
people and the possibilities of his situation. Telemachus wisely
stops Odysseus' extravagant idea of testing the whole servant
population of the island, but one purpose of all the lying tales
(38) is severely to test the disposition of the listeners.

In particular, he has been told in Hell and encouraged by
Heaven to test his wife. The wonderful thing is that he gets to
do no such thing. She turns the tables right away, and it is he
who is tested, exhaustively. But she knows who he is all along
(45), so what is she testing? She is the female incarnation,
Odysseus' counterpart, of the spirit of Homer's deepest distinction, that between gross fact and subtle truth.

She starts the grand game played about these two poles
when Odysseus tells her the tale, made up specially for her, in
which he, the stranger, claims to have made Odysseus' acquaintance twenty years ago, before the siege of Troy. He practically sets himself up, and she seizes the opportunity: "Now
I think I will in fact test you, stranger." What then was Odysseus wearing? He describes it with improbable exactitude:
The tunic was soft and glistened like an onion skin, and many
women gazed at it in wonder. He doesn't know if Odysseus
wore it at home, or was it a gift from a comrade or a stranger?
For verisimilitude he throws in Odysseus' best friend, the herald
—older, dark skinned, round shouldered, curly haired, a sharply
drawn figure who appears twice in the *Iliad* and vanishes. He
describes in loving detail a golden brooch, artfully crafted with
a hound pinning a fawn that is writhing to get away. "I will

tell you how my heart pictures it," he says (19). He is teasing, of course, about the gazing women and the tunic-giving comrades. Surely she herself gave him the tunic and, as she admits weeping, the brooch.

Whatever *his* cause for a suspicion induced by others, she has more, arising from the facts: Where has he been all these ten years? Telemachus had already let slip something about Calypso, but what she really cares about is the mutuality of their memory, expressed in that familiar appeal-inquisition: "Do you remember the ring [or bracelet or necklace or . . .] that I gave you ages ago?" His heart pictures it as if it were yesterday. And so he passes the Test of the Brooch brilliantly —a great moment for them both.

But not the yet greatest. Penelope's crucial and final test is administered after the repossession of the palace. She can't yet look him full in the face. There is a secret sign between them by which they will know better each other's mind. Odysseus restrains Telemachus' impetuous intervention in his own behalf. The wedding music he has ordered begins, sweet song and fine dancing, led by the palace minstrel he has saved from the slaughter. He is now bathed and Athena has restored his looks; he is, for the moment at hand, beautiful with Athena's sheen. Still Penelope holds back. Now he reproaches *her* for being iron hearted and offers to go and lie by himself. She denies that she is either magnifying her own importance or overly amazed by him; she well knows "what manner of man you were" *before* you left Ithaca. She orders Eurycleia to bring out his bedstead and to make up his bed for him outside her bridal chamber, their master bedroom—which he himself had built. "So she spoke, testing her husband."

He blows up—and passes the Test of the Bed with a totally, deeply satisfactory mark.

Test of the bed

his bed, about which Telemachus had already made
er anxious by suggesting that it might by now be cov-
er⌐ ith nasty spider's webs (this boy does not understand
the kind of spinning that is going on in his mother's apartments)—this bed is no ordinary piece of furniture. It is part
of a rooted growth. Odysseus had built his and Penelope's bed
chamber around a large vigorous olive tree, trimmed to serve
as the bedpost of their marriage bed; the bed he had planed
straight and smooth, and it was inlaid with gold and silver and
ivory:

> So I manifest to you this sign, and I don't know
> If the bed is still firmly in place for me, woman! Or if some
> Man has by now put it somewhere else, cutting it from its olive
> foundation.

When Penelope hears this angry, heartfelt outburst, *her* "iron"
heart melts, and she bursts into tears and throws her arms
around him and kisses him and even begs his pardon. At this
great moment Helen comes to her mind, and she speaks of her,
not quite coherently—Homer has a way of making heroic
hexameter convey the utterance of a woman in the throes of
feeling (35). But her associations are clear enough: Paris seduced her cousin into a rootless, placeless, loveless marriage
without natural foundations; she has to avoid that miserable
fate which can befall a woman even with her own husband.
And of course, Helen is the cause of all her troubles to begin
with, troubles now coming to their end.

The test he has passed for her is not a test of valor or vigor;
he had passed that earlier in the day when he strung the bow
with ease. Recall that the Test of the Bow was also *her* idea.
The test he has passed now is one of identity in its literal meaning, self-sameness: He is still the manner of man he was be-

She needs "living proof"

fore he went to Troy, her husband who has returned steadfast in his memory-laden, ineradicable love for his wife and his loyalty to the naturally rooted institution of marriage. That is what she needed to know and what she cares about; I doubt she minds all the women she is about to hear more of.

So they go to their hypernaturally long wedding night (48), for which Homer produces his most amazing simile: She comes to him as a shipwrecked sailor comes to land (42).

Odysseus, having been tested and found sound, expresses his new priorities clearly: first going to the "much loved bed," then securing his possessions, finally meeting his father.

Laertes, the old retired king, is a somewhat mysteriously recessive player in the *Odyssey*. Odysseus learned from his mother in Hades of his father's self-banishment to an outlying farmstead; we know he no longer comes to town. That is perhaps understandable, but why had he, alive and not old, abdicated his kingship to Odysseus even before the Trojan expedition? It is an unusual action; Nestor, for example, hangs on into very old age, over three generations (23). Homer simply takes the situation as given, but we may speculate.

Laertes is not an assertive soul to begin with, given to passive dejection and depression; he may well have preferred the farm to the palace in any case. Penelope, the daughter of Icarius, is the niece of Tyndareus, both of whose daughters married into the most powerful families in Greece, the Atreidae of Argos: Helen is married to Menelaus and Clytemnestra to Agamemnon, the overlord (24). We know that this clan was none too happy to see one of their women go off with an obscure crown prince of unillustrious family, governing a rocky island whose one asset is that it can be "clearly seen" (38). Myth outside the *Odyssey* has it that they tried to stop the marriage, but Penelope chose to follow Odysseus. They have certainly tried to convince her to remarry, to take the most generous wooer. We also know that Menelaus hoped to get Odysseus to resettle in Argos (24).

So, I imagine, the great families made it a condition of Penelope's marriage—they must have known she had the steadfast spirit to elope with Odysseus—that Laertes should hand off the kingship to Odysseus, who was in any case better suited for it (3), to everyone's satisfaction.

This is the old man whom Odysseus, here once more and for the last time the tester, now puts—that is the truth of it—to the torture of his inquisition. When he and his tiny band arrive at Laertes' well-ordered farm, he tells them all to go and fix dinner. He finds his sad father alone, bent over, digging around his vines. He is wearing old leathery work clothes, lovingly described by Homer: gloves, shinguards, goatskin cap; had the Greeks worn boots one would see the pair painted by van Gogh.

Should he kiss the old man or test him? He decides to test. He compliments him on his orchards, figs, vines, pears, and tells a last lying tale (38). He claims to have come looking for a guest he once entertained, the son of a certain Laertes, son of Arceisius. He has just met a man who wasn't quite in his right mind and wouldn't tell him if Laertes was in fact on the island. With this story he brings his father to the point of weeping and asking about Odysseus. His own nose begins to sting, and then he reveals himself: "That one

Van Gogh, A Pair of Shoes.

you ask about, I am myself, Father." But now Laertes is not ready, and Odysseus has to show his scar and name by count the trees in the orchard Laertes gave him when he was a child. When he knows the signs, Laertes faints around his son's neck.

What is the object of this prolonged testing? "The man not quite in his right mind" may be the clue: Odysseus has to know whether his father is sound of mind as well as able-bodied, because he, Odysseus Ithacesius, is about to face the Ithacan nobles *en masse*. But it is a harsh, strained, dubious moment, this first meeting of son and father that makes the family complete. In this epic the reunion of the whole family is not the climactic finale. That event is now to come as the three generations of the Laertidae stand together to meet in battle the fathers of the slain suitors. Now Laertes can joyfully exclaim:

What a day this is for me, dear gods! I am truly glad!
My son and my son's son are holding a contest of excellence.

How even that final battle is something of a fadeout has been set out before (14). At any rate, it is not the final effort Odysseus' Return requires of him (48).

47
TIME CHASMS

BEFORE RELEASING ODYSSEUS to his peaceful and prosperous future, I want to take note of Homer's way with the past. The gods *elevate* the ordinary human scene by the grace of their watchful presence (1). Similes *project* harsh human events onto a distant horizon of art and nature (20). Besides height and horizontal distance, the Homeric world also has depth: The stories embedded in the epic telling *deepen* the human situation by opening up its foundations in the past beneath it. They are time chasms.

Neither Homer nor his heroes hesitate to interrupt the action with a long, a really long, story. Isn't the odyssey itself such an interruption in the bare plot of the *Odyssey*, told on the brink of a long-delayed Return? The heroes tell of their youthful exploits—Nestor is the specialist here (23). Or they tell of their lineage—so Diomedes the Argive and Glaucos from Lycia stand still in the midst of battle for a long colloquy during which they discover that they are "guest friends," whose families have offered each other hospitality; clever young Diomedes uses the occasion to propose an exchange of armor to which the slow-witted but good-natured Lycian agrees, "giving golden for bronze, a hundred-head of oxen for nine"— a bit of deadpan fun much rarer in the *Iliad* than in the *Odyssey*.

Nestor in particular is unstoppable. When Patroclus fatefully turns up to gather news for Achilles who is *hors de combat,* self-disabled (9), Nestor launches into a long heroic tale whose immediate relevance is merely this: In my lusty youth, I wouldn't have acted like Achilles. The tale serves to underscore the heroically excessive youthfulness of Achilles' conduct and to express what might be called the admiring disapproval of the elders. In fact, all these time-out stories, these old histories, do illuminate the action, though sometimes quite obliquely.

In the *Odyssey* two embedded stories seem to me particularly to call for reflection. By attending to their *content* we learn something about the current situation into which they are injected, but by thinking about the *embedding itself* we learn how the past figures in Homer's world.

In novels, which have replaced epic for us, flashbacks take us back in time to bring us up to the novel's present having learned what we need to know. In the epic poem the embedded stories serve the same purpose. The memory either of one of the people in the poem or of the poet himself is mobilized to give a temporal foundation to the poem's present. In Homeric epic these stories have the air of a deliberate loss of focus, of a mind wandering with intentional leisureliness, taking time for purposes of recollection: Time out.

Yet what characterizes some of these embeddings is just that there is *no* time out. A sudden cleft, a rift opens in the flowing time of the narrative. We are given a deep look into the events behind the present, but when the chasm closes we are at the opposite brink of present time with not a moment lost, though freighted with new knowledge of old matters: Time has been cloven to disclose the grounds of the present.

The stories of which that is true are those Homer himself tells. When the heroes tell a story it is part of the current ac-

tion: The man telling it is taking time out of the work at hand
to reminisce, but this telling is part of the real, running time
of the action; when the story is finished it is later in the hour
for everybody. When Homer tells it no time passes for the people in the poem. The time chasm has great depth but next to
no breadth; from one brink to the other it is but a moment,
or less.

The two stories to be considered are about Odysseus, about
his mark and his weapon, the Story of the Scar and the Story
of the Bow.

Odysseus knows—as does his wife—that when Eurycleia
washes his feet she must recognize him. The scar is *his* mark,
by which he will later reveal himself to his other faithful servants. Between her feeling the scar in the shadow to which he
has withdrawn and the clatter of the basin being upset by his
foot as she drops it, the story is seamlessly inserted: "Right
away she knew the scar, which once a boar had . . ." We are
immediately wafted back some fifty years or so to Odysseus'
birth, shortly after which his maternal grandfather Autolycus
arrives in Ithaca. It is Eurycleia herself who hands him the
newborn baby to name. She actually shyly suggests a name,
Polyaretos, "Much-prayed-for" (like Arete of Phaeacia). But
Autolycus, "Wolf-Himself," that self-willed rogue, perversely
chooses for the baby as his "eponymous"—that is, his signifying—name, Odysseus, the "Hated" (21); "because I have
come here much hated (*odyssamenos*) by men and women all
over the all-nourishing earth"; no wonder; he is a wolfish thief
and cheat. All the other meanings, active and passive, "Pain-
giver," "Man of Wrath," "Woe-man," "Sufferer," are no more
apt for this man who is loved by all women and many men all
over the earth and who does less outright harm than most heroes. To be sure, he suffers and inflicts pain, but he prevails
and ends well (48). Perhaps wily Autolycus has given him

an apotropaic name, one that turns off evil by anticipatory naming—perhaps. But he does promise gifts when Odysseus comes to manhood.

In the second part of the story, twenty years or so later (and thirty years before the present), Odysseus has come of age; he is at the stage that Telemachus has reached just now. Telemachus' initiatory test will come tomorrow, when he will fight his first battle. Odysseus' test was an encounter with a great wild boar, tracked down after a wonderful hunt including a steep climb up Parnassus. Parnassus is the mountain sacred to Apollo and Muses: "To climb Parnassus" is an English phrase for writing poetry, but that is, to be candid, pure serendipity. Still, we know that there is a poet in Odysseus, and that he should receive his distinguishing mark on the Muses' mountain is a wonderful thought. He makes his kill, but not before the boar charges and gores him in the thigh and slashes his leg. When Autolycus and his sons have healed the wound he is sent back to Ithaca with his marking scar and his glorious gifts, and "his father and lady-mother rejoiced in his return and asked him about everything, and he made a good story of how he got the wound and how the boar charged . . ."—a story whose circular telling can go on *ad infinitum.*

This embedded story does at least two things: It turns the scar from a mere identifying mark into a significant emblem of his nature. And it is long-deferred confirmation to us that he is indeed often naming himself surreptitiously when he uses words for hating and grieving.

The second story is much briefer. Athena has put it into Penelope's mind to get Odysseus' bow (46). With lovely, leisurely circumstance Homer follows her going for the key, the bronze key with its ivory handle, and on her way to the distant strongroom where among the treasures lies "the back-bent bow . . . which . . . ," and the story of its acquisition begins. Even

Odysseus has always been the same

...g Odysseus was already the man to carry out labors (5), and he had been dispatched by Laertes and the Ithacan elders to Lacedaimon to recover a flock of stolen sheep. There he met Iphitus, who gave him the great bow, that Odysseus "would never take with him on the black ships when going to war, but it lay in his halls as a remembrance of his foreign friend, and he carried it in his own land."

And then we are back with Penelope shooting the bolt of the treasure chamber, making her way through the chests to the peg where hangs the unstrung bow in its case, sitting with it on her knees, weeping as she uncases it, going back to the hall to address the wooers—holding her veil before her face—and offering herself as the prize in the Contest of the Bow.

Between the insertion of the key and the throwing of the bolt, one moment in Penelope's pensive, long, unswerving way, we see into Odysseus' youth, that he was even then the man for all missions that he is now, that like his son, he made a friend in the Peloponnesus, and that his bow is not merely a fine piece of equipment but a memento of a dear dead friend—for Iphitus has been killed by Heracles.

The time lines of these embedded stories, especially the Story of the Scar, are actually more complex than the figure of a time chasm conveys. But two diagrams looked at in conjunction will make them clear.

1 We can read Homer's account one-dimensionally, linearly, as it is spoken. By my watch this takes perhaps ten minutes, thirty if I try it in Greek. This linear reading looks as it would if someone within the epic were telling the story:

Eurycleia finds the scar	The Story of the Scar	She drops Odysseus' foot

2 We can, however, take in the same account two-dimensionally; that reading does not register on a watch. The nar-

ration of the foot washing does not miss a beat, but a line, a
second dimension, descends into the depth of time between the
moment Eurycleia recognizes Odysseus and the moment his
foot clatters into the basin.

This line goes fifty years back to Odysseus' birth and then
twenty years forward to his coming-of-age. At these stations
the vertical line into the past develops two horizontal lines of
its own, representing the story of his naming, which took, perhaps, a few minutes, and the story of his visit to his grand-
parents, the hunt, wounding, healing, and telling of the story
to his parents, which altogether took perhaps a month:

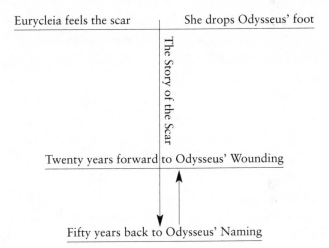

I would swear that this poet knows what he is doing—not,
of course, that he had in mind anything so skeletal as a dia-
gram, but that he would have laughed at the notion that these
stories might be mere exuberant excrescences brought on by
narrative naïveté.

This is the way the past is inserted into the present of the
poem's world. But that world itself has a past, is *of* a past, in
the sense that Homer is generally thought to be relating stories telling of a real Trojan plain, a real Argive dynasty, a real

Mediterranean sea world, even a real Ithaca. Much keen effort has gone into discerning what the real time of the Homeric world is: Does it depict that epoch with fair verisimilitude, or does it mingle in a preponderance of elements from Homer's own time, or is it perhaps a never-never world that is far more invention than history, as Homer's language owes more to art than to ordinary speech? The remote past is that strange tissue of facts that we believe to be perfectly knowable in themselves but acknowledge to be hopelessly unavailable for us. It is therefore merely an irresistible speculation, weird and wonderful, if on putting down the *Odyssey* I ask myself: Have I just been in the world of 1173 B.C., ten years after the traditional date for the fall of Troy? Or in the Greece of the eighth century B.C., one of the suggested centuries for Homer's lifetime? Or in a realm of Homer's imagining that never was? Or always is?

48

TWICE TOLD, THRICE DEAD

IT IS THE NIGHT BEFORE THE FINAL BATTLE (14). Penelope and
Odysseus are about to go upstairs to their unseveredly natural marriage bed. But not before he has told her that "*we* have
not yet come to the limit of our labors." He reports to her Teiresias' mystifying injunction to fulfill one more duty, which will
take him away from home one last time; she demands the details and he gives them. And since it has been tactfully con-
veyed—in the first person plural and right away, before they
retire for their night together—she receives the disappointing
news with equanimity and hope: "Hope (*elpore*) there is then
that this *will* be the escape from evils." Meanwhile Eurynome
has made up their bed, and now they ascend by torchlight.
Telemachus stops the dancing, and he goes to a victor's sleep
in his hall together with his two new brothers—the swineherd
and the cowboy—his little army:

> We few, we happy few, we band of brothers;
> For he to-day that sheds his blood with me
> Shall be my brother; be he ne'er so vile
> This day shall gentle his condition.

This is just the reward King Odysseus promised these serfs.
And now upstairs.

Odysseus + Penelope
are perfect together

They are a pair. Greek has a "dual," a special grammatical form for speaking of two that go naturally together; it could be the two eyes in the head, two eagles wheeling in tandem, two friends being received together. But the poignant use is here where the two "enjoy lovely love," and then "take delight in stories, relating them to each other"—the verb "relating" is the same with which Homer invoked the Muse in the first line of the poem (*enepontes, enepe*). She tells of all she had to bear at home and—for all her dismay, perhaps not without a touch of pride—of the cattle, sheep, and wine consumed in the wooing of her.

He tells her his odyssey, all twelve adventures in order from the Ciconian point of departure through the magic islands to the Phaeacian place of emergence and the treasure he has brought home. One unhad adventure he throws in; he had actually avoided the Clashing Rocks, the route of the Argonauts (33). Some details that might hurt her he no doubt leaves out, for example, Agamemnon's warning against her in Hades. Others he relates with the proper emphasis to please her, such as his refusal of immortality and agelessness from Calypso. One event he most wonderfully omits—not a word of the young princess who dreamed of having him as a husband and asked never to be forgotten (35). His silence betokens both his delicacy toward his wife and his kept promise to the princess.

This night is probably the first chance Penelope has had to relate her penelopeia, the story of her suffering and bravery. But it is Odysseus' *second* telling of his odyssey, which he had first shaped into a tale among the Phaeacians. It is now a twice-told tale, yet it is a private, interior story which will never become a myth among public myths (32). Perhaps Telemachus will hear it and the grandchildren, when he puts Helen's gift of a bridal gown to use (24). Of course, the Muses know it, and they have told Homer who has told us of Odysseus' telling. In the treatment of time or the telling of tales, Homer is nothing if not cagey and complex.

This night is a full night of relieved weeping, lovely love, long talk, and "sweet sleep that loosens the limbs." Athena has made sure there is world enough and time by holding back golden-throned Dawn on the banks of River Ocean. When morning does come, Odysseus sets off with his little band to meet his father and to face the bereaved Ithacans. Penelope is to go upstairs and let no one in. It is the last we see of her on earth, though her fame will soon resound in Hades (31).

THRICE DEAD

This night she bravely urges Odysseus to tell her what labor is taking him away so soon, and so she elicits from him the details of that strange mission enjoined by Teiresias in Hades. He calls her "Amazing woman!" for her discerning eagerness and repeats to her the seer's words.

This aftermath-labor no longer gives him an adventurer's thrill, though it requires him once more to visit a great many cities of mortals, just as he was doing in the first lines of the *Odyssey*. This time he is to carry in his hands a well-fitted oar until he comes to men who neither know the sea nor put salt in their food nor know about ships and "the well-fitted oars that serve as wings to ships." No more islands—he is clearly traveling inland, on the continent, and the sign that he has arrived at his destination will be that he falls in with another wayfarer who will say that Odysseus has a winnowing shovel

on his stately shoulder. There he is to fix his oar in the earth
and to make a first sacrifice to Poseidon. Then he is to depart
for home to offer sacrifices to all the other Olympian gods in
order. And a gentle death in old age shall be his.

Homer has actually told us what the Ritual of the Oar signifies, though it was by indirection and nearly five thousand
seven hundred lines ago (30). In fact, during his visit in Hades,
Odysseus was asked to perform the ritual for one of his crew-
men just before he spoke with Teiresias (an attentive listener
could have put two and two together, right then). We must
now recall Elpenor, the "Hopeful." Wonderfully, Penelope herself, when she has heard of this last labor, unwittingly calls
on us to remember him: She says "Hope (*elpore*) there is
then . . ." Recall that this poor hopeless boy fell to his death
from Circe's roof in a stupefied hangover just as they were
leaving for Hades; his soul had got to Hades before Odysseus
and extracted the promise of a proper sailor's burial. As soon
as Odysseus got back he fulfilled this promise by burying the
boy's body and armor and erecting a memorial mound. And
"on top of the mound we fixed his well-fitted oar," as the
young sailor had requested in Hades.

So what Odysseus is bidden to perform by Teiresias is a fu-
nereal ritual. Inland, far away from the sea, he is to bury the
sailor that he was, while acknowledging Poseidon's empire
symbolically on land. For we know that this resentful god lays
angry claim to a part interest in the earth. It is a virtual death
that Odysseus dies and a cenotaph that he raises. His oar
marks not the site of a sailor's pyre, but the laying to rest of a
sailor's life and the beginning of his Return for good.

When he had come back from the house of Hades, which
had never yielded up another man except Heracles, Circe
called Odysseus "twice-dead" (*disthanes*). Now he has added

a death and must be called "thrice-dead"—one descent to Hades, one symbolic burial, and finally one consummating death in happy old age. In the seer's words:

> ". . . And then the Periods
> Of all thy labors in the peace shall end
> Of easie death, which shall the lesse extend
> His passion to thee that thy foe, the Sea,
> Shall not enforce it, but Death's victory
> Shall chance in onely-earnest-prayr-vow'd age
> Obtained at home, quite emptied of his rage,
> Thy subjects round thee, rich and blest.
> And here has Truth summed up thy vitall rest."

PICTURE CREDITS

Front cover:

Blinding of Polyphemos by Odysseus and his companions. Protoattic amphora from Eleusis, circa 670 B.C.

Kassandra threatened by Ajax. Hydria, circa 480 B.C.

Achilles. Amphora, circa 445/440 B.C.

Penelope beside her unfinished weaving and her son, Telemachus. Circa 440 B.C.

Achilles and Ajax playing a board game. Amphora attributed to Exekias, circa 540/530 B.C.

Pages iv–v: *Achilles slaying the Amazon Queen Penthesileia.* Kylix, circa 455 B.C.

Pages 72, 73: Attic Black-figure amphora attributed to Exekias; later sixth century B.C. Courtesy of DEVOS.

Page 131: Sherd from the Athenian Marketplace published by the author. Copyright © Agora Excavations 19, American School of Classical Studies at Athens. Cartoon reconstruction by the author.

Page 290: Vincent van Gogh (1853–1890). *A pair of shoes,* oil on canvas. Paris, 1886. Courtesy of Amsterdam, Van Gogh Museum (Vincent van Gogh Foundation).

REFERENCES

Translations of the *Odyssey,* the *Iliad,* and all other works are the author's, except where noted. Sometimes the author has translated the same line in different ways to bring out particular meanings.

References to the *Odyssey* and the *Iliad* cite the Greek text from the Loeb Classical Library editions of the epics.

Capital Roman numerals refer to books of the *Iliad,* lower case Roman numerals to books of the *Odyssey.* Arabic numerals refer to line numbers in the original Greek text. (Thus, XX 273, 322 refers to the *Iliad,* Book 20, Lines 273 and 322; i 36 refers to the *Odyssey,* Book 1, Line 36.)

ACCOUNTING FOR THE TITLE

7   all the "Returns": i 36; hos e- phath': i 42; "I feel indignant . . .": Horace, *Poetic Art* 359

8   that same shield: XX 273, 322

13   Swift's Gulliver in fact was: Plato, *Apology* 41a; Swift, *Gulliver's Travels* III 8

15   *promachoi:* III–VIII, XI–XVII, XX–XXII; "And, as imagination . . .": Shakespeare, *Midsummer Night's Dream* 5.1.14; "And like a poppy . . .": VIII 306

16   than the *Iliad:* Aristotle, *Poetics* 1459b; Socrates bans the poets: Plato, *Republic* 391

17   "purification of affections . . .": Aristotle, *Poetics* 1448b, 1449b; "the leader (*hegemon*) . . .": Plato, *Republic* 605d, 595b; tragic myth: xi 271, 543, 409; epic pleasure: Aristotle, *Poetics* 1462b

19 "the spontaneous overflow . . .": Wordsworth, "Preface" to the *Lyrical Ballads*

20 "The house was quiet . . .": Wallace Stevens, "The House Was Quiet and the World Was Calm"

21 "You sodden with wine, . . .": I 224; "as one knowing . . .": XXIII 305; old man's shirt: IX 490

22 "noble naiveté, silent grandeur": Johann Winckelmann, *Reflections on the Imitation of Greek Works in Painting and Sculpture* IV (1755); "that old quarrel . . .": Plato, *Republic* 607b

23 and their opposites: xi 203, iv 111, xiii 332, xxiii 13

27 "Achilles, swift of foot": IX 196

28 courtly obeisance: IX 276

29 second such actuality: Aristotle, *On the Soul* 412a; "actually" be doing: XVIII 95, 97

30 they were beautiful: xiii 399, xvi 15

32 *to philomython:* Longinus, *On the Sublime* 9.12

34 "In drama . . .": Aristotle, *Poetics* 1455b

1. THE GODS

35 "But, o Friend, we come too late . . .": Hölderlin, "Bread and Wine"

36 "willing suspension of disbelief . . .": Coleridge, *Biographia Literaria* XIV; "because they believed not . . .": Ps. 78:22; "that I am He . . .": Isa. 43:10; "the substance of things . . .": Heb. 11:1

37 "am I beyond gods . . .": VIII 27; manifest to human eyes: xvi 160, x 573; Odysseus' vice regent: i 105

38 and their calves: XIII 371; "follow the footsteps . . .": ii 406, iii 30, v 193, vii 38; about Odysseus' return: iv 799; their own shape: vii 201; "and the folk . . .": XVIII 518; *ichor:* V 339

39 an unforgettable singling-out: V 381; and hyacinth: XIV 347; charming maiden: vii 20; "female he-gods": VIII 7; "It is hard, goddess . . .": xiii 312

40   *theoeides:* xv 271, iv 628, i 113; "Living lightly": iv 803, v 122

41   "unquenchable laughter": I 599, viii 326; a sweet smile: xiv 465, xx 301, xxxiii 111; "are like to die": xviii 100; "Dog-fly": XXI 489, 421; death is not a prospect: V 401, 417; "Oh dear, oh dear . . .": i 32

44   "Talkative, anxious . . .": W. H. Auden, "Progress?"

2. ODYSSEUS: HIS LOOKS AND TRANSFORMATIONS

46   close to bald: xviii 353; "Ruddy-Blaze": VIII 185, xix 183; bandy-legged: viii 136, xviii 68

47   "physical shape" closely: III 208; "like winter-snowflakes": III 208, 202; mind is vacant: viii 162, 176; only to Philoctetes: viii 219

48   with Athena's help: XXIII 774; impersonation of a beggar: xiii 401; "I know, I get it . . .": xvi 136, xvii 193, 281

49   head and shoulders: vi 232; she puts rags on him for safety: xiii 429; "No, I am not . . .": xvi 187; leaning on a stick: xvi 456, xvii 202; powerful physique: xviii 70; out of Odysseus' cup: xxii 1; cached nearby: xxii 101; magic of all the moments: xxiii 153

50   *daimonie:* xxiii 166, 174; ambrosial cosmetics: xviii 188; this minute awaiting her: xviii 196; for the Laertidae: xxiv 369; "Be silent! . . .": xix 42

3. ODYSSEUS: HIS NATURE

51   "twice-dead when . . .": xii 22

52   "What better antidote . . .": Theodore Weiss, *Poets on Poetry* (1966), 212; "pied-planning": xxiii 293

53   *polyphron:* i 83, xxi 204, viii 297, 327; "on the wine-tinted sea . . .": v 221; "Eumaeus, surely this is . . .": xvii 264

54   "From Ilium . . .": ix 39; get some treasure together: xi 356; cloak for the night: xiv 462; at the suitors: xx 302

55   "who endows with grace . . .": xiv 435, xv 319; "In your own heart . . .": xxii 411

56   sold into serfdom: xi 103, xiv 138; *"Father* Zeus, . . .": v 7; "what kind of a man . . .": iv 681; in abeyance: ii 26

57   "I am Odysseus, . . .": ix 19

4. HEROES

58   "then, hero, approach . . .": x 516; noble among noblemen: iv 303, 312; there are no "heroines": xi 227; called "Greek heroes" by Athena: i 272; blind Phaeacian singer: viii 483; she weaves his shroud: xix 144

59   at Troy and in Hades: xxiv 68, X 416, xi 629; Achilles' domain: Aristotle, *Meteorologica* 352b

5. ODYSSEUS AT TROY

60   Ajax's at the other: VIII 224; twelve ships: II 637; crew of fifty: II 719; assembly and adjudication: XI 5, 805; center of the expedition: IX 180

62   best-loved hero: X 460, 245; every detail he knows: X 314; Thracian horses: X 500

63   a hundred ships: II 577; infamous night expedition: X 120, 240

64   fleeing to the ships: II 171; Diomedes, observes: X 245; Diomedes steps in: IX 27; Odysseus prevents it again: XIV 74; his savior Odysseus: IV 338; Odysseus or Ajax: I 137; set right with Achilles: XIX 216; he runs away: VIII 94; honorably wounded: XI 437; kind Menelaus: XVI 26; an outstanding archer: viii 219

65   mother's skirts: VIII 271; stinking wound: II 721; "Bowman, No-account, . . .": XI 385; Apollo's darts: XXI 278; Phthia: XI 767; "Hades is so unsoothable . . .": IX 157; "If you hate Agamemnon . . .": IX 300

66   *philophrosyne:* IX 256; Thersites (possibly meaning "Nervy"): II 212; "of unmeasured wordage": II 246

67   calling them She-Greeks: II 235; this unlovely man: II 266; "No way will . . .": II 203; "The heavens themselves . . .": Shakespeare, *Troilus and Cressida* 1.3.85

68 "May I no longer . . .": II 260; "For he who stays . . .": II 292, 298; "Let the Greeks not . . .": XIX 160, 225

69 "the son of Capaneus": IV 403, V 319; among the great ones: XIV 112; "a well-preserved senior": XXIII 791; an incomparably distinguished man: Aristotle, *Politics* 1284a

6. AJAX THE SILENT

70 the living visitor Odysseus: xi 543; "baleful equipment": xi 554; his friend's funeral pyre: xi 547; so grimly foretold: XXII 63; like a turreted wall: VII 219, 245; "bulwark" of the Greeks: III 229

71 as it slowly gives way: XI 558, 546; in one breath: I 138; being offered seven: IX 637; when he is wounded: XI 463; equal prizes: XXIII 725

73 Agamemnon's shield: XI 36

7. BRIEF ACHILLES AND ENDURING ODYSSEUS

76 comradeship of the young: XVII 651; for guile: viii 75

77 fairly small fleets: II 685; with Patroclus' approval: XIX 297; who love their wives: IX 340; cries in his grief: XIX 321; he returns to battle: XVI 282; Penelope's husband: II 260, IV 354; missing him: xi 200

78 mama's boy: I 348, 417, XVIII 95

8. HEPHAESTUS' WORLD: THE SHIELD

79 a big solid man: XVII 210, viii 366; "a wonder to behold": V 725; "First he wrought . . .": XVIII 478, 608

80 continual quarrels: I 590, XVIII 395; "unquenchable laughter": I 599; faithless in bed: XXI 420, viii 266; twenty of them: XVIII 376

81 her son is to die young: XVIII 434; Achilles will lose: XVIII 482; proposal to the Trojans: XXII 117

82 this bloody poem: III 146, VI 466; "How long ago . . .": Frances Cornford, "Parting in Wartime"

83   shield-world: XVIII 601; "Ah, happy, happy boughs! . . .": Keats, "Ode on a Grecian Urn"

84   youths and maidens: XX 269; River Scamander: XXI 241; "from the fair . . .": XXII 313; "She looked over his shoulder . . .": W. H. Auden, "The Shield of Achilles"

9. PATROCLUS THE FRIEND

88   gentle and softhearted: XVII 670; Achilles makes gentle fun: XVI 2; the healing art from Achilles: XI 831; mission of mercy he undertakes: XI 604; his man in battle: XIII 604; Eumaeus: xiv 165; we, the readers: xv 697; "so you, Patroclus, . . .": XVI 754, 585, 812; "My Fanny": Jane Austen, *Mansfield Park*, chap. 48

89   "the helpless fool": XVI 686; makes him foolhardy: XVIII 305; Antilochus cries: XVII 695; in her captivity: XVIII 29, XIX 295; Zeus pities them: XVII 426; "When they saw . . .": Constantine Cavafy, "The Horses of Achilles," trans. Rae Dalven

10. ACHILLES THE UNWITTING LIAR

90   "For hateful to me . . .": IX 312; the sophist Hippias: Plato, *Lesser Hippias* 365a, 370c; "On the third day . . .": IX 363

91   "Now I shall go . . .": I 169; Achilles of Athens: Plato, *Apology* 28c; "Socrates, on the third day . . .": Plato, *Crito* 44b; "is to perish . . .": XXIV 86; "Mother, since you . . .": I 352; "My child, why . . .": I 414; "minute-spanned": XV 612

92   one's proper fate: XVI 860; no seizing will bring back: IX 378; "For Mother, the goddess, . . .": IX 410; pertinent question: XVI 36; "if he is evading . . .": XI 794

93   "Zeus-born Patroclus, . . .": XVI 48; *ton apolesa:* XVIII 82; the same wordplay: xiii 340

94   devastating news: XVIII 9, 80; *apopthimenoio:* XVIII 34; "Be dead! . . .": XXII 365; He says it repeatedly: XVIII 115; "Xanthus, why are you . . .": XIX 419; land of his fathers: XXIII 150; "mingle in love . . .": XXIV 129

11. HECTOR THE HOLDER

95   women and the families: XVI 832, XVII 223; pusillanimous elders: XV 721; compared to Achilles: XX 435; drink on duty: VI 264; stays to save his men: XVI 362; keeps his distance: VI 360, 521

96   her lost freedom: VI 455; Achilles has killed: VI 429; undone and exposed: XXII 465; the wronged husband Menelaus: VII 119; Achilles well knows: XVI 850, XIX 414; "It is not . . .": XV 496; desecrating his corpse: XXIII 185; Patroclus urgently tells Achilles: XXIII 71

97   "The race is ended . . .": Edwin Muir, "Hector in Hades"; so many heroes: I 4; "spoil for the dogs . . .": XXII 353

12. THE PLAN OF ZEUS

98   "Argos and Sparta, . . .": IV 52; Achilles, the swift-fated: I 493, 511; Patroclus has died: VIII 477

99   "It is not destiny . . .": XVI 707; fulfilled his prayer: XVI 250; "but what is the pleasure . . .": XVIII 80; "But Zeus does not . . .": XVIII 328

13. ACHILLES **AS** HADES AND ACHILLES **IN** HADES

100   nectar and ambrosia: XIX 347; "killing and blood . . .": XIX 214; a golden cloud: XVIII 205; a blaze of fury: XIX 16; Achilles' death: XIX 407; as he emerges: XXI 300

101   the Ruddy River: XXI 342; "A man in no way . . .": XX 467; it has become inviolable: XXIV 11; "great in his greatness": XVIII 26, xxiv 40; He talks to dead Patroclus: XXIII 105, 137; will remember Patroclus: XXII 389; for evermore dead: I 234; not to be soothed: IX 158; the dead below: XV 188; "He had made up . . .": XXIII 176

102   courtesy—or booby—prize: XXIII 890; steal Hector's body: XXIV 24; divine condemnation: XXIV 157; "But for me, . . .": XXIV 246

103   "stretch forth . . .": XXIV 506

104   marvel at each other: XXIV 629; Cassandra, the seeress: XXIV 699; creature and returned: VIII 367

105 "Do not extenuate death . . .": xi 488; "How did you dare . . .": xi 475; "For before, when . . .": xi 484; "Not all the wealth . . .": IX 406

106 "Better to reign in Hell, . . .": Milton, *Paradise Lost* 1.263

14. BEGINNINGS AND ENDINGS

110 "sings words taught . . .": xvii 518; With Calypso: i 14

111 *anti-theos:* i 21; their own fault: i 32; taboo on Olympus: iii 310; her island, Ogygia: v 14; palace gate in Ithaca: i 84; the assonant verb: i 62

112 "reversal and recognition": Aristotle, *Poetics* 1432a; unity and concentration: Aristotle, *Poetics* 1459a

113 the wooden horse: viii 492

114 "Pallas Athena, . . .": xxiv 547; "Made weak by time . . .": Tennyson, "Ulysses"

15. THE RETURNS

116 "Reading the wall . . .": Edwin Muir, "The Return of the Greeks"; "his own soul": i 5

117 "Odysseus far away . . .": xxiii 68

16. THE POET OF THE ODYSSEY

118 "Homer deserves praise . . .": Aristotle, *Poetics* 1460a

119 "Tell me now, . . .": II 484; "Difficult is it . . .": XII 176; "took away his divine song . . .": II 595

120 "Goddess, daughter of Zeus . . .": i 10

121 "the Muse who teaches, . . .": viii 488; "moved by the god": viii 499; "Self-taught am I": xxii 347; the gods listen: i 152

17. NAÏVETÉ AND INSIGHT

122   "Being without any familiarity, . . .": Friedrich Schiller, "On Sentimental and Naïve Poets" (later title, "On Naïve and Sentimental Poetry") (1795)

18. BEAUTY AND CRAFT

124   "in hollow caves, . . .": i 15, ix 30, xxiii 334; "navel of the sea": i 50; "A great fire . . .": v 69

125   "Be not afeard . . .": Shakespeare, *The Tempest* 3.2.132; bowl of ivy wood: xiv 78; "O Father . . .": xix 36

126   Phaeacian cityscape: vii 45; shish kebab deftly prepared: vi 306, xviii 108, viii 336; "Heard melodies are sweet . . .": Keats, "Ode on a Grecian Urn"

127   "I never doubted . . .": XVIII 82, XXII 104, xiii 340; "much-designing" Odysseus: ix 414; an ugly one: xxii 174, 192

19. VISIBILITY AND VISUALITY

129   may be blind: i 153; sweet song: viii 62; "Aye, on the shores . . .": Keats, "To Homer"; "My heart envisions . . . ,": xix 224

130   "mental image-making": Horace, *Art of Poetry* 361; Ezra Pound, *ABC of Reading* IV I; observed by Aristotle: Aristotle, *Poetics* 1455a

131   his own armor: XVI 64; Achilles has returned: XVI 281; it is only Patroclus: XVI 656, 724; helped to kill: XVI 793; "a wonder to behold": XVIII 83; hurled from the walls: XXII 63; as father killed father: *Little Iliad* 3

132   "Never now can I . . .": XXII 126; "as in a dream . . .": XXII 199; "In front . . .": XXII 158; "And in that space . . .": Edwin Muir, "Ballad of Hector in Hades"

133   "Now my spirit . . .": XXII 252; "There are no oaths . . .": XXII 262

20. SIMILE: THE DOUBLE VISION

134   "*As* a Carian . . .": IV 141

135   "What light through . . .": Shakespeare, *Romeo and Juliet* 2.2.3; "Sweet sleep, . . .": xxiii 342

136   "And like a poppy . . .": VIII 306; piled up in clusters: XI 113, 305; XII 433; XVII 746, 755

137   "As in heaven . . .": VIII 555; "As when a man . . .": xx 25; beggar's food, evidently: xviii 120; "so Odysseus was befouled, . . .": xxii 401

138   "As the snow melts . . .": xix 204

21. NAME TAGS AND SPEAKING NAMES

142   employment as a farm hand: xviii 356; second line on: xxiv 119; aspects of one nature: x 330

143   ak*ach*izein, *Ach*illeu: xi 486; *Ach*eron: x 513; *odyromenos kai acheuon:* ii 23, iv 100; "Why do you . . .": i 62; the "Hated": xix 407; *odyromenon noston:* v 153, xiii 219; "He has gone . . .": i 242

144   the Greek wail *aiai:* Sophocles, *Ajax* 905

22. TELEMACHUS AND HIS TELEMACHY

145   the incidents that Aristotle: Aristotle, *Poetics* 1455b; full attention immediately: i 114; ineffective viceroy: ii 225

146   "Dad": xvi 130; Odysseus' sister Ktimene: xv 363; "no clean" death: xxii 462; trussed and strung up: xviii 339, xxii 175

147   candidly admits it: xxii 154; make very attractive: iii 305; Neoptolemus of Phthia: xi 506; "Few sons are equal . . .": ii 276; "This is my son, . . .": Tennyson, "Ulysses"

148   father might harbor: i 215; Telemachus was born of us two: xxiii 61; Orestes who avenged his father: i 298; the luscious Calypso: i 198; father had got there: ii 328, i 259

149   a bad lot: xx 246; of his whereabouts: xiii 417; news of his father: iii 82; large public consequences: iv 315

23. NESTOR AT HOME

150   a timely return: ii 372; "And the wind . . .": ii 427

151   her favorite among men: iii 52; "the shrill Ranter": I 248, II 246; with Athena right there: iii 145; "Telemachus, what a word . . .": iii 230

152   given the regency: iii 194, 267; "he unwilling . . .": iii 272, v 155; murder of Agamemnon: Aeschylus, *Agamemnon* 1417; IX 145; the usurper's funeral: iii 311; "They say he has . . .": iii 246; irritatingly interfering: X 164; Patroclus' funeral games: XXIII 305; at inconvenient times: XI 668

153   "your father, . . .": iii 122; mourned in Pylos: iii 112; "We can boast . . .": xv 196

24. HELEN AT TROY AND HELEN AT HOME

154   prize of the Trojan War: III 91; ends of the poem: III 236, xi 298, xxiv 199, i 329

155   on guard against: xxiii 218; artful vanity: III 125; self-forgetful faithfulness: ii 93; you hold back: XXII 226; "the Trojan boast": II 160; "all-over-beautiful" maiden: XVI 85

156   makes you shudder: XIX 325; "Would Helen's clan . . .": xiv 68; bringing a dowry along: III 70, 91; "the *husband* of fair-haired Helen": III 329; Priam . . . emphasizes: III 164; "serviced his troublemaking lust": XXIV 30; "Beauty-Hill": XX 53; the war then and there: III 67; piece of curiosity: III 139; "chattering like cicadas": III 151

157   being utterly undone: XXII 467; "lovely women-friends . . .": III 175; "All Greece reviles . . .": Hilda Doolittle, "Helen"

158   solid big brother: VI 344; "woman-crazy": III 39, XI 385; captivating as a lover: III 437; in an excited state: III 375; take care of him: III 406; "Was this the face . . .": Marlowe, *The Tragicall History of Dr. Faustus* 5.91

159 Hector foretells that death in dying: XXII 359; wedding music: iv 8; Achilles says outright: XIX 326; mattered more to Helen: III 174

160 Clytemnestra's funeral: XXIV 765, iii 305; fifth century B.C.: Herodotus, *The Persian Wars* 2.113; common piratical venture: VI 290

161 men who died at Troy: iv 93; "No one has cared . . .": Janet Lewis, "Helen Grown Old"; "So far the poet . . .": Rupert Brooke, "Menelaus and Helen"

162 whisper to Peisistratus: iv 71; "where there is no snow . . .": iv 561; "My mother says . . .": i 215; Odysseus as missing: iv 115, viii 85

163 "dog-faced me": iv 140; self-inflicted blows: iv 244

164 live near Sparta: iv 171; "I take no pleasure . . .": iv 193

165 "pain-killing and wrath-reducing": iv 220; one Greek's mouth: iv 274; several-years-old news: iv 557; Menelaus, smiling: iv 594

166 denouement at the palace: xv 10; diminished palace treasure: xv 19; he wants to get up and go: xv 46; a bridal gown: xv 125; she is right: xv 160

167 "So may Zeus . . .": xv 180; seeing her cousin: xvii 143; "but take a bath . . .": xvii 46; ships or comrades: xvii 143

25. THE STATIONS AND SIGHTINGS OF ODYSSEUS' ODYSSEY

169 Thrinacia: i 7; sealed world: iv 558, xvii 143

170 "Why should I . . .": vii 244, xii 542

26. ASLEEP ON THE WATCH

171 home to Ithaca: x 31, xii 338, xiii 79

172 scared of a snare: x 232; the barking monster: xii 226; tired and hungry: xii 280, xix 211

173 "Sleep, the brother of Death": XIV 231; "I knew in my heart . . .": xiii 340

27. THE POET OF THE ODYSSEY

174 "Enclosed Coast": xiii 160

175 fame of warriors: IX 186; "not a seducer . . .": xi 363

176 "who has learned . . .": xvii 518; a smart wrestler: xviii 90, XXIII 763; where it belongs: viii 215; "it sang beautifully . . .": xxi 406; his lyrelike bow: vi 162, xxi 258; caught Aphrodite and Ares: viii 266; way to take Troy: viii 73; Trojan Horse: viii 492; fat boar's back: viii 477

177 Phaeacian boys: viii 256; Ithacan wooers: i 150, xxii 344; "Seek the light . . .": xi 223; *mythologein:* xii 450, 453

28. THE FAME OF MEN AND WOMEN

178 *klea andron:* IX 189; Achilles has slain: I 366, VI 416

179 "For my own . . .": Michel de Montaigne, "Of Glory," *Essays* 2.16

180 "Come hither, . . .": xii 184; *aïstos, apustos:* i 242; "I am Odysseus, . . .": ix 19

181 he truly loves: IX 343; "the fame (*kleos*) . . .": xxiv 125, 196; "If he would . . .": xviii 254; "for your fame reaches . . .": xix 108

29. ODYSSEUS' ODYSSEY I: FIRST THROUGH SIXTH ADVENTURE

183 twelve ships: II 637, ix 159

184 "Like things produced . . .": Wallace Stevens, "The Sail of Ulysses" 6; "What shall I . . .": i 10, ix 14; on Odysseus' account: xiii 159; "I for one cannot . . .": ix 28

185 tacit apology: vii 312; "From Ilium . . .": ix 39; deliveries of wine: II 846, X 559, IX 71; "much wine is drunk": ix 45

186 bread-eaters: ix 89; "Hateful is the dark-blue sky, . . .": Tennyson, "The Lotos-Eaters" 4

187   "Circle-eyes": ix 105; "that I may test . . .": ix 174; judgments nor customs: ix 215

188   "No-one, *Outis*, . . .": ix 366

189   alinguistic semihermit: ii 150, xxii 376; so puny a creature: ix 508; prophecy about him: x 330, xiii 172

191   Aeolia, "Squall Isle": x 1; back to Aeolia: x 30; "I endured . . .": x 53

192   "Roughpelts": x 86; "dread goddess giving voice": x 135

193   "Friends, not yet . . .": x 174; "but no effective action . . .": x 202; a "miserable" drug mixed in: x 235

194   *moly:* x 305; "once it has passed . . .": x 328; butcher-ready hogs: x 390

195   "I think that Circe . . .": Xenophon, *Memorabilia* 1.3.7; "he will tell you . . .": x 539

196   "to keep off . . .": Ezra Pound, *Canto* I; "Hero": x 516; Cimmerans: xi 14; sleeping off a drunk: x 552; his rower's oar: xi 51

30. ODYSSEUS IN HADES: SEVENTH ADVENTURE

197   "he himself is . . .": xi 602

198   yet another voyage: xi 90, 121; though not dreaming: xxiv 12

199   the shade himself: xi 387; "very womanlike women": xi 225

200   a daughter of Neleus: xi 285; "whose fame (*kleos*) . . .": Thucydides, *Peloponnesian War* 2.45; Queen Arete interrupts: xi 335

31. THE WOOERS IN HADES

201   "Cyllenian Hermes . . .": xxiv 1

202   Autolycus: xix 396; "who lends grace . . .": xv 320; tombless fate: xxiv 24; mourned discreetly underwater: xxiv 54, XVIII 38

217   she is Penelope: v 216; his time with her: i 14, 50; iv 557; vii 244; xiii 333

218   "For I know . . .": v 423

35. PHAEACIA THE ARTISTS' COLONY: TWELFTH ADVENTURE

219   "far from wage-earning men": vi 4

220   "The gods . . .": vi 20; "So now, having suffered . . .": v 377; dreamless restorative sleep: v 487

221   "Papa dear": vi 57; "the female cry . . .": vi 125

222   "Milady": vi 149; by Apollo's altar: vi 162; *homophrosyne:* vi 181

223   rings with this sound: vi 244, 246; "and when we . . .": vi 262; "Child": vii 22; "Athena": vii 80

224   the occasion is right: xvi 186

225   ever was Calypso's: vii 311; "there will I pray . . .": viii 467

226   "I am Odysseus, . . .": ix 19; he tells the odyssey: ix–xii; "a sleep much like death": xiii 181

36. THE LOCALES AND SETTINGS OF HOMER'S ODYSSEY

228   "navel of the sea": i 50; "concealed all around": xiii 152

37. THE LIAR'S GODDESS

230   "I am never . . .": X 280; "I have never yet . . .": iii 221; "carrying a man . . .": xiii 90

231   to his homeland: Porphyry, *On the Cave of the Nymphs* 35; "a wonder to behold": xiii 108; "Oh to the land . . .": xiii 200

232   "But everything trite . . .": Edwin Muir, "The Return of the Greeks";
       well-loved man: xi 356; "You are a fool . . .": xiii 237

233   "land of his fathers": xiii 251; "Dangerous man, . . .": xiii 291

234   "Yet you didn't . . .": xiii 299; "but you don't care . . .": xiii 336

235   "Booty-Bringer": xiii 359; "if you would stand . . .": xiii 389

236   "I sent him . . .": xiii 422

38. THE CRETAN LIAR

238   poison for his arrows: i 261; *First Tale:* xiii 256; generation at Troy:
       XIII 361

239   *Second Tale:* xiv 1; "and her clan . . .": xiv 68; "And quickly
       you . . .": xiv 131; "Hateful to me . . .": xiv 156, IX 312; "Old
       man, . . .": xiv 167

240   maternal and paternal grandfathers: xiv 199

241   with his comrades: xiv 379

242   how Odysseus got the teller: xiv 462; calling him "Dad": xvi 60; but
       his wife: xiv 227; *Third Tale:* xvii 415

243   "Nothing feebler . . .": xviii 130; "Many things . . .": Sophocles,
       Antigone 332; *Fifth Tale:* xix 75; *Sixth Tale:* xix 165

244   "I am indeed . . .": xix 118; prognosticated for Nausicaa: xix 137;
       "wandering through . . .": xix 170; "Ruddy-Blaze": VIII 185, xix
       180; to emanate from it: xviii 355

246   liar was with Calypso: xxiv 269; the "Hated": xxiv 304; Ephyra:
       i 259; herself been kidnapped: xv 415

39. LYING TALES VERSUS FAIRY TALES

248   "as imagination bodies forth . . .": Shakespeare, *A Midsummer
       Night's Dream* 5.1.14

40. TELEMACHUS RETURNS

250 "I am of Ithaca . . .": xv 267; "Odysseus begot me . . .": xvi 119

251 unsettled palace: iv 114, xvii 6, xvi 147, xvii 71; he recites his tale: xvii 124; error of an attempt: xxi 128; "This is no public house . . .": xx 264; "The door flapped open . . .": Edwin Muir, "The Return of Odysseus"; "I observe and know . . .": xx 309; Antinous: xxi 95

252 "you care for me . . .": xvii 397; expects more of him: xviii 175, 217; *sophrosyne:* xxiii 30; "Her word remained . . .": xvii 57

253 in the house: xx 129; "No other woman . . .": xxiii 97; impracticality of the move: xvi 311

254 the familiar son: xiv 29, xvi 5; the young master: xvi 12

41. ODYSSEUS AND TELEMACHUS: CONVERGENCE

256 gift of recognition: viii 468, iv 138; magical sea world: xi 397, iv 520; on the same day: viii 244, ix 29, xii 448, iv 521; shepherded by Athena: xiii 221, xv 1

42. PENELOPE THE KINGLY QUEEN

257 "Sole at the house's . . .": Edwin Muir, "The Return of Odysseus"; spins and unravels: ii 96; balances hopes and chances: xiv 372

258 *kouroi:* xix 141; before she does: iv 742; "Taking apart . . .": John Hollander, *Powers of Thirteen: Poems* 115

259 "weaving a design": ix 422, xiii 303; of the Laertidae: xi 188; "be in service . . .": xviii 254, xix 127; "I would not wish . . .": xix 143

260 to make herself up: xviii 172, 180; yield to him: xi 386, 434; xv 422; xxiii 166; ward off her captivity: viii 523; "the sea supplies . . .": ix 20; xix 108, 113

261 heaps about the hall: xix 535; the dream geese: xv 161; "As welcome . . .": xxiii 233; *Kakoïlion:* xix 260, 597; xxiii 19; "Prompted by some god, . . .": xxiii 222, xiv 68

288 his mother's apartments: xvi 35; "So I manifest . . .": xxiii 202; Helen comes to her mind: xxiii 218

289 "much loved bed": xxiii 354; no longer comes to town: xi 187, i 189; most generous wooer: xv 16

290 decides to test: xxiv 238; "That one you . . .": xxiv 321

291 "What a day . . .": xxiv 514

47. TIME CHASMS

292 "giving golden . . .": VI 235

293 acted like Achilles: XI 655

294 Story of the Scar . . . Bow: xix 392, xxi 17; other faithful servants: xxi 217; "because I have come . . .": xix 407

295 reached just now: xix 413; "his father and lady-mother . . .": xix 466

296 "would never take . . .": xxi 42

48. TWICE TOLD, THRICE DEAD

299 he gives them: xxiv 248; "Hope (*elpore*) there is . . .": xxiv 287; "We few, . . .": Shakespeare, *Henry the Fifth* 4.3.60; promised these serfs: xxi 215

300 "enjoy lovely love": xiii 301; Ciconian point of departure: xxiii 310; penelopeia: xiii 302

301 "Amazing woman!": xxii 264; "the well-fitted oars . . .": xxiii 272

302 spoke with Teiresias: xi 77; "on top of . . .": xii 15; interest in the earth: XV 193

303 "And then the Periods . . .": George Chapman, *Twenty-four Bookes of Homer's Odisses* (1614) xi 170

Oft of one wide expanse had I been told
   That deep-browed Homer ruled as his demesne;
   Yet did I never breathe its pure serene
Till I heard Chapman speak out loud and bold:

Then felt I like some watcher of the skies
    When a new planet swims into his ken;
Or like stout Cortez when with eagle eyes
    He stared at the Pacific—and all his men
Looked at each other with a wild surmise—
    Silent, upon a peak in Darien.

—John Keats, "On First Looking into Chapman's Homer" (1816)